The Sky Barons

THE
SKY BARONS

Neville Clarke and Edwin Riddell

Methuen

First published in Great Britain in 1992
by Methuen London, Michelin House, 81 Fulham Road, London SW3 6RB

Copyright © 1992 Neville Clarke and Edwin Riddell

The authors have asserted their moral rights

A CIP catalogue record for this book
is available from the British Library
ISBN 0 413 63680 1

Photoset by Deltatype Ltd, Ellesmere Port, Cheshire
Printed and bound in Great Britain
by Clays Ltd, St Ives PLC

Contents

List of Illustrations

Acknowledgements

We are deeply indebted to Ann Mansbridge at Methuen for her unstinting support and advice and to David Watson for his invaluable assistance in the preparation of the manuscript. To Bernard Ostry in Canada, Raúl Trejo Delarbre in Mexico, Luis Ezcurra Carillo in Madrid, Bruce Gyngell in London and Helmuth Runde in Germany for the insights they gave us into the nature of the Sky Barons and their baronies. Neil Watson at *Screen International*, Louise McElvogue and Richard Zahradnik at *The Hollywood Reporter* and Harry Dennis gave generous advice on many points of detail. Finally, we acknowledge all those broadcasters past and present who provided us with both facts and opinions on an astonishing range of matters.

We are grateful to those who have generously granted us permission to quote from previously published material, which, so far as is possible, we have acknowledged in the text and in the bibliography.

Introduction

From geostationary orbits in space, unblinking military satellites survey the globe's surface. They are able to pick out an object the size of a handkerchief. Deep in the Amazon rainforest, a mobile satellite dish relays pictures of primitive tribes to suburban parlours. In the once-forbidden city of Beijing, a television reporter talks back to the London studio as she reports on the fearful massacre taking place around her. The enormous changes in Eastern Europe's political systems and boundaries have been fuelled by the new mass medium of cross-frontier television. Communications, increasingly in the hands of a few powerful corporations, are beginning to shape the future.

In the mid-1980s, when we began seriously to chart the rise to prominence of a new breed of global entrepreneurs – the 'Sky Barons' as we have chosen to call them – the main economies of the West were in the full flush of *laisser-faire* economic monetarism. In the countries of the Eastern bloc, the iron grip of Marxism was only just beginning to be loosened by the ideas and policies of Mikhail Gorbachev.

A few short years on, the world that had existed since 1945 has been turned upside down. The subject states of the old Communist world have one by one thrown off their Marxist past. In their place, new nation states are emerging, some in what is turning out to be a baptism of fire. In the Middle East, countries that had formerly been sworn enemies joined in an extraordinary alliance against the Iraqi invasion of Kuwait and agreed to discuss the possibility of a lasting settlement between Israel and its Arab neighbours. South Africa, long the pariah of international affairs, looked to have turned its back once and for all on its apartheid past.

It is not our present purpose to analyse in close detail the role of the new communications media in bringing about these political revolutions. Some aspects of the relationship are illuminating to our story. We would be surprised, however, if historians of the future do not rate that role to have been very significant.

What is certain is that these events have taken place under the light of unprecedented media coverage. The Gulf War brought the new power of men like Ted Turner, who owns the international Cable News Network (CNN), into true perspective. As the leadership hierarchies in Eastern Europe began to unravel, so did the extraordinary multiple life led by Robert Maxwell, who had scuttled about the world stage in ever more frantic manoeuvres.

Against this background, the rise and fall of some of our principal characters has been undeniably dramatic. Who could genuinely have predicted the scandals and revelations that have accompanied the downfall of the likes of Maxwell, Alan Bond and Giancarlo Parretti?

Maxwell himself had become fond of predicting that by the millennial year of 2000 there would be just a handful of media corporations dominating the flow of ideas and information throughout the world. If that is true, as we believe the evidence demonstrates, it will be an entirely new phenomenon.

Governments, aided by the limited broadcasting range of land-based transmitters, had previously been able to control the medium of television through restricting it within particular state boundaries by international agreement. The invention and development of the communications satellite has changed all that. With the aid of satellites, it is possible to leapfrog boundaries of nationality and time zones, offering the possibility of global networks for the first time. Many of today's Sky Barons cherish the idea of such empires.

The new media empires traverse the boundaries of the old nation states with something approaching impunity. The traditional public service broadcasters, with roles defined in relation to old boundaries, have watched helplessly as the new Sky Barons exploited their freewheeling international status. In the United Kingdom, for example, we shall see how a combination of ineptitude on the part of those controlling television and the shrewdness of Rupert Murdoch and a handful of close advisers ended the 'cosy duopoly' of the system of British broadcasting that had stood for thirty-five years.

The history of great newspaper and publishing empires, of film studios and television organisations, is largely the history of the personalities who created and ran them. The purpose of this book is to describe how the handful of great modern communications organisations that dominate the global flow of ideas and information came into being. What kind of men are their rulers? What are their backgrounds? What do they believe in? Who will inherit their empires when they are gone?

In an age when governments are relinquishing their traditional monopolies in the market place or losing them to the imperatives of new technology, the Sky Barons wield power undreamt of by their predecessors.

We have chosen to call them 'Sky Barons' for good reason. The satellites on which their operations depend are located high beyond the reach of government and the law, in equatorial station some 23,000 miles above the earth's surface. Those who control the major media corporations possess power comparable to that held by feudal barons within their fiefdoms. Men like Murdoch, Turner, Berlusconi and the Brazilian Roberto Marinho hold the keys to the views of billions of their fellow citizens.

These men – so far there are no sky baronesses – are not elected by democratic vote. They are accountable only to their shareholders, their bankers and their own consciences. By no means do we suggest that those who control today's global media machines are bereft of ideals beyond the market place. Nor do we claim they necessarily have unhealthy pretensions to world domination. We do however point out the extreme fragility of our rights and freedoms in the face of their enormous economic and technological power.

The Sky Barons control the flood of words, images and data that pumps incessantly round the globe carrying the information, ideas and entertainment which are the lifeblood of man's freedoms and liberties.

This book traces the history of communications media and recounts some of the abuses to which their control has been prone in the past. It examines the motivation and behaviour of the handful of people who today dominate the world's entertainment and information. It looks at their backgrounds and their qualifications to exercise such power. It reveals the sources of their wealth and describes the complex web of alliances, rivalries and enmities between them.

The nature of modern communications systems is such that only the richest and largest multinational corporations can afford to buy and exploit them. In most cases, however, there is a single individual or dynasty behind each of the giant corporations. Are these latter-day barons tomorrow's overmighty subjects? Or are they, like the Hollywood moguls and press barons before them, 'great monsters of the deep', doomed to extinction as the flood of mergers and takeovers inevitably leads to giant grey corporations, to be run in an Orwellian future by faceless administrators and bureaucrats?

In attempting to answer these questions, we have travelled to North and South America and most of the Western European countries, visiting the headquarters of the empires and interviewing their senior executives. We have spoken to hundreds of people from five continents both inside and outside the organisations concerned, recording the views and utterances of the Sky Barons themselves as much as possible. We have also drawn on a wealth of existing material in order to give balance to our own conclusions. We have viewed and assessed their channels, programmes and films.

In the English-speaking world, where the television and film industries find their main focus, the actions and utterances of men like Rupert Murdoch and Ted Turner have long since become the daily fodder of the international gossip machines. Their power is at least matched by the Brazilian Roberto Marinho and the Mexican Emilio Azcárraga and their respective family empires. The Sky Barons we have chosen to discuss in detail represent different aspects of the concentration of power that has been taking place in the last few years. We do not pretend to provide a comprehensive survey of all the world's media empires. We have concentrated instead on the motives and characteristics of the most prominent players on the world scene and how they achieved and used their power.

I

The Field of Battle

Robert Maxwell set out as a penniless Jewish refugee from Czechoslovakia and created a publishing empire based on contacts made as a British Army officer in postwar Berlin. Today, Maxwell's heirs watch the dismantling of the edifice their father built and reflect on his oft-repeated promise that he would leave them nothing when he died.

For some time before his mysterious death in 1991, Maxwell had become obsessed with a messianic idea. In a BBC radio interview in the summer of 1987, he said: 'I am a candidate from Europe to build one of the ten great corporations in this field which will help make a great deal of money for my shareholders, provide an enormous number of jobs at home and abroad, and give Britain and Europe an influential place at the top table of information and communication.' This, he went on, 'is at the heart of everything, whether it is peace or war or new technology or entertainment or quicker solutions to such problems as cancer'. Not long after, the Maxwell Communications Corporation made its fatal bid to enter the major league by acquiring the US publisher Macmillan for $2.5 billion.

When the American publishing group Time Inc. announced its proposed merger with Warner Communications in 1989, Time's president Nick Nicholas said: 'We believe there will emerge on a world basis six, seven, eight vertically integrated media and entertainment mega-companies. At least one will be Japanese, probably two. We think two will be European. We think there will be a couple of American-led enterprises, and we think Time Inc. is going to be one.'

With due allowance, the remarks of both men seem to have

been prophetic. The tide of mergers and takeovers across film, television, publishing and newspapers is leading inexorably to a world whose major communications and information services are controlled by a small group of individuals and corporations.

The young Robert Maxwell had lost most of his family in the Nazi holocaust. His mother Chanca who taught him to read and write at the age of four-and-a-half and to whom he was particularly attached, his father, three sisters, one brother and his grandfather all perished in Auschwitz. At first he took vengeance on the Germans. In March 1945, having just learnt of the death of Chanca, he wrote to his wife Betty the day before he received the MC, 'As you can well imagine, I am not taking any prisoners and whatever home my men occupy, before I leave I order it to be destroyed.'[1] One can only speculate whether this psychological trauma coupled with his determination to sup at the top table may have led him to believe that the end justified any means, including the criminal.

Roberto Marinho, nearly in his nineties, is master of Brazil's media. In 1925, Marinho went to work as a journalist at the *O Globo* newspaper just founded by his father in Rio de Janeiro. It was the year in which Hitler published his prison memoirs *Mein Kampf* and the Charleston reached England. It was the year John Reith, Managing Director of the British Broadcasting Company, called for the removal of the prohibition on news broadcasting before 7 pm. The year in which the BBC's radio services claimed an audience of 10 million and John Logie Baird was perfecting his system of transmitting moving pictures by wireless.

One day, shortly after he had started at the office, the young Roberto returned home with his father, who had been taken ill. In a matter of hours, and just twenty-three days after launching his newspaper, he was dead. The day after, at the age of only nineteen, Roberto Marinho became the editor and sole proprietor of what is today Brazil's largest national daily.

It is a scenario that could be taken from Orson Welles's *Citizen Kane*. The teenage Marinho was filled with a determination to

[1] Quoted in Joe Haines, *Maxwell*.

build his father's venture into a force to be reckoned with. Today, the Globo press and broadcasting empire founded sixty-seven years ago on that early newspaper is still owned and controlled by the Marinho family. They retain an iron hold on a communications empire spanning thousands of square miles from the snowcapped Andes headwaters of the Amazon to the grassy pampas of Uruguay. The Globo organisation has an almost total grip on what Brazilians read, see and hear.

The idea of men inspired to great achievements by the untimely death or betrayal of a father has a venerable Hollywood tradition. The teenage Marinho's sudden translation from tyro journalist to newspaper proprietor has parallels in the rise to power of other of our Sky Barons.

In 1920, five years before the young Marinho went to work for his father at the newspaper in Rio, the son of a Scottish Presbyterian minister who had emigrated to Australia in the 1890s became editor of the *Melbourne Herald*. The *Herald* was the first of a string of titles that Keith Murdoch was to acquire and pass on to his son Rupert. Sir Keith, as he was later to become, was forced by an Australian monopolies tribunal to sell the paper which had laid the foundations for today's giant News Corporation. It was a perceived injustice Rupert Murdoch never forgot, and which he finally righted in 1987, when, after a long and bitter battle with rival press barons John Fairfax and Robert Holmes à Court, he bought back the *Herald*.

Ed Turner was a salesman from Mississippi who founded a small outdoor advertising business in Atlanta. In 1960, his son Ted went to work for his father after being expelled from Brown University. Three years later, Ed Turner committed suicide, depressed by debts and the untimely death of his beloved daughter. It is told that Ted, still only twenty-four, refused to hand over the billboard leases to the creditors who wasted no time in pressing for an early settlement of the debts. Turner threatened to burn the company's records, build competing billboards and starve out the competition. The prospective buyers dropped the deal in exchange for stock in his company. Today Ted Turner controls the biggest international television news organisation in the world and is spoken of as a future President of the United States.

In 1970, Turner acquired a small UHF television station WTCG Channel 17. The four other Atlanta stations, all larger, were on the VHF standard and many set owners could not receive the WTCG signal. Later he was to change the station's call sign to WTBS for 'Turner Broadcasting System' and merged his billboard and television activities under the grand title 'Turner Communications'. One of his first coups was securing the rights to televise the games of his favourite baseball team, the Atlanta Braves. Now he owns them. From these early beginnings, Ted Turner built the world's first satellite-fed cable network 'The SuperStation that Serves the Nation' and later the world's largest privately owned television news service.

While the young Ted Turner was following in his spare time the fortunes of the Atlanta Braves baseball team, the son of a Milanese bank official was a no less avid supporter of AC Milan. AC was then less fashionable than Inter, the more successful of Milan's two soccer clubs. Today, Silvio Berlusconi not only owns AC Milan, European champions in 1990, but also presides over Italy's three main private television networks, a share of the country's first pay-TV channel, the giant Standa retail chain, the Mondadori publishing house, film and TV production studios, a cinema chain, extensive insurance and banking interests plus a stake in TV networks in Germany and Spain.

'Television,' says Berlusconi, 'like the advertising which supports it, is an attractive fable where everyone is beautiful, everything is elegant, and all the children love father and mother and are loved in their turn.' That philosophy, affirms Berlusconi, 'is fundamental to everything I do'.

Louis B. Mayer had created the original dream factory at MGM. 'I wanted warm stories, sentimental entertainment,' he once said. The films made at MGM were for the cinema-going family. 'Make it Good. Make it Big. Give it Class' was the studio's motto. It was what the people wanted. It was corn, as Mayer himself admitted, but he added: 'What's wrong with good corn?' Silvio Berlusconi has enthusiastically adopted the Mayer formula.

Metro Goldwyn Mayer was perhaps the most illustrious of all the Hollywood studios. In the 1980s its incomparable film library was purchased by Ted Turner, a move appreciated by Rupert Murdoch, who followed suit by buying the library and studios of Twentieth-Century Fox. Both Murdoch and Turner saw that such libraries would play an important part in founding the new television empires. MGM's studios eventually fell into the hands of an Italian financier, Giancarlo Parretti, who managed to persuade the French state-owned bank Crédit Lyonnais to loan him a reported $1.3 billion for the purchase, despite his record on financial matters.

Of the original seven principal Hollywood film studios, six are now part of huge international conglomerates. MGM-UA is controlled by the Crédit Lyonnais bank, which has lent to several other Hollywood production companies. Warner Brothers is part of the Time-Warner combine in which the Japanese Toshiba and C. Itoh now have strategic stakes. Twentieth-Century Fox is owned by the Australian-born Rupert Murdoch. Columbia Pictures is entirely owned by Sony. MCA-Universal is likewise a subsidiary of Matsushita. RKO ceased separate production in 1953. Only Paramount, owned by the Gulf & Western combine, is still left entirely in American hands. It is however being eyed by the Hitachi Corporation.

A similar fate has befallen the major record companies. The CBS label, with its artiste roster from Bob Dylan to Michael Jackson, was Sony's first major 'software' acquisition. The various labels under the PolyGram heading are part of the Dutch-owned Philips conglomerate. The huge German publishing organisation Bertelsmann, which now has extensive TV interests, bought the BMG and Ariola labels.

The Walt Disney Corporation has built its first theme park in Europe, centred around the 'Castle of the Sleeping Beauty' at a site near Paris from whence the publicity men claim the Disney family originated. With the 1992 European Single Market in mind, Disney is also making a concerted push into Europe in film and TV production and distribution. Disney is one of the main partners in the Sunrise consortium (now known as Good Morning TV) that outbid the incumbent TV-am for the UK breakfast television franchise.

Until recently, Britain was regarded as having the best system of broadcasting in the world. In January 1992, the international consultancy Peat, Marwick McLintock, which had advised the majority of the applicants for new ITV licences, predicted that by 1995 virtually the whole of UK commercial television will have passed into foreign hands.

By the beginning of 1989 the firm of Bertelsmann in West Germany, which started life as a small town family publisher of hymnals, had become the world's largest media concern. It was overtaken in March 1989 when Time Inc. and Warner Communications announced their proposed merger. Gerald Levin, Vice-Chairman of Time-Warner, said: 'This is not a transaction for the purposes of 1989 or even the 1990s. It is for us to be positioned for the next century.'

In Italy, Silvio Berlusconi's aims always seemed more prosaic. When he acquired the country's largest retail chain Standa, he unashamedly announced that he would use his three television channels to advertise and boost his supermarket sales. At the same time, the Italian government watched with concern as Giovanni Agnelli's Fiat motor car, truck and defence conglomerate extended its media interests from newspapers to television, and latterly through its RCS Rizzoli subsidiary to film and video.

The French publishing group Hachette is fifth in the world league table of media giants. It is headed by Jean-Luc Lagardère, majority shareholder in the electronics and armaments concern Matra. In 1988, Hachette sold 650 million copies of seventy-four different magazines in ten languages. Hachette's ambition for a television outlet was realised when it purchased a majority stake in the ailing French TV channel La Cinq. In 1991 Hachette set up a film and video division, but discovered before the year was out that television is very different from publishing as La Cinq filed for insolvency. Nothing deterred, Lagardère is now intent on merging Hachette and Matra.

Australian-born but American-naturalised Rupert Murdoch

owns an alarming share of the British press as well as the majority interest in the six satellite channels of British Sky Broadcasting which are beamed at the UK. In the United States, Murdoch's Fox television network, to acquire which he surrendered his Australian citizenship, is fast bidding to overtake the top three national networks. Murdoch's media interests are of course world-wide and would appear to have survived the debt crisis resulting from the stock market crash of 1987 and subsequent recession, which badly hit many of the new communications empires.

In the UK, Rupert Murdoch used his influence and newspapers to campaign tirelessly for the government break-up of the so-called BBC/ITV 'duopoly'. Murdoch stands to be the biggest gainer from the likely decline of an ITV system hamstrung by having to find an estimated £232 million a year for the British Treasury under the cash bidding system for the new Channel 3 TV franchises introduced by Mrs Thatcher.

In the meantime, Murdoch's Sky Television is slowly digesting its onetime rival, BSB. Sky, together with the operators of the Astra satellite from which it is transmitted, has also been at the forefront of the lobby against the European Commission's costly plans for HDTV (High-Definition Television) development.

Brazilian billionaire Roberto Marinho, head of the Globo empire, retains a foothold in Monte Carlo beaming programmes to Italy and is expanding into the Iberian peninsula via new television stations in Portugal. The Mexican Emilio Azcárraga has set up shop in Madrid. His giant Televisa conglomerate also has its eye on Spain. Azcárraga already has a solid foothold in the United States with its rapidly growing Hispanic population. Spanish is set to become the second most-spoken language in the world by the end of the century. Azcárraga's Televisa was the key element in the pan-Hispanic satellite link-up between Spain and Central and South America inaugurated in April 1992, the year of the Barcelona Olympic Games and the 500th anniversary of Columbus's voyage to the New World.

Mikhail Gorbachev's policies of *glasnost* and *perestroika* encouraged Sky Barons including Ted Turner, Richard Branson, Silvio Berlusconi and Robert Maxwell to slip behind the iron curtain while it was still in place. Music and sport led the way. With the curtain dismantled and rusting away, Western television and advertising are following fast. Virtually no country in the world is immune from the cultural revolution now taking place.

II

Precursors:
The Press and Hollywood

In 1878, an impressionable young American, Edward Willis Scripps, camped out under the stars close to the ruins of the Coliseum in Rome. Lost in thoughts of grandeur, he had a dream.

> I decided that I would establish a little kingdom such as Rome was in its prehistoric beginning. I decided that I would extend this kingdom of mine, which would consist of my first newspaper, to another and then another newspaper, and I determined so long as I lived to go on extending my kingdom into perhaps an empire of journalism.

The power of communication has always fascinated and at times frightened people. Throughout history people have sought to control information as a means to domination and a route to riches. For centuries, the Church had jealously guarded the written word as its sole prerogative until the invention of the printing press allowed that power to escape.

For nearly two thousand years, there had been little change in popular communication from the time of the ancient Roman *Acta Diurna*, a chronicle of daily events compiled by government officials and posted up in the streets, and the *Notizie Scritte* issued by the government of the Venetian republic in the sixteenth century. This latter publication had remained handwritten long after the invention of printing, so that the censors could keep control of its contents. Private presses in Europe, mainly in those parts influenced by the Protestant Reformation, had begun issuing newsletters from time to time in the sixteenth century, developing into what is generally agreed to be the first regular weekly newspaper, the *Frankfurter Zeitung*. In England, the first regular weekly newspaper was the *Weekly Newes*, which appeared in 1622.

If the invention of printing let the genie out of the bottle, there have been countless attempts to stuff it back. Governments quickly came to recognise the importance of controlling information disseminated by the press. Henry VIII, in 1529, began the process of issuing proclamations against particular publications, and the compulsory licensing of books for printing began in England in 1538.

Despite the poet John Milton's eloquent plea for freedom of publication in *Areopagitica* (1644), the freedom of the press in England did not get legislative support until Parliament refused to renew the Licensing Act in 1694. This did not prevent successive governments from harrying authors and printers through the means of warrants issued under the common law. Another means of control existed through the Stamp Act of 1712, imposing a tax on news sheets, which remained until 1855. The measures against the press in Britain were typical of those adopted in other countries and nearly all the great strides in newspapers came in the late nineteenth and early twentieth centuries.

Control of the press was accompanied by restrictions on theatrical performances introduced in the middle of the sixteenth century in England and remaining in substantial force until 1843, when censorship of the theatre became the responsibility of the Lord Chamberlain. In the twentieth century, these restrictions have been added to by censorship codes in the cinema and broadcasting.

The eighteenth-century economist Adam Smith was among the first to perceive that good communications were the foundation of all important improvements. Smith recalled how counties near London had violently opposed the extension of the turnpike roads on the grounds that this would enable areas further away from London to undercut their prices for grass and corn. Despite the protests of the Home Counties, the roads were built. 'Since that time,' Smith loftily observed, 'their rents have risen and their cultivation has been improved.'

Information and its control is as essential to commerce as it is to governments. It was the key to the early fortune of the Rothschilds, whose information network was faster than - Wellington's couriers in bringing news of victory at the battle of Waterloo in 1815 to the City of London. The Royal prerogatives on the mail were perhaps the most successful of the early attempts to monopolise communications for profit. Today no corporation can ignore the importance of gathering, storing and communicating information.

Edward Willis Scripps fulfilled his particular dream of empire by founding the United Press international news agency. The Scripps-Howard League eventually became the second largest newspaper chain in the United States. Scripps was if anything more awe-inspiring than that other prototype of the press baron, William Randolph Hearst. Visitors to Miramar, Scripps's desert retreat outside San Diego, were met by 'a hulking, bearded figure clad in a skull-cap, rough clothes and rawhide boots'.

It is said that at the height of the Spanish-American War in 1898, Hearst had cabled his illustrator at the Cuban front. The illustrator was none other than Frederic Remington, the celebrated painter of the Wild West. Remington had complained that there were no pictures to send back. In a classic riposte, Hearst wired Remington. 'You make the pictures. I'll make the war.' Hearst's papers were instrumental in stirring up American public opinion for the war with Spain. Hearst, the original Citizen Kane, is of course the prototype of the misuse of press power.

In 1878, when E. W. Scripps had his vision of a new Roman Empire founded on the power of the press, the family firm of Bertelsmann in the quiet north-west German town of Gütersloh was still an obscure publisher of religious books. Today Bertelsmann – known locally as 'the sleeping giant' – is the world's second largest media corporation, controlling print, publishing, record companies, television and radio.

At that time other hopeful emigrants from the Old World were seeking their fortunes in the newly opened frontier of the USA and Mexico. These were the Goldrush days. In 1881, the city which was to become the birthplace of the motion picture industry had a struggling frontier newspaper. The *Los Angeles Times*, driven by a water powered press, periodically stopped because the pipes were blocked by fish. The paper was bought by its editor, Harrison Gray Otis. An early practitioner of the school of unleveraged buyouts, Otis ruthlessly brought the paper to profitability and a circulation of some 30,000 by 1900. It was to be the basis of a multi-million dollar corporate empire constructed by his son.

In 1960, the *Los Angeles Times* became the first of the great private American newspapers to become a public company. Today it rules supreme following the demise of its last rival the *Los Angeles Examiner*, Hearst's old flagship paper. The *Examiner* was legendary for its crime reporter Aggie Underwood, who liked to fire a revolver at the ceiling on slow news days. Following the *Examiner*'s closure on 1 November 1989, Los Angeles joined twenty-three other major cities in the US which had only one newspaper.

Weetman Dickinson Pearson, later Viscount Cowdray, was a young structural engineer from England. Pearson had been involved in massive construction projects in Mexico in the 1890s. He had worked on the drainage of the lake on which the sprawling metropolis of Mexico City now stands and the vital rail link between that city and the east coast port of Vera Cruz.

It is unlikely that Pearson would ever have noticed a poor young country boy collecting newspapers as they were thrown from the train as it passed through a small village near Vera Cruz. Miguel Alemán used to supplement the meagre family income by delivering the papers. Like the Hollywood actor Ronald Reagan, Alemán would one day become president of his country. His son, also Miguel, was one of the men who built and controlled the giant Hispanic communications empire, Televisa.

Pearson grew rich in the Mexican oil business. Built on this wealth acquired in the New World, other generations of the Cowdray family created *The Financial Times* in the UK. The 'FT' – now partly owned by Rupert Murdoch's News Corporation – is part of the Pearson conglomerate with interests in publishing, newspapers and satellite television.

At the same time as the early press pioneers were laying the foundations of their empires, other ambitious men were creating the beginnings of a potent new medium. A village near Los Angeles was to become the centre of world production of first silent and then talking pictures.

At the outset of the First World War in 1914, the USA was producing about half of the world's films. The rest were made in Europe, mainly in Italy and France, where the latter in particular had established the successful beginnings of a film industry. The war put a stop to that as the front remorsely swallowed up men and money. By 1917, film production was almost totally in the hands of Hollywood. Producers, directors and actors – many of them from Europe – flocked to Los Angeles. The result was an enormous hike in the salaries of the top performers as America caught onto the fever of the movie houses that were being built all over the country.

When the First World War ended in 1918, the majority of people in Britain and the United States were already going to 'the pictures' at least once a week. 'Chaplin and Pickford were at the head of an ever-lengthening galaxy of stars who became the darlings of a world-wide public. World-wide it was, for until speech was added the film was a truly universal medium. Captions were kept down to the minimum needed for following the story and they could be translated into any language.'[1]

When the moguls of Hollywood sought to extend their empires, their model was that of the oil corporations. The epitome was Standard Oil. Standard was one of the first oil companies to combine the hitherto separate functions of refiner, distributor and retailer – a process that would now be called 'vertical integration'. The heads of the early Hollywood companies like Warner, Rank and MGM consciously modelled themselves on the oil tycoons. They not only controlled the cinema chains but also developed corporate models for their activity – the so-called studio system with its in-house writers, producers, actors, directors and stars.

[1] Vivian Ogilvie, *Our Times*.

The 'stars' were a new phenomenon. 'Up to 1909,' wrote Egon Larsen, 'film actors, in striking contrast to stage actors, had been anonymous, the reason being that the producing companies wished to avoid paying big salaries.'[2]

The producers knew of course that an anonymous actor was in no position to extract large fees and had to take what was offered. 'Mary Pickford, for instance, had been thrilling thousands of cinema-goers week after week in her heart-rending films before she was given a name, and that was not her own – not at first, anyway. For in England the exhibitors, faced with the problem of advertising the news that another film with "that girl" was being shown, invented a name for her – Dorothy Nicholson. Love-letters and marriage offers were sent to Miss Nicholson, but they never reached Mary Pickford, as no one in England knew her real name; and Mary herself had no idea that she had become England's sweetheart under an alias.'[3]

Carl Laemmle, then the leading independent producer, decided to break with the tradition of anonymity and moved his operations to a quiet village with an unremarkable name situated close to Los Angeles. Mary Pickford was the first of the hundreds of 'stars' that Hollywood was to launch upon the world.

The 'star system' was one of the key steps on the road to the studio system, by which the Hollywood producers gradually began to control the activities of both production and distribution. Those early stars – Pickford, Douglas Fairbanks and above all Rudolph Valentino – held millions in their thrall. When Valentino died at the age of thirty-one, a number of young women committed suicide. His lying-in-state at a Broadway undertaker's in New York attracted crowds stretching for eleven blocks.

In 1927, the age of the silent movies had come to an end when in *The Jazz Singer* Al Jolson unintentionally spoke cinema's first line of dialogue: 'Come on Ma, listen to this.' Twelve years later, in 1939, the cinema produced its first technicolor blockbuster. *Gone*

[2] Egon Larsen, *Spotlight on Films*.
[3] Ibid.

With The Wind was later to inspire a young advertising man called Ted Turner who was born the year before the picture's release.

When Greta Garbo's first 'talkie' appeared in 1930, the publicists had no need of superlatives. 'GARBO TALKS' was enough to send thousands flocking to the cinema houses to see *Anna Christie*. What they heard, delivered in that incomparable husky drawl – 'Gif me a viskey, ginger ale on the side, and don't be stingy, baby' – was no disappointment.

The story lines of the most popular movies of the twenties showed their addiction to the Victorian melodrama – a tradition of unscrupulous landlords or the idle rich exploiting poor but honest workers and homesteaders, particularly where that exploitation focussed in on the threat to the virtue of a young woman.

If the screenwriters were tapping an ancient spring with their stories of exploiter and exploited, what a well of human emotions they could draw on with sex!

> The movies . . . drawing millions to their doors every day and every night, played upon the same lucrative theme. The producers of one picture advertised 'brilliant men, beautiful jazz babies, champagne battles, midnight revels, petting parties in the purple dawn, all ending in one terrific smashing climax that makes you gasp'. The vendors of another promised 'neckers, petters, white kisses, red kisses, pleasure-mad daughters, sensation-craving mothers . . . the truth – bold, naked, sensational'.[4]

As the author wrily admitted: 'Seldom did the films offer as much as these advertisements promised.' Yet the promise was enough for the moral brigade. In 1926, the child welfare committee of the League of Nations met to consider 'the effect of the cinematograph on the mental and moral well-being of children.'

'Of all the arts, for us cinema is the most important,' Lenin had

[4] Frederick Lewis Allen, *Only Yesterday*.

declared in 1922. Calls for films with an educational and moral purpose were nevertheless heard increasingly on both sides of the Atlantic. The Hollywood moguls were sufficiently attuned to the gathering climate of official if not popular opinion to decide on self-regulation. Ten of the leading producers got together and invited a member of President Harding's cabinet to advise them.

Will Hays, an elder of the Methodist Church, became president of the Motion Picture Producers and Distributors of America. The Hays Office had no official powers but merely 'advised' producers if their scripts were likely to run into trouble with the state censorship boards. In reality, Hays was all-powerful. Through its indirect but all the more insidious censorship it tried to bring about a film world of artificial moral endings, a kind of mom-and-apple-pie assertion of values that often lay ludicrously at odds with the artistic content of the film itself.

Much the same approach was evident in the British arrangements. The British Board of Film Censors was established by the cinematographic trade and operated a self-regulation that for all its absurdity and inconsistencies had the desired effect of keeping the government at bay.

The power of the press barons and the Hollywood moguls reached its apogee during the 1930s. It was extremely rare for owners of newspapers to venture into the film business, an exception again being William Randolph Hearst who founded Cosmopolitan Pictures largely in order to provide roles for his girlfriend, Marion Davies. The films were in competition with each other to draw the largest possible audiences, but the cinema's visual monopoly was not to be challenged seriously until the advent of television in the 1950s.

III

Precursors:
Radio and Television

It was the development of radio that first introduced the idea of broadcast entertainment – and then somewhat by accident. The author James Laver, on leave from France in 1918, recalls how sitting in the lounge of Brown's Hotel in London he had listened to a performance of *Yes, Uncle* currently running in the West End. The performance was relayed not over the airwaves but down a telephone line.

This was a new phenomenon. Although the public were already used to going to the new cinema houses, as they had gone to the theatre and music hall, the idea of entertainment conveyed to the home or the comfortable sitting-room of an hotel was an entirely new one. Until that time, as one author wrote: 'Cultural and educational opportunities for adults came from lectures, reading, and evening institutes. . . . In villages a sing-song in the village hall or the pub, perhaps some remnant of old-time country dancing on the green, maybe a lecture by the vicar on his travels in Switzerland, sufficed as recreation for rural communities who still lived close to the soil.'[1]

Marconi had transmitted a message over the ether across the English channel as long ago as 1899. The advent of the thermionic valve in 1904 was a turning-point for radio. The same valve was later to be used in the development of television, and again nearly fifty years after its invention, in the early models of the computer. These valves made it technically possible to transmit sounds as well as signals. The First World War speeded up the development of radio technology. Yet it was not until the Marconi company's

[1] Leslie Baily, *Scrapbook for the Twenties*.

experiments in 1919 that the notion of 'wireless' gained wider footing.

By the beginning of the 1920s, the British government had licensed some 6,000 radio experimenters. Those early crackling transmissions from Chelmsford – 'Writtle testing, Writtle testing' – were concerned with technical quality rather than content. It was only when the announcer got tired of reciting lists of railway stations that the tenor voice of a Marconi worker, Edward Cooper, and another amateur singer, Winifred Sayer, were heard by the possessors of the crystal sets. The first professional performance in Britain was in 1921 when the *Daily Mail* sponsored a broadcast by Dame Nellie Melba.

In the United States, things at first had moved not much quicker. The first radio station – KDKA in Pittsburgh – had been opened by the Westinghouse company on 2 November 1920, to broadcast the results of the Cox-Harding presidential election. As usual, the worthy – in the form of religious services, concerts and politics – preceded the truly popular.

It was not until Jack Dempsey fought Georges Carpentier for the world heavyweight boxing title in July 1921 that the true potential of the medium became apparent. Three reporters barked their comments into ringside telephones and the fight was relayed to some eighty points throughout the US. By the winter of 1921, while Britons entertained themselves with 'wireless', everyone in America was talking about the new 'radio'. Stations began to spring up in towns and cities everywhere. It was essentially a commercial enterprise.

Meanwhile, in Britain, a lull in the radio test transmissions from Chelmsford had led to a public outcry. In 1922, the manufacturers of the sets approached the government with a proposal to run their own programme. The British Broadcasting Company Ltd was set up with the six largest manufacturers as its shareholders and began a daily service on 14 November 1922.

By the end of 1923, just a year after the start of the first BBC regular service, several hundred thousand British listeners had taken out licences. The first wireless sets were rather basic in design and reception was patchy. Gradually, the ubiquitous

headphones and 'cat's whiskers' began to be replaced by loudspeakers. Mains power was used instead of batteries. Those who
had slung elaborate aerial arrays from poles in their gardens or
chimney-tops started to install indoor aerials in lofts and attics.

> 'Listening-in' was a solemn ritual, like television in later
> years. Crystal sets and headphones could be bought for
> only a few shillings, and a complete set for under ten
> shillings. The wireless set was accepted as a feature of the
> average house, and soon the coils, wires, loudspeakers and
> controls of the primitive sets were combined into one box
> or cabinet.[2]

The moment had come and now needed only the man.

> At nine o'clock in the morning of December the 30th,
> 1922, a very tall Scotsman walked into the B.B.C.
> doorway in London. The liftman showed him up to an
> office . . . no one was there . . . a chair, a table, a
> telephone, an empty desk. . . . The tall man, whose name
> was John Reith, was left there alone. The newly appointed
> Managing Director of the B.B.C. had arrived.[3]

Fearful of the power it had unleashed into private hands, the
government bought out the shareholders in the British Broadcasting Company. On 1 January 1927, the British Broadcasting
Corporation was incorporated under a Royal Charter. Reith was
its first head and he laid down the public service principle which
guided British broadcasting for sixty-five years. By opting for
state control and public service in radio, the British authorities
had deliberately chosen a diametrically opposite route for the new
medium to that of the United States. That pattern was to be
repeated in television, and its consequences have been far
reaching.

[2] John Montgomery, *The Twenties*.
[3] Percy Edgar, *Scrapbook for 1922*.

Reith had strong religious views. He also had firm opinions about correct social behaviour and insisted that the BBC announcers, unseen by their audience, should wear evening dress. He was determined that broadcasting should be conducted as a national service, with definite standards. He wanted the service to reach the greatest possible number of homes, and to provide 'all that is best in every department of human knowledge, endeavour and advancement'.[4]

By contrast, in the United States, the beginnings of radio were marked by a mad scramble for frequencies and an almost total lack of regulation. In his history of broadcasting *Radio, Television and Society* (1950), Charles Siepmann wrote, 'all the virtues and defects of unfettered enterprise were exemplified in the mad rush to develop the new market – rapid expansion, ingenious improvisation, reckless and often unscrupulous competition, in which the interests of the consumer (and, in the long run, of the producer also) were lost from sight.'[5] In spite of the passing of the Communications Act of 1934 and the creation of the Federal Communications Commission as a regulatory body a proposal to 'reserve and allocate' one-fourth of all radio broadcasting facilities to non-profit stations was defeated and the future of broadcasting was set firmly on strictly commercial lines.

It was the beginning of what Newton F. Minow, President Kennedy's 'New Frontier' chairman of the FCC, was to describe three decades later as 'a vast wasteland' of 'game shows, violence, formula comedies about totally unbelievable families, blood and thunder, mayhem, violence, sadism, murder . . . and most of all boredom.'[6]

The BBC became the greatest broadcasting organisation in the world. That position was largely won through the strength of its leaders and the talent of its programme makers. The Corporation was also extraordinarily successful in persuading successive

[4] John Montgomery, *The Twenties*.

[5] Quoted in John Witherspoon and Roselle Kovitz, 'The History of Public Broadcasting', *Current Newspaper*, 1987.

[6] Speech to the National Association of Broadcasters, May 1961.

governments until the 1950s not to allow the advent of commercial competition. In this respect the BBC was virtually unique amongst the public broadcasting organisations of the leading countries of the Western nations. The famous Reithian troika of founding principles was 'information, education and entertainment'. It is striking that those same public service principles were to find their way into the legislation when commercial television was finally established in Britain in 1954.

The power of radio had been amply demonstrated in 1938 when a broadcast by Orson Welles of *The War of the Worlds* panicked the population of America. Its potential in politics was established in the 'fireside chats' given by Stanley Baldwin in his election contest with Ramsay MacDonald. By the 1940s, radio had become the universal medium of communication. Yet it was still possible to confine the flow of information within national boundaries.

In the summer and autumn of 1936 the foreign and especially American newspapers had been full of speculation about the relationship between King Edward VIII and the American divorcee Mrs Wallis Simpson. Under a 'gentlemen's agreement' the British press had agreed only to report the facts of the divorce case in Ipswich. The American press had no such inhibitions. 'King's Moll Reno'd in Ipswich' was one unforgettable headline. It was only when it came to the final act of abdication itself that the BBC made arrangements for Edward's last message to his people to be relayed from Windsor Castle. Cinemas and theatres interrupted their performances to carry the speech. At 10 pm Sir John Reith, Director General of the BBC, announced: 'This is Windsor Castle. His Royal Highness Prince Edward.' A door was heard to close, and then the former king spoke: 'At long last I am able to say a few words of my own. . . .'

As James Laver notes, the early histories of the radio and the cinema were intertwined in a curious yet complementary way. 'For a generation people watched moving pictures without speech, and for almost as long people listened to radio without sight.'[7] Sound came to the cinema in the 1920s but it was to be

---

[7] James Laver, *Between the Wars*.

another generation before television was invented in the late 1930s and another generation after that before it became widely available.

Long before the days of the cinema, the idea of using 'the persistence of vision' had been exploited by early experimenters with moving pictures such as Paul Nipkow, the German inventor. Nipkow is credited with the idea of scanning a picture to break it up into small elements of light and darkness. In the 1880s, Nipkow had designed a primitive disk scanner with punched holes through which light from an illuminated picture reached a forerunner of the photoelectric cell known as a 'selenium cell'.

Various other experiments followed, including those of another Scotsman, John Logie Baird, who successfully demonstrated a scanning system in 1925. Baird's system had the advantage over that of Nipkow of being able to use the new thermionic valves to amplify the current variations, as well as new types of photo-electric cell. Baird's first 'televisor' consisted of a circular cardboard disk cut out of a hat box in which he pierced two spirals of small holes with scissors. A darning needle served as a spindle, and bobbins supplied the means of revolving the disk. Experimenting in 1923 with this Heath Robinson contraption at borrowed lodgings in Hastings, Baird shone a powerful electric lamp through a bull's eye lens on to a little cardboard cross casting a shadow on to the disk then via a selenium cell and an amplifier was able to reproduce a picture a few feet away. On Friday 27 January 1926, Baird demonstrated his new invention to more than forty distinguished members of the Royal Institution in full evening dress. One managed to get his long white beard caught in the disk but was rewarded by seeing the image of his face transmitted.

John Reith was sufficiently impressed by his fellow countryman to allow Baird to use the BBC's London station in 1929 to relay signals on medium wavelength. In 1936, the BBC set up the first regular television service in the world. But Baird's original system was quickly superseded by the development of the Marconi-EMI system of electronic line-scanning by means of the cathode ray tube.

The new technologies of sound and colour in the cinema were accompanied by advances in the transmission of images on the small screen. The thirties saw the birth of television but its development came to a virtual halt during the Second World War. The development of radar during the 1939–45 war advanced the technology of television whilst holding back its availability to the public. This was the era of great film journalism – of the news magazines of Movietone, Pathé and Gaumont – which was to set the style for television.

The arrival of television with its seemingly limitless power for the instantaneous communication of word and image to a mass audience gave both democratic and totalitarian governments pause for thought. As in the early days of the printing press, the power of the new medium was to be contained by licence and censorship and where possible guarded as a prerogative of state. Such it has remained until very recently.

The legendary film studio heads – Zukor, Goldwyn, Mayer, Fox, Warner – were as determined as they were flamboyant. The ineffectual attempts by the US government in the 1930s to control Hollywood studios via the anti-trust legislation provide an instructive comparison for those who would seek to control the infinitely more powerful and complex world-wide media corporations of today.

The Sky Barons seek to emulate the power of the great studios in their heyday. 'Vertical integration' has been carried to its logical extreme by Silvio Berlusconi in Italy, who controls Europe's largest communications empire. Berlusconi not only owns the most powerful commercial TV networks and makes the programmes for them, he also possesses the advertising agency that produces the television commercials for the products sold in his huge Standa retail chain – which of course are advertised on his own stations.

On a truly world-wide scale, Sony Corporation of Japan makes a myriad forms of consumer hardware – including televisions, radio sets and hi-fis. Sony went a long way to fulfilling the software needs for these products with the purchase first of CBS Records and then of Columbia Pictures.

Despite the interruption of 1939–45, television, radio and cinema were the bricks on which a whole new generation was to build its empires. The new generation included entrepreneurs prepared to exploit the increasing convergence between films, music, broadcasting, journalism and publishing – a convergence speeded up by technology and given world-wide scope for monopoly by artificial satellites.

The 'global village' predicted by Marshall McLuhan, in *The Medium is the Massage* (1967), is spurred ever nearer by a dozen or so world-wide corporations whose activities encompass not just production of programmes, but manufacture of electronic hardware, ownership of satellites and communications channels, newsprint, broadcasting stations, record companies and publishing corporations.

IV

The Satellite Age

On 10 July 1962 NASA, the US National Aeronautics and Space Administration, successfully launched the first communications satellite into orbit from Cape Canaveral. At the receiving station in Goonhilly Down, Cornwall, British engineers saw their NASA counterparts at the control centre in Andover, Maine, in flickering, ghostly images bounced across the Atlantic via the Telstar satellite. Unlike today's satellites anchored in synchronous orbit with the earth, Telstar continuously circled the globe and had to be 'caught' for the brief periods when its orbit made it visible to both continents.

In the event, the French receiving station at Pleumeur Bodou managed to lock on first and Goonhilly only came on line for the final minute of the brief but historic transmission which included a message from the chairman of the American Telephone and Telegraph Co., which had built Telstar. Later it was Europe's turn to speak to America. The French sent live pictures of Yves Montand singing, the British, more prosaically, a test card and an official greeting.

It was the year that the United States put their first astronaut John Glenn in orbit aboard Friendship 7 and the year that the world came close to the brink of catastrophe over the October Cuban missile crisis. The age of satellite television had begun. In the future such events would be relayed simultaneously to audiences around the globe.

Arthur C. Clarke, the science writer, had predicted the advent of communications via satellite as long ago as 1945. It was not until 1959, however, that the Soviet Union succeeded in launching the first satellite, Sputnik, into an orbit around the earth.

Once again it was to be military rather than civilian considerations that were to provide the spur to new developments in communications technology – just as the First World War had advanced radio and the Second World War had done the same for television through the developments in radar.

Both the Russians and the Americans knew that satellites in fixed orbit round the earth would be the key to developing the military technologies that would dominate the rest of the century. The so-called 'Space Race', with its artificial competition to be first to land a man on the moon, was a by-product of the strategic and military importance of space, both for future weapons systems and for intelligence-gathering.

As early as 1929 Frank Whittle, a young graduate from the RAF's Cranwell College, had suggested that aircraft might be driven not by propellers but by jet propulsion. Ten years later, in 1939, Whittle succeeded in building a prototype of an engine in which air was sucked in at the front, compressed and heated up. Fuel was injected into the combustion chamber and ignited, the result being the huge backward thrust associated with a rocket. The rockets to be used in the space programme, however, would be propelled not by jet engines but by liquid fuel.

Wernher von Braun and a group of fellow German military scientists were captured by the Americans along with the V2 rocket site at Peenemunde in Northern Germany, from which the deadly missiles had been targeted at London. By the 1950s it was business as before when von Braun worked on the US ballistic missile programmes such as Juno and Pershing. But von Braun also led the group that orbited Explorer I in 1958. As deputy administrator at NASA, he developed the Saturn V rocket used in the Apollo programme in the sixties and seventies.

At 3.56 am Central European Time on 21 July 1969, Neil Armstrong, commander of the Apollo 11 space mission stepped from the lunar module, Eagle, onto the surface of the Moon's Sea of Tranquillity and said: 'That's one small step for a man, one giant leap for mankind.' His image and his words were relayed instantaneously to an audience of hundreds of millions throughout the world via a Westinghouse camera built to withstand heat, cold, shock, meteorite bombardment and particle radiation. The signals were received at earth stations in the Mojave Desert in the USA and in Australia and Spain, passed to Mission Control in Houston and then on by satellite and terrestrial relays across the oceans and the continents.

At the EBU headquarters in Geneva where the Eurovision retransmission was coordinated, the wives and children of the multinational staff gathered together to watch cheered wildly. In a corner, the Swiss photographer hired to record the moment for prosperity snored gently, exhausted by the long wait.

Von Braun has rightly been called the father of the space age. The Second World War however had also seen the important development of radar and the practical use of primitive computers. Notable here was the machine developed by Alan Turing, the brilliant young Cambridge mathematician who was brought to Bletchley Park to help break the German Enigma codes. By the end of the war, thousands of people were involved in the Bletchley Ultra project, many painstakingly working on the 'electro-mechanical computing machines'.

That work today would be performed by a microscopic printed circuit, thousands of times smaller but essentially the same in the principles of its construction as the bulky old Ultra machines. The Space Race compressed everything. Scientific developments that would have taken decades to unfold were achieved in months because of the overwhelming fear – particularly on the part of the US after the Russians had succeeded in putting a man in orbit before them – that the enemy might be one or even two steps ahead. Nowhere was this super-accelerated development more marked than in the sciences of rocketry and computers.

The historical point at which the two disciplines of rocket technology and computers meshed was the Apollo programme. Von Braun had contributed the Saturn rocket to get the craft into space. In order to land a space module on the moon, however, it was essential that the ship had its own onboard computer as it would need to pass out of range of mission control in Houston. Computers at that time took up an area the size of an average room. The work pioneered at Pennsylvania on a machine to calculate gunnery tables had produced a computer that weighed 30 tons, occupied 1,500 square feet and contained more than 18,000 of our old friend the thermionic valve. The demands of the Apollo programme – and in particular the requirement of Apollo 11 – were for a computer that could fit inside the tight confines of the space module.

The successful development of the small-scale computer by IBM meant that in future any spacecraft – whether stationary or mobile – could be fitted with such an instrument to manoeuvre it in space. That development was also of immense commercial benefit. It led directly to the personal computer which today is a standard item of equipment used by practically every office and many households in the Western world. In the hands of an author, it is an invaluable instrument capable of juggling paragraphs and text for a whole book within the confines of a plastic disk measuring 3.5 inches square. A simple connection to a telephone line allows the machine to become a means of delivering articles from London to a newspaper in Los Angeles 6,000 miles away in a matter of a few seconds, as computer talks to computer via a telecommunications satellite thousands of miles above our heads.

As in the past, the technology for the communication of information and ideas is often shared with the military and is vital to modern warfare. In 1988, the US was faced with domination of the high-definition television (HDTV) industry by the Japanese and Europeans. The Pentagon decided to spend millions of dollars to encourage the development of HDTV in the United States. It was a move designed to safeguard an industry considered essential for the development of the defence of the United States and in particular its 'Star Wars' SDI programmes.

Later that year, on 11 December, Europe's first direct broadcast satellite Astra soared into orbit on a French-built Ariane rocket launched from the Kourou Space Centre in French Guiana. It was cocooned in an aluminium and fibre container alongside Skynet-4B, a UK military satellite destined to provide communications between the British Admiralty and its surface vessels and submarines at sea around the world. Astra was also the means by which Rupert Murdoch was to launch Sky Television, his direct attack on the television market of the UK.

Military spy satellites were instrumental in both the Falklands War and the Gulf War. Their ability to observe minute detail on the earth's surface was a major factor in persuading the USA and USSR to conclude nuclear weapons agreements. Because of satellites and high-resolution photography, it is no longer possible to conceal large weapons systems on the ground.

During the Gulf War against Saddam Hussein's Iraq, Western television viewers were given a grandstand view of cruise missiles flying down Baghdad streets mapped out earlier by satellite, and of 'smart' bombs that could be delivered down ventilation shafts photographed from space. Reporters from Ted Turner's Cable News Network (CNN) provided the pictures, uplinked by satellite, of missiles delivered with the aid of in some cases the same satellite.

Again, during the abortive coup of August 1991 against President Gorbachev in the Soviet Union, US spy satellites were able to seek out his whereabouts under house arrest in the Crimea. Telephone intercepts using key words such as the President's name were set up to determine what was happening.

More importantly, the old-style Stalinists who led the failed putsch appeared to have no inkling of the new power of TV and satellite media. Together with open-line telecommunications, these were used by the supporters of Gorbachev and Boris Yeltsin to nullify dictates handed down through the ossified communications systems of the Communist Party.

Within hours of the pronouncement of the coup, forces of resistance mobilised across the Soviet continent. Even as the plotters were attempting to impose some form of media control, viewers in Byelorussia and Georgia were able to get outside information via CNN, beamed in via satellite under the policies of glasnost promoted by Gorbachev and his close ally Alexander Yakovlev. The early braggadocio prediction of CNN owner Ted Turner – 'We're gonna be all over the world' – appeared finally to have come true.

In June 1954 the first successful experiments in exchanging programmes between the UK and Continental Europe had taken place. Broadcasting organisations in seven countries founded the Eurovision system: Britain, Italy, West Germany, Switzerland, Belgium, Italy and France.

Eurovision had a network of forty-six television transmitters. If the Italian state broadcaster RAI wished to televise a programme from London, the BBC sent the programme by landline to Dover, from where it was transmitted by radio across the Channel to France. The programme then went via a series of relay transmitters across France, through Switzerland, over the Alps and down through Italy.

The technical and organisational problems involved in such exchanges were considerable. The early Eurovision employed some 4,000 miles of radio circuits, while the equipment needed comprised as many as 25,000 valves. Aerials has to be sited in remote mountainous regions such as the Jungfrau.

Having crossed the English Channel and the Alps the search was on to cross the Atlantic. It was to be another eight years before the launch of the first communications satellite, Telstar, brought about the potential means of simplifying such programme exchanges to the point where today they can all be carried via a single object in space.

'Science, already, has achieved marvellous things,' Claude Graham White had written in 1930. 'We can talk by wireless telephone across immense distances. Soon, perhaps, we may be able to see, as well as to hear, anyone on the other side of the Atlantic to whom we may be speaking. And with the perfection of the long-range high-speed flying machine it will be possible for us not only to annihilate distance with words, and even with scenes transmitted by television, but to travel ourselves at such a pace that oceans will be crossed in hours, and a journey to the most distant part of the world will not occupy more than a few days.'[1]

As White had prophesied: 'That is what the future holds forth; that is what we shall obtain as our final conquest of the air. We

---

[1] Claude Graham White, *Flying*.

shall have a "magic carpet" which will span oceans and continents between dawn and dusk, shortening Jules Verne's eighty days circuit of the globe to not more, probably, than about eighty hours.'

The new satellite technology took the conjectures of fantasy into the realms of possibility. The magic carpet was ready to fly – what use would the Sky Barons make of it?

V

The Old School: Murdoch

The engineers located Siding 29 of the Canadian Pacific Railroad where the gold of the Prairies met the indigo of the Rockies and the going got tough. Today the siding serves the township of Banff which lies eighty miles west of Calgary. The railway came to Banff in 1883. Cornelius Van Horne, Canadian Pacific's Vice-President at the time, said: 'If we can't export the scenery, we'll import the tourists.' In a day it is easy to see a dozen or more glaciers. In the surrounding Alberta foothills the slopes are rich with spruce, alpine fir, Douglas fir, Lodgepole pine, Engelmann spruce and whitebark pine. A far cry from the vanishing forests of Brazil.

Banff is bear country. A pensioned and peaceful elk is on call to graze outside tourists' windows but grizzly bears (*ursus arctos horribilis*) come down from the mountains in spring and early summer to the lush foothills to raise their cubs and if disturbed may maul the children of local citizens. In June 1980, Banff was terrorised for a week by a grizzly which attacked three and killed one of its inhabitants. Bear warnings issued by the Canadian Ministry of the Environment advise: 'make a wide detour or leave the area'.

There was a bear warning out the week in June 1989 that Roberto Marinho came to Banff. He came at the invitation of the Annual Banff Television Festival to accept the festival's award for 'Outstanding Achievement' for his Brazilian television network Rede Globo. Past recipients of honours from this once struggling but now popular and respected festival include Britain's Granada Television and Channel 4 as well as Gregory Peck, now honorary president of the festival's international advisory board. Peck described Banff as 'one of the best, most interesting, most civilised events I have ever attended'. Other laureates have included Lord Olivier, Ed Asner and Peter Ustinov.

The keynote speaker at Banff was Andrew Neil, at the time both Editor of Murdoch's *Sunday Times* and Chairman of Murdoch's Sky Television. Neil's lecture was sponsored by the Canadian Broadcasting Corporation, under threat like its British cousin the BBC from financial cuts, government pressure and the new wave of private, commercial broadcasters.

Murdoch's lieutenant is sometimes referred to on the *Sunday Times* newsroom floor as 'Rambo'. In this genteel atmosphere of public service and quality broadcasting, Neil's arrival was not unlike that of a grizzly in the placid streets of Banff. In a soft, mid-Atlantic Scots, Neil proceeded to lay about the assembled representatives of what he called 'the established broadcasters' with only the faintest suggestion of contempt.

Neil's main target was the BBC. He savaged their 'tortured accents', their 'costume department led drama' and their 'class attitudes'. It was a speech that turned out to be a dress rehearsal for the MacTaggart Memorial Lecture Rupert Murdoch himself was to give later in the year at the Edinburgh Television Festival. A speech which in the event was reported by the *Sunday Times* across six columns on the leader page with its message 'In every area of economic activity in which competition is attainable, it is much to be preferred to monopoly.' Especially in television, the piece might have added. Neil likened the attitude of the established broadcasters towards the television revolution with that of the Duke of Wellington to the advent of the railways. In 1883 Wellington had complained in the House of Lords: 'These contraptions will enable the working classes to move about.'

At the time, Murdoch's Sky Television was about to become locked in a bitter struggle for the UK satellite television market with British Satellite Broadcasting.

Like his father's contemporary Roberto Marinho, Rupert Murdoch is first and foremost a newspaper man. His has been an astonishing career, owing as much to the determination that is innate as well as to the ability to grasp the reality of the new communications world.

One episode from Rupert Murdoch's early career in Australia serves to demonstrate this determination. When Murdoch inherited his father Sir Keith's Melbourne press empire he set to work tirelessly to expand it and devoted himself to the task of beating the opposition. This crusade soon brought him into conflict with Sir Frank Packer. Rupert Murdoch was looking to expand from Melbourne to Sydney. He began with the purchase of a small local newspaper group operating in the northern and western suburbs of the city.

In the early 1960s three families ruled the Sydney press – the Fairfaxes who owned the *Sydney Morning Herald* and the *Sun*; the Packers who owned the *Daily* and *Sunday Telegraph* and Ezra Norton who owned the *Mirror*. In addition, John Fairfax was the largest stockholder in Sydney's Channel 7 television and the Packer group controlled Channel 9. In Melbourne, Fairfax joined with the *Herald* and *Weekly Times* to control Channel 7 there and Packer allied himself with Electronic Industries which controlled Melbourne's Channel 9, creating the beginnings of two national networks.

Norton sold the *Mirror* to his closest rivals the Fairfaxes, thus avoiding shifting the balance of power in Packer's favour. But the *Mirror* proved to be a drain on finances and, in 1960, Fairfax sold it to the twenty-nine-year-old Rupert Murdoch. He remodelled the paper on the lines of the UK namesake which he had admired when at university in England. It was a success but that very success brought Murdoch up against Frank Packer.

Already alarmed by Murdoch's sortie into the Sydney suburban paper field, Sir Frank Packer had decided to merge his own suburban papers with those of another group. Frank's eldest son Clyde was put in to run the operation and they used downtime, when the presses were idle, at the Mirror Newspapers to print additional copies. In May 1960, with Murdoch's acquisition of Mirror Newspapers, that downtime was no longer available.

Clyde Packer found an alternative printing establishment. He was friendly with Francis James, the publisher of a weekly paper, *The Anglican*. James had fallen on hard times and his printing works was in the hands of a receiver who had called for tenders for the business. Clyde told James he intended to approach the receiver to make a deal. James, anxious not to lose control, tipped Murdoch off. On 7 June, while dining at a restaurant in Killara, about twenty kilometres from the Anglican Press premises, James received a telephone call from the receiver informing him that he had been ejected and that a band of six men led by Clyde Packer and his brother Kerry had occupied the printing works and were in the process of changing the locks. James's lawyer advised that possession was, in the circumstances, nine-tenths of the law.

James, the son of an Anglican clergyman, had been a wartime RAF pilot. Shot down over Germany, he later escaped from a prisoner-of-war camp on his third attempt. He went back to war. Dashing home, he changed into a tracksuit, made a quick call to Rupert Murdoch and set off for his printing works.

Murdoch rapidly despatched photographers to the site of the impending battle and contacted Frank Browne, the *Sunday Mirror*'s sports columnist who mustered a group of heavies on the steps of Sydney Town Hall. By this time Murdoch's photographers had their first picture of Clyde Packer holding the print works manager by the collar, about to throw him out into the street.

At one o'clock in the morning the attack began. James led one group to the rear of the building where they gained entry through an unguarded lavatory window while Frank Browne's forces led the frontal assault. By 2.30 am it was all over. A battered Kerry Packer led out his brother Clyde and their defeated troops while James led his supporters in prayer.

That morning's *Mirror* ran the headline 'KNIGHT'S SONS IN CITY BRAWL'. The story was liberally supported by photographic evidence. Later in court, James won the day and supported by Murdoch cash kept his business afloat. It was an event which Murdoch might well have recalled twenty-six years later during the notorious battle of Wapping with the British Fleet Street unions.

Like Marinho, who was one of the first of the old press barons to move into electronic media, Murdoch often recalls his father when speaking about his own career. 'As you know, my whole life has been with newspapers,' he said at an address to the International Institute of Communications in Washington in 1988. 'So was my father's. You could say it was my destiny to be in love with newspapers. One of my earliest recollections of my father was seeing him early in the morning, sitting in bed, the covers scattered with newspapers.' Murdoch continued: 'Articles would be ringed; facts underlined; page margins filled with shorthand queries. Why didn't the *Sun* have that story the opposition made so much play with? Why was the final edition front page such a mess? Who was that bright young writer another paper was featuring? Could someone have a quiet word with him?

'It was an original and exhilarating, grandstand introduction to the art of newspapering,' said Murdoch, 'and I suppose it is no surprise that I never had the slightest inclination to try my hand at anything else.' Except television, films and publishing (to name but three), he might have added.

Murdoch himself tackled the charge of 'empire-building' in Washington. 'A great deal,' he told his audience, 'has been written and said about the concept of the possibility of global networks. . . . My company, News Corporation – probably because we already cover a wide range of media and entertainment across four continents – is frequently mentioned. Indeed every time we make a new acquisition, no matter how modest, analysts are quick to suggest that it is just another step in our ambition to build some sort of global communications empire.' Murdoch continued: 'Last month, when we announced our $3 billion purchase of *TV Guide* and Triangle Publications, a *Wall Street Journal* headline dutifully recorded: "Move will balloon Murdoch's debt but help fulfil his vision of a global media empire." Well, I've got news for the *Wall Street Journal*'s headline writer,' said Murdoch firmly. 'Our debt won't balloon. . . . Buying *TV Guide* was an opportunity no mainstream publisher could possibly resist, regardless of visions.' Murdoch left his audience in no doubt where he stood on the issues of world-wide media monopolies. 'I believe that there will be global media networks. I believe they will be demand-driven by multinational marketing companies, the IBMs, Sonys, Toyotas, Volvos, Coca-Colas of this world.'

The policy of buying up so much had seemed logical enough in 1988. 'Is a global communications network a reality?' Murdoch asked rhetorically. 'My answer unequivocally is "yes". Are there really going to be world-wide media networks? My answer is "yes", both print and electronic. Is it really going to be possible for an advertiser to achieve, in practice, a single order with the media of his choice across the world? Again my answer is "yes".'

As we now know with hindsight, News Corporation's debt did in fact balloon as it became clear that Murdoch, like other Sky Barons, had found too many media opportunities too hard to resist. But Murdoch's survival of that crisis, the crash of BSB and the outcome of legislation in the UK affecting ITV – all in the short time since 1988 – have left him in a position much stronger than even he could have hoped for.

On 26 March 1992, Rupert Murdoch made another major address, this time to the Business of Entertainment conference in New York. The venue was the Pierre Hotel in Manhattan. To those who had heard Murdoch's speech some four years earlier in Washington, it was impossible not to reflect on the astounding changes that had taken place in the intervening period – the end of the Eastern Bloc, the Gulf War, the move towards majority rule in South Africa. It was also impossible not to reflect that Murdoch's vision of a global media empire, despite some hair-raising financial moments, had now come to pass.

In typically self-deprecating style Murdoch, who seems increasingly aware of the passing of time, recalled how a year earlier he had celebrated his sixtieth birthday – 'if celebrating is the word for what you do on that occasion.' He had spent much of the previous year restructuring his company's finances and decided to take a break. 'So, although appeasing my puritanical Scottish ancestors by mortifying myself at an Arizona health spa, my wife and I felt justified in escaping into the desert for a night at the movies.'

It was wholly characteristic of Murdoch's mordant streak that the choice for this touching tryst was not some romantic melodrama but Jonathan Demme's unnerving psycho-thriller *Silence of the Lambs*. 'I thought this was pretty tolerant of us,' added Murdoch. The reason for this, he explained, was that *Silence of the Lambs* had just replaced *Home Alone* as the US all-time top grosser: 'And at Fox, we don't just watch *Home Alone* we worship it.'

With tongue firmly in cheek, Murdoch went on to explain how he had a personal interest in the *Silence of the Lambs* star, Anthony Hopkins: 'Before he starred in *Silence of the Lambs*, where he played a homicidal, cannibalistic lunatic, he had attracted a lot of attention in a British play called *Pravda*, where he portrayed a maniacal colonial newspaper tycoon, allegedly based on me.' Murdoch paused while his audience waited. 'So I suppose he's in danger of being typecast.'

Result, one disarmed audience. The comment was even more piquant to the audience of film executives and journalists, since earlier in the month Murdoch had watched the departure of his Twentieth-Century Fox chief Barry Diller and joined the ranks of movie moguls by taking over personal control of the historic studio. In a brief anecdote, Murdoch had demonstrated not only that here was a person acutely conscious of his role and reputation, but also one who could apparently be trusted not to get carried away with the quite awesome power bestowed upon him.

It was equally characteristic, however, that the full extent of that power was then rolled out in the manner of one of the old-style May Day parades in Moscow. 'We have assembled, acquired or invented an absolutely unique collection of media assets in almost every phase of the business,' said Murdoch, listing the activities of News Corporation, including its recent entry into the electronic database business. Turning to the company's news operations, he noted that in this same month (March 1992), his UK satellite operation BSkyB had for the first time moved into operating profit. 'But at the same time, one of its channels, Sky News, has quietly, if expensively, become the first building block of what we envision will become the premier world-wide electronic newsgathering network anywhere. Ask anyone in Europe, and particularly at the BBC,' he went on, 'and you will be told that Sky News has added a new and better dimension to television journalism.'

Murdoch continued pointedly: 'Taking nothing away from CNN, which has done an outstanding job, I would point out that Sky News, the Fox [his US television network] news service and the News Corporation's combined reach – which have together over three thousand journalists spread over every continent and every country – leave us with an army of newsgatherers second to none both with regard to their access to news and ability to bring news from anywhere into people's homes.'

As in Washington four years earlier, Murdoch made his intentions quite clear. 'Because of our uniquely independent and international situation, we will have the flexibility to more fully integrate all our media operations and respond to new technologies as they become available in the years ahead.' Then, aware of the implications of this, he added: 'Just as we have learned over the last three years that political freedoms cannot be separated from economic freedoms, neither can they be separated from freedom of information.'

Murdoch went on to outline a vision of a global news and entertainment supply based on freedom of choice, the supremacy of the consumer and the Americanisation of everything.

Murdoch is the archetype of our Sky Barons. More than anyone else, he has been able to operate as a citizen of the twenty-first century, transcending national boundaries and breaking old dominations. We shall see more of his career as our story unfolds, from the early challenge to the Australian press barons like the Packers through to his systematic attack on the old TV duopoly of the BBC and ITV in the United Kingdom and his creation of a network to challenge the three giants in the United States.

VI

Captain Courageous: Turner

On 11 December 1938, the producer David O. Selznick ordered the burning of forty acres of old and outworn exterior sets on the backlot of his Hollywood studio acquired from RKO-Pathé. It was one of the first scenes to be filmed for *Gone With The Wind* – the burning of Atlanta.

Robert Edward ('Ted') Turner III was born in Cincinnatti, Ohio earlier that year. There was Irish, Dutch and German blood on his mother's side and English, Scottish and French on his father's. The mixture was to prove explosive.

Ted Turner was born in troubled times. In 1938, the Spanish Civil War was reaching its climax, Hitler marched into Austria to consummate the Anschluss, the Japanese bombed Canton and Shanghai, Chamberlain spoke of 'peace in our time' and Orson Welles panicked the population of the United States with his radio broadcast of H. G. Wells's *The War of the Worlds*.

On 3 September 1939, Selznick and his director Victor Fleming were filming the titles for *Gone With The Wind* ('the four greatest words since *Birth Of A Nation*') word by giant word. During a break in filming, the crew heard on the radio of Britain's declaration of war on Nazi Germany. They returned to their task. 'Wind', as the film was known, was to premiere in Atlanta before Christmas. There had been wars before and there would be wars again and it was predicted that the film would gross at least nineteen million dollars.

Selznick's production, based on Margaret Mitchell's epic saga, went on to win a record eight Oscars. MGM, *Gone With The Wind* and the city of Atlanta were all to play key roles in the infant Ted's later life. MGM, indeed, runs through the story of the Sky Barons like a crimson thread.

Turner's father was a native of Mississippi. A salesman by trade, he later set up a billboard business in Savannah, mother city of Georgia – the thirteenth and last of the original colonies. Savannah was founded in February 1733 when James E. Oglethorpe sailed up the Savannah river aboard the good ship *Anne* and established what was to be America's first planned city. The sea and the sense of adventure were to be another formative influence on the young Ted.

Three hundred miles to the north-west of Savannah lies Atlanta – capital of the South. It was here during the Civil War that the ruthless Union commander General Sherman had puffed on his ever-present cigar as his troops put the city to the torch. The ensuing firestorm more or less razed the original city. It was to Atlanta that Ed Turner moved his family and set up another billboard business, Turner Outdoor Advertising. For a while the firm prospered, so much so that the young Ted Turner was encouraged to return to Atlanta to join his father's firm after a spell of two years in the Coast Guard.

Ted's real ambition had been to attend the prestigious US Naval Academy in Annapolis. His record was not altogether unblemished. He had been thrown out of Brown University on two occasions. The first suspension was for setting light to his room. The second was for 'repeatedly breaching dormitory rules concerning women in the rooms'.

Instead of joining the Navy, Ted settled for the humbler Coast Guard. 'I, who would one day affect the destiny of the nation,' he said later, 'was cleaning crap.'

Ted joined his father in 1960. It quickly became apparent that the business, far from thriving, was up against the wall. Three years later, depressed by mounting debts and the tragic death of Ted's sister, Ed Turner committed suicide after first arranging to sell the business.

Ted set out to rescue what was left of his inheritance. He refused to hand over the billboard leases that were part of the sale arranged by his father before his death. He threatened to burn the company's records. He said he would build competing billboards. He threatened court action. In the face of this onslaught, the would-be purchasers gave in. They forgot the sale and took stock in Turner's company instead. Still only twenty-four, Ted had been thrust in at the deep end.

The influence of fathers on sons is one of the more fascinating aspects of our story of today's Sky Barons. Whatever faults Turner's father may have had, his son clearly felt he owed him a debt. When Ted Turner's picture finally appeared on the cover of *Success* magazine, he held up a copy to the heavens and asked: 'Dad? Do you see this? I made the cover of *Success* magazine! Is that enough?'

Turner's base remained firmly in Atlanta. His original HQ was located in a Southern-style mansion on Techwood Drive where he now has a garden of sixteen satellite dishes connected by five miles of optical fibre cables with the modern CNN headquarters in downtown Atlanta.

Atlanta is the geographical hub of the south-eastern United States. It was the terminal for the Western and Atlantic Railroad and has always been associated with the latest in transportation, trade and culture. By the 1980s it was rapidly becoming the satellite technology capital of America.

Atlanta is home to Coca-Cola and RJR Nabisco as well as Turner's enterprises. 'Drawn by low land prices and cheap non-union labour, new businesses proliferated and the big banks, hoteliers and international investors moved in. From the glittering galleries of Peachtree Street to the commuter county golf courses with their $15,000 initiation fees, it was a rip-roaring, all American yarn of enterprise, opportunism and fast bucks,' wrote the *Guardian* (22 January 1990). No one in their right mind would have put an international news network there.

Today the bubble threatens to burst. Rapid development and population expansion have led to environmental and pollution problems and the city is threatened with a water shortage by the year 2010. Atlanta is also facing a huge skill shortage and an incalculable wastage of potential workers. But all this remains well below the surface, even in the newly created 'Underground Atlanta'. Located at the historic birthplace of the city and forming its natural centre, the subterranean development comprises shops, restaurants and entertainment ranging from 'Fat Tuesday' (New Orleans gumbo and po-boy sandwiches) to the 'Teryaki Temple' and 'Udderly Cool'.

The Coca-Cola company has plans to build a 45,000 square foot pavilion to be known as 'The World of Coca-Cola' complete with interactive displays and exhibits of memorabilia to enable visitors to learn about the beverage that was first served in Atlanta more than a hundred years ago. 'Underground Atlanta' is actually the city's original street and railroad level hidden beneath modern viaducts. It is a six city block area covering twelve acres. Atlanta will also host the 1996 Olympic Games.

Many places in Atlanta bear the name Peachtree after the Civil War battle of Peachtree Creek only four miles to the north of the city on 20 July 1864. A few blocks downtown from the Peachtree Centre with its glass façades and banks, along International Boulevard, stands the CNN Centre.

The building went up in 1976 and was acquired by Turner in 1986. From the lower level which was once an ice skating rink there towers a fourteen-storey glass roofed atrium decorated with the flags of the nations. The complex includes the Omni Hotel with 470 luxury rooms all with balconies onto the atrium, the Omni Coliseum, home of the Atlanta Hawks and 17,000 seat venue for circuses and pop concerts, cinemas, offices, consulates and 'Reggies' – 'an authentic British pub'. 'Reggies' was founded by a descendant of Lord Cornwallis, Reggie Mitchell, ex Royal Marines and Punjab Frontier Force. Reggie sports a Ted Turner lookalike moustache and serves a potent cocktail of rum, orange juice, *crème de banane* and lime known as 'Turner's Triumph' in honour of Ted's America's Cup victory.

No visit to Atlanta is complete without a guided tour of the CNN studios, billed as a forty-five minute 'walking experience through CNN and Headline News'. After paying the $4 entrance fee, the visitor mounts from the ground floor of the vast atrium with its *Gone With The Wind* boutique selling mementos of the film on a seemingly endless escalator reminiscent of Charles de Gaulle airport near Paris, to be greeted at the top by a giant cutout of Ted Turner himself, surrounded by his yachting trophies and memorabilia.

The tour guide has a machinegun delivery, punctuating his commentary with repeated warnings to 'watch your step'. The visitor is clearly on dangerous territory. Statistics fly in a staccato monotone: twenty-seven bureaus, eighteen international and nine national, received in ninety countries, over two hundred affiliates throughout the world, sixty million households in America. Only the North and South Poles it seems are beyond Turner's reach. 'Don't worry,' says the guide, 'one day Ted will get there.'

From a glass-lined corridor the visitor looks down on the CNN newsroom with its three 'anchor' sets and a vast assignments desk stretching down the centre of the room. Other circular desks reminiscent of a piano bar or baccarat table are known as writer/producer 'pods'. The writers sit on the outside with producers and copy editors assigning and checking stories on the inside.

The female presenters, likened unkindly by some to 'Barbie Dolls', are smart and coiffured. The men wear jackets, ties and shirts up top but jeans and trainers from the waist down. As well as the CNN and Headline News services, the Hispanic network Telemundo transmits a CNN news service in Spanish to an audience of thirty million Spanish speakers in the United States and Latin America.

On the way out the guide points out the North Tower where the executive offices are located. With reverence he indicates Ted Turner's own suite high up on the fourteenth floor looking down on the flags of the nations and the *Gone With The Wind* boutique.

Irving Thalberg, who had headed production at MGM since its founding days, had initially advised Louis B. Mayer against 'Wind'. 'I'm too tired to burn Atlanta,' Thalberg had reputedly said.[1] David Selznick had signed over the distribution rights for 'Wind' to Metro Goldwyn Mayer in exchange for the services of Clark Gable. At the time Gable was under contract to MGM, the

[1] Peter Hay, *MGM – When the Lion Roars.*

studio owned by Selznick's father-in-law, Louis B. Mayer. Selznick had originally wanted Errol Flynn to play Rhett Butler.

Both Flynn and Clark Gable were, in casting terms, 'dangerous men'. 'The dangerous man,' wrote Ethan Mordden, 'is sexy and tough, often an outlaw but honourable once you get through to him.'[2] Darryl Zanuck outlined the type more cynically: 'Women love bums.'

Ted has always been a ladies' man and was named number one in *Playgirl*'s list of the world's ten sexiest men. 'I'd like to introduce my girlfriend, Jane Fonda,' Ted told an assembled crowd of journalists at Cannes. What the fiery Miss Fonda – once taunted by the American press as 'Hanoi Jane' for her stand during the Vietnam war but seen by some as a potential First Lady to a future President Turner – said to her consort afterwards can only be guessed at. Turner soon amended this to 'my fiancée' and later in 1991 the couple married.

Turner has been likened to an amalgam of Errol Flynn and Clark Gable. His moustache matches that sported by Flynn in *The Private Lives of Elizabeth and Essex*. He has been dubbed 'Errol Flynn in grey flannel'. But clearly Gable was his model down to that famous last line so nearly censored by the Hays Office: 'Frankly, my dear, I don't give a damn.'

Turner had won the America's Cup in 1977 at the helm of the *Courageous*. He had survived and come first in the notorious Fastnet Race of 1979 when just 87 out of 306 boats finished the course and nineteen lives were lost. At the victory press conference after the America's Cup, Turner fell over backwards – drunk.

Ted Turner has a sense of history. In Las Vegas in 1989, he told the Video Software Dealers Association that television and films could make profound social and behavioural changes. 'That's why I have a moustache,' he declared. 'I'm just as cornball as anybody else.'

Atlanta, the Civil War and *Gone With The Wind* led Ted to name his third son Beauregard after Pierre Gustave T.

[2] Ethan Mordden, *The Hollywood Studios*.

Beauregard, the Southern hero who designed the battle flag of the Confederacy with its white stars embedded in a blue cross of St Andrew on a field of red. His second son was to be named Rhett and rumour has it that it was only his then wife who dissuaded him from naming his youngest daughter Scarlett and blessed the child instead with the more mundane Sarah Jean. His first daughter was called Laura Lee. The first-born was, of course, destined to be Robert Edward IV.

In 1978 he called his salesmen to his 5,000 acre plantation in Savannah, aptly named 'Hope', for a conference. Pacing the living room as if it were the poopdeck of a pirate ship, he told them: 'I am your captain, we're going to go out and raid all the other ships on the ocean. We want their advertising and we're going to get it!' This was the authentic voice of the swashbuckler from Atlanta, known throughout the USA as Scallywag City.

In 1967, Turner acquired an ailing AM radio station in Chattanooga and then added two more stations. But the empire really began to take off in 1970. By this time Turner had consolidated his father's businesses and amassed sufficient funds and credit to buy the Atlanta UHF television station WRJR – Channel 17. It was the smallest of the five Atlanta television stations and the only one on UHF. There were few sets tunable to UHF, the standard VHF being almost universal.

In Turner's own words, his station was run by 'a bunch of hippies . . . and they ran the few commercials we did have in black and white, upside down, but nobody was watching, so it didn't matter.' On one occasion, Bill Tush, the anchor, introduced a dog sporting a shirt and tie as his co-anchor. On another occasion, Tush donned a gorilla suit to introduce a report on guerrilla warfare.

Turner changed the WRJR call sign to WTCG, merged his billboard and broadcasting holding and renamed his company Turner Communications. Later, WTCG was to become WTBS – Turner's super station and the springboard for the Turner broadcasting empire. The empire grew rapidly. In 1976, Turner bought the Atlanta Braves baseball team and, in 1977, the Atlanta Hawks basketball team. In 1979, the Turner Communications

Group became the Turner Broadcasting System Inc. And in 1980, CNN – the first twenty-four hour news channel in the world – was launched with a subscriber base of 1.7 million.

For years Turner was sometimes scorned, sometimes derided and seldom taken seriously. European public service broadcasters saw him as a joke unique to the United States, one of those oddballs who could only exist in America's Deep South. The smartass nicknames proliferated: 'The Mouth of the South', 'Terrible Ted', 'Captain Outrageous'. His Cable News Network (CNN) was dubbed the 'Chicken Noodle Network'. Many of those who dismissed him in the early years came to fear him or become his ardent suitors a few years later.

There is a watershed in most men's lives. Turner's came in 1985. In sociological perspective, the moustache belonged to the buccaneering Errol Flynn and *Captain Blood* until 1985 and to the Southern gentleman modelled on Clark Gable's Rhett Butler thereafter. The fact is that Turner had the physique and the looks for either role. 'Salt and pepper hair, close cropped moustache, leathery complexion, a trim and muscular six foot two . . . the temperament of a guerrilla,' gushed one author. 'To some he was obnoxious, a bully. To others, he was a rascal, a gambler. Above all he was combative, a survivor.'[3]

'As I grow older, I've become less desperate,' he said. 'I've decided to be more statesmanlike. I'm going to be a gentleman.' Ted Turner was forty-seven. As it happened the gentler role was partly forced upon him when he had to admit representatives of the cable operators onto the board in exchange for refinancing desperately needed after the stock market crash of October 1987. Like Berlusconi in Italy, Turner waged continuous guerrilla warfare against the broadcasting establishment. But Turner chose to use a weapon that Berlusconi had no intention of using – the leveraged buyout, or LBO, backed by junk bonds. Berlusconi's fight, as we shall see, had to be carried out through guile and politics.

In 1985, when we began charting the role of the Sky Barons in

[3] Douglas K. Ramsey, *The Corporate Warriors*.

detail, Ted Turner's fiefdom already stretched across the United States, Canada and Mexico and into Europe, Australia and Japan. He was in negotiations with the Soviet Union and Communist China. On 30 September 1985, the CNN 'world-wide' channel via satellite was launched in Western Europe. Robert Wussler, Executive Vice-President of the company and a former CBS executive, said at the time that Turner wanted his company to be 'as global as possible'. Explained Wussler: 'Ted is an internationalist. He believes very strongly in one world, that we are all citizens of the planet Earth.'

Journalists at CNN were specifically forbidden from using the word 'foreign' on direct orders from Turner and told to use the word 'international' instead. Wussler adds: 'He wants to prove that private industry can sometimes do things quicker, better and easier than governments can, because governments sometimes have traditions that can't be overcome.' Little did Wussler foresee the significance of these words and the role Turner's news network CNN would play in the weeks surrounding 15 January 1991, when the allied forces operating under United Nations mandate went to war with Saddam Hussein's Iraq.

Perhaps of all the present-day Sky Barons, Ted Turner has the greatest claim to the adjective 'global'. His news service was available in embassies, newspapers, offices and hotel rooms across the world before the word 'glasnost' entered the Western vocabulary. Like Robert Maxwell before him, Turner sees himself as a healer between East and West. Turner had established a personal friendship with Fidel Castro – 'my Commie pal' he liked to say – and boasted of duckhunting exploits with the figure who until Iraq's Saddam Hussein and Libya's Colonel Gadaffi was Bogeyman No. 1 with the American press and public.

In December 1984, Ronald Reagan had romped to victory in the US presidential elections and Mikhail and Raisa Gorbachev met the British Prime Minister Margaret Thatcher in London. In March of the following year Gorbachev took over from Constantin Chernenko as head of the Soviet Communist Party and by November was sitting down with Reagan in Geneva for what the American president described as a 'fireside summit'. 'The world,' Gorbachev said, 'has become a safer place.'

Ever in the forefront of moves to promote better East–West understanding, Ted Turner had gone to Moscow to announce the 'Goodwill Games', an alternative to the 1984 Olympic Games in Los Angeles which the Soviets were boycotting. It was the day that the news broke of his purchase of the MGM library of 3,300 films. But first Ted had other fish to fry. 1985 was to go down as the year Turner made his biggest play yet, the year in which, as Turner put it, 'the guppy tried to swallow the whale'.

The whale in question was CBS. Later, Turner was to say with relish: 'What a play that was!' It was said that Turner's motto in his Ahab-like quest for CBS was: 'Go full ahead until you hit something.' It was Fastnet and Captain Courageous all over again. But in 1985 instead of landing his whale, Turner hit rock.

In the heart of Manhattan, on 6th Avenue between 52nd and 53rd Streets, there rises a sleek, slim skyscraper faced in black granite brought all the way from Quebec. It is the only skyscraper ever designed by the architect Eero Saarinen. 'Black Rock', as it inevitably became known, was the headquarters of CBS, the Columbia Broadcasting System and of its founder and first president, William S. ('Bill') Paley, who had created the company in 1928. The building was completed in 1965, four years after the premature death of Saarinen at the age of fifty-one.

CBS News was a legend. The greatest broadcasting news organisation ever, it was said with some justice, and with the most respected body of broadcast journalists in the world. Edward R. Murrow, Fred Friendly, Charles Collingwood, Walter Cronkite, Eric Sevareid are just a few of its illustrious alumni. It seemed that it would be easier to topple Saarinen's skyscraper than to remove CBS from its pre-eminence in the field of news. But in 1984 things started to go wrong. There were internal upheavals, but that was nothing new. Far more threatening was a lawsuit brought by the retired General William C. Westmoreland, commander of the US forces in Vietnam from 1964 to 1968. The suit concerned a documentary about Vietnam fronted by Mike Wallace, star of the

CBS flagship *60 Minutes*. The documentary, 'The Uncounted Enemy', had been transmitted in 1982.

Essentially the programme alleged that Westmoreland had conspired to misrepresent Viet Cong strength to President Johnson, to Congress and to the American people. Westmoreland called the programme 'a preposterous hoax'. He accused Wallace of staging 'a star chamber procedure with distorted, false and specious information, plain lies, derived by sinister deception– an attempt to execute me on the guillotine of public opinion'.

Such outbursts were taken less seriously in the United States than in other countries, but the problem was compounded by an article in *TV Guide* entitled 'Anatomy of a Smear'. The article made serious charges about the techniques used in making the programme and had a credibility that demanded attention. One of its authors was Sally Bedell Smith, a highly respected reporter, who was about to join the *New York Times* as chief television correspondent. Van Gordon Sauter, CBS News President, ordered an internal enquiry. The ordeal that followed was to be called 'CBS's own Vietnam'. The enquiry was conducted by a CBS news executive of the old school, Bud Benjamin.

Sauter's report was dynamite. It found eleven major flaws in the programme. The report was kept internal. For the public, a memorandum was issued, which, while accepting that the programme had some faults, meant that CBS News stood by it.

In September, Westmoreland filed a $120 million libel suit against CBS. The pre-trial period was to last two years and was filled with acrimonious charges flying between the two sides. The action finally reached a New York federal court on 9 October 1984. After eighteen weeks of what proved to be a media circus, Westmoreland and CBS reached an agreement. No money was paid to Westmoreland but CBS issued a statement acknowledging his services to his country and said that they had never intended to impugn his patriotism or loyalty. 'We won the case,' CBS Chairman Tom Wyman was to say later, 'but we came out of that case with a somewhat damaged image – and all the research we did proved it.'

In the middle of the Westmoreland affair, CBS faced another

libel action against *60 Minutes* and this time Dan Rather, the CBS evening news anchor, who was on an annual salary of $2 million for ten years. It was yet another media circus and CNN, which at that time reached about 30 million viewers, put cameras in the courtroom for live coverage of Rather's testimony. Supremely smooth, confident and authoritative as an anchorman, Rather was less assured on the witness stand. CNN's rating rose 20 per cent during the trial. Again CBS won the case but to borrow a phrase from Wall Street, the reputation of CBS as a news organisation had been 'put into play'.

Soon CBS was to be put into play for real. The ground for a takeover bid was laid in January of 1985. Three men from North Carolina formed a group called Fairness in Media and filed papers with the Securities and Exchange Commission. Their aim was to purchase enough stock in the company to be able to exert influence on CBS. The controversial right-wing Republican Senator for North Carolina, Jesse Helms, came out in support of the campaign with the slogan 'Become Dan Rather's boss'.

Fairness in Media claimed there was 'a liberal bias in [CBS] news reporting and editorial policies'. There was little evidence to support the charge. 'By the 1980s when Conservative chic was in full flower,' wrote Peter J. Boyer, 'CBS was about as left-wing as the Cedar Falls chapter of the American Legion.' The *New York Times* columnist William Safire described Dan Rather as 'a red- blooded Texas centrist and something of a sentimental patriot.'

But Fairness in Media supporters were not the only ones buying CBS stock. In February it was disclosed that the arbitrageur Ivan F. Boesky and a group of speculators had acquired 8.7 per cent of CBS's stock thus becoming the largest stockholders in the company. A year later Boesky was arrested for other activities on the stock market.

Black Rock was worried. Suit was filed against Fairness in Media on the grounds that the action brought by the group was essentially political fund-raising. The group did not gather the support it had hoped for. By March it had dropped its plans for a proxy fight to gain seats on the board. Rumours of a takeover continued. It was suggested that the General Electric Company was interested in a friendly merger. The rumour was denied but GE was later to buy CBS's rival NBC. Another candidate suggested was the publishing conglomerate Gannett Company. In March, Capital Cities Communications Inc. agreed to acquire the American Broadcasting Companies (ABC) network for $3.5 billion. It seemed communications stocks were undervalued. The networks were up for grabs and rumour piled on rumour.

In April, Wall Street and the broadcasting establishment were rocked as Ted Turner announced a $5.4 billion bid to purchase 67 per cent of CBS stock – the amount required to take over the company. At the time he held less than half of one per cent of the outstanding shares.

The bid was based on stockholder notes and bonds worth approximately $175 per share. The notes and bonds were to be redeemed in five to twenty years. The market price of CBS stock in April was around $90. Later, in his successful 1985 bid for MGM, Turner was to turn to Drexel Burnham Lambert, whose whizz-kid financier Michael Milken was the specialist in the use of 'junk bonds' based more on hope than on assets.

Turner proposed to finance his offer by selling off all of CBS's assets (its record, toy, radio and publishing divisions) and keep only its television operations. To comply with Federal Communications Commission requirements he would also sell WCAU – CBS's Philadelphia station. In a leveraged buyout such as this the transaction is financed mainly by borrowing against the assets of the company being taken over. Eventually the debt is paid off by money derived from the company's operating income as well as from the sale of the assets. High interest is offered on the bonds – 15 to 16.5 per cent – and there are onerous penalty clauses.

Financial analysts were briefed by Turner in a ballroom at the Park Lane Hotel on Central Park South. Reactions were mixed. Turner was seen as a determined bidder but his offer was described as a 'creative package that might appeal to investors who put greed before other things'. Some had reservations about Turner's personality: 'He is a wonderful businessman, but he is a maverick.'

Turner told journalists: 'We have been very interested in joining forces with one of the three networks because of our desire to be No. 1 in our business.' Turner revealed that CBS had previously tried to buy CNN and that he had responded by suggesting a merger since he did not wish to separate CNN from the rest of his company nor surrender editorial control. One of the CBS executives who discussed the matter with Turner, Bill Leonard, later recalled that Turner's parting shot had been: 'Someday I'm going to own you, you bet I am. Remember I told you so.'

Now he had made his play. It would, the experts said, be like a mouse swallowing an elephant. Turner preferred his maritime analogy: 'a guppy swallowing a whale'. The figures made no sense. In 1984, CBS earned $212.4 million on revenues of $4.9 billion. In the same period Turner earned $10 million on revenues of $281 million.

Board member and former FCC chairman Newton Minow later said he thought Turner's offer was 'dead on arrival'. But publicity forced CBS to take the matter seriously. Bill Paley, the network's founder, was shocked. 'He was very upset. He didn't want to have his child kidnapped.'

Paley made a statement: 'CBS is strong. CBS is healthy. But that strength and health are the products of more than half a century of careful, concerned nurturing by a great many very dedicated people. To throw this away would be a tragedy. To risk its loss would be to trifle recklessly with the company's future and with the public interest.'

If history was against Turner in his attempt to buy CBS, it also did him a favour. After failing to take over CBS, Turner was by necessity channelled down a different route, one which made him an innovator in two critical areas. In the first place, he decided to build up his own cable network, the Super Station. And, as we shall see, he was more determined than ever to build the CNN channel into a world-wide news force that would one day overtake CBS itself.

The direction in which the seafaring Turner's plans now lay was MGM, the distributors of the original *Gone With The Wind* that had been such an influence on his early life. It was apt that the director of 'Wind', the underrated Victor Fleming, had also been the maker, in 1937, of a sea saga called *Captains Courageous*, based on a novel by Rudyard Kipling. Needless to say, *Captains Courageous*, too, had been a production of MGM.

VII

The Pope of Television:
Berlusconi

In the spring of 1945, following General Mark Clark's slogging campaign up the Italian peninsula, the US Fifth Army finally ground out victory over a 200,000-strong German defence force. In a macabre footnote to the end of the fascist empire, North Italian partisans recaptured the escaped dictator Benito Mussolini near Lake Como. Together with his mistress, Clara Petacci, and a handful of remaining supporters, Mussolini was summarily shot. The bodies were taken to Milan and put on display. For several hours, an enraged mob trampled and spat on the once revered dictator and his mistress. In a final indignity, the corpses were suspended upside down from a telegraph pole at a filling station in the Piazza Loretto.

It was fitting that the scene of the gruesome obloquy of the new Roman emperor Mussolini should have been Milan. For it is Milan and the North that has been the engine room of Italy's postwar renaissance. Likewise it is probably no accident that Milan is also the birthplace and headquarters of one of the most remarkable new communications empires in the world, that of Italy's so-called 'Pope of Television', Silvio Berlusconi.

It costs about 450 dollars to have someone killed in Milan. In the cafés and restaurants of the city, journalists at the daily *Italia Oggi* discuss the going rate. In Italy, home of the Mafia and Camorra, of kidnapping for ransom and of political instability, such knowledge is commonplace. No wonder that Berlusconi, the man who revolutionised Italian television, always takes a different route from his magnificent eighteenth-century villa at Arcore outside the city to the headquarters of his holding company, Fininvest. Berlusconi is constantly shadowed by a phalanx of anxious, sharp-suited aides and even sharper-shooting bodyguards.

The seventy-room Villa San Martino stands in its own secluded 250 acres. It was purchased by Berlusconi from the heirs of the Marchese Casati, who committed suicide after shooting his wife and her lover. Today the villa has a private park, helicopter pad, stabling for horses, indoor and outdoor swimming pools, gymnasium, sauna, steam bath, jacuzzi and a special area fitted with large television screens. Inside, the walls are hung with one of the finest private collections of Rennaissance art in the world. When working at home, as he frequently does for security, Berlusconi keeps a closer eye on the screens than the pictures. For these relay the channels of his own three networks as well as those of his competitors – chief among them the state-owned RAI.

At a dinner with Berlusconi in his villa, the president of international sales at Paramount Television was curious to note that every half-hour a white gloved servant would bring his master a folded note. It turned out that the messages contained not the prices of the stock market but the latest half-hour ratings for Berlusconi's TV stations.

It would be hard to find another individual – save perhaps for his American counterpart Ted Turner – who more aptly represents the rise of the modern Sky Baron than Berlusconi, known in Italy as *la sua emittenza* ('His Transmittence'). The career of this supremely smooth, confident and daring entrepreneur is almost an exemplar of the cult of the individual against state bureaucracy, and the way in which the wily string-puller can play off politicians to the greater aggrandisement of an empire.

On the opening Sunday of the MIFED international film market in Milan in October 1991, Berlusconi was in unusually relaxed mood. Normally, his demeanour is dynamic to the point of jumpiness. A small, energetic man with an ever-ready and quite dazzling smile, Berlusconi joked with journalists quizzing him about his future intentions for the enormous Fininvest empire which spans his interests in television, advertising, insurance, publishing and retailing. His staff joked too. Their master was always in a good mood, they said, when the soccer team he owns, AC Milan, had won, as it had earlier that day. Ever the showman, Berlusconi is wont to arrive at home games in the breathtaking San Siro stadium by helicopter, to the accompaniment of 'Ride of the Valkyries' played over the PA system.

At MIFED, Berlusconi went out of his way to scotch the persistent rumours that he was planning to take the privately owned Fininvest onto the international stock market. Instead, he said, Fininvest would spend the next three years digesting the enormous meal it had taken in the form of the Mondadori publishing empire. Berlusconi did not, however, rule out his interest in bidding for the Channel Five television franchise due to be advertised in Britain in 1992 – 'That number five is lucky for me,' he said with a chuckle.

Berlusconi had another reason to be pleased with himself. A few days earlier, he had realised one of his longest cherished ambitions. On 26 September 1991, a remarkable event took place – one unprecedented in the history of Italian television. The public TV channel RAI-3 joined with its arch private rival, Berlusconi's Canale 5, to air a five-hour marathon against the Mafia and its still growing power in Italy. From 8.30 pm to 11 pm, the programme was broadcast from a theatre in Palermo, Sicily, by RAI-3, the channel run by the former Communist Party. From 11 pm to 1.15 am, Berlusconi's Canale 5 took over with a special edition of the popular Maurizio Costanzo show, live from a Roman theatre.

The show was billed as a tribute to Libero Brassi, a Sicilian industrialist killed by the Mafia in the summer of 1991 for refusing to pay protection money. The broadcast was widely acclaimed by all but the Christian Democratic Party, who condemned it as 'Stalinist'. Many of those who took part in the show openly accused Christian Democrat government ministers of connivance with the Mafia. Gianni Pasquarelli, Director General of the RAI organisation, and a Christian Democrat appointee to boot, went so far as to accuse the programme – made it should be remembered by one of his own channels – as a series of 'summary trials against people, institutions and political parties'.

For Berlusconi, the key mover in postwar Italian media, the event had special significance. It was the first big test of his newly won right to broadcast live news programmes, withheld for years in the bitter struggle waged with the supporters of the state TV corporation RAI. It was another snook cocked by the Milanese upstart against the centralising power of the Rome based RAI.

To Berlusconi's evident delight, and some surprise, the broadcast reached a record audience for factual programmes transmitted by the two channels, exceeding even those during the war in the Gulf. Over 20 million people tuned in at some stage to the five-hour marathon.

After the Mafia programme, Berlusconi called Costanzo the following day to congratulate him on his success. Like many of our Sky Barons, Berlusconi is essentially a hands-on operator. He raps out orders to his staff in clearly enunciated, crisp phrases – harking back to his days as an MC and entertainer.

Berlusconi provides an interesting comparison with the old Hollywood moguls, or those early TV pioneers in Britain such as the tapdancing Grades, who came from a background of theatre and burlesque. Visitors to San Martino are sometimes treated to an impromptu Berlusconi rendition on the piano. Berlusconi, the man from chic Milan, is almost alone amongst the Sky Barons in having trod the boards of show business – not the only characteristic he shares with the early film and TV pioneers. Like the old studio heads, Berlusconi was prepared to immerse himself completely in the new medium of his day – in his case, that of television rather than the movies. But Berlusconi is also a university graduate in law and in many ways a typical example of the postwar European technocratic entrepreneur. The legal training in particular was to stand him in good stead.

To the outside world Milan in 1960 was already the hub of Italy's postwar industrial renaissance. But its role in communications was limited to newspapers and publishing. Television and radio were held in a vicelike grip by the state corporation RAI, based in Rome.

Appointments to RAI were then, as now, made on political grounds. So much so that the heads of the three RAI networks are selected to give each of the three main political parties a network. Thus, RAI-1 is identified with the Christian Democrats led by Giulio Andreotti, RAI-2 with Bettino Craxi's Socialist Party and RAI-3 with the former Communists, now the Party of the Left.

Berlusconi was born in 1936, two years earlier than his contemporary Ted Turner. Like Britain's Richard Branson, however, Berlusconi came from a middle-class background, the son of a banking official. Like Branson, too, the young Berlusconi showed early entrepreneurial tendencies. At school he sold cribs to his classmates, which he had written and copied out himself. His university thesis was an analysis of contracts for TV advertising.

In his spare time, the teenage Silvio got together a band. Berlusconi of course took the role of lead singer and master of ceremonies, appearing at Adriatic resorts. For a season, he was the entertainment director on Costa Line cruises in the Mediterranean. While still at college, Berlusconi and a group of fellow students also banded together to sell household appliances at the Milan Fair. He entered as a partner in a construction company, and with a loan from his father's boss started dealing in the booming Milanese property market of the early 1960s. In 1968, Berlusconi used his father's connections to help purchase a large tract of land outside Milan. There he built a new development, known as Milano Due. One of Berlusconi's promotional slogans in selling the apartments at Milano Due was 'Commit now and get a bigger bathtub'. Those who were prepared to sign in advance on the dotted line got an apartment with more luxurious fittings.

Whilst working on the Milano Due project, Berlusconi had another brainwave. Why not, he conjectured, offer a further inducement to potential purchasers? Cable television was already established in US cities such as Atlanta. Berlusconi decided to incorporate a cable network into his 'satellite city' of the future.

Business thrived. It was only a short step from providing the cable to providing the programmes. Berlusconi bought a slate of Hollywood films and TV series, until then virtually unknown on the rigidly controlled and culturally elitist RAI. Viewers loved it. Gradually, Berlusconi started to buy up other local TV stations, eventually establishing his first network, Canale 5 – five is now his lucky number – in 1980. Canale 5 was so called because the Milanese publishing giant Mondadori had itself already established a fourth network, Rettequattro.

In 1983 Berlusconi started his second channel, named Italia Uno. That same year the financially troubled Rettequattro, owned by Mondadori, ran out of money and programmes. Berlusconi was mentioned as a possible investor. Mondadori's directors ruled him out when it emerged that he had been secretly negotiating to buy Rettequattro through an Italian holding company, Aqua Marcia. Mondadori broke off negotiations with Aqua Marcia in July 1984, a day before the deal was due to be signed, vowing to go it alone.

Within a month, Mondadori had meekly surrendered Rettequattro to Berlusconi. At a meeting held at their futuristic headquarters near Milan, the Mondadori clan announced their capitulation. In a deal reportedly priced at the firesale figure of 15 billion lire (then worth about $7 million), Berlusconi took control of Rettequattro, and brought all three networks under his Rete Italia programming arm.

Mondadori itself was ultimately to fall into the hands of the man from Milan, after a protracted and bitter battle with the entrepreneur Carlo de Benedetti. For the time being, Berlusconi was content to be the effective sole owner of all national commercial television in Italy.

For eight years, Berlusconi along with other commercial operators had broadcast his TV channels in the absence of any legal framework. The 1970s and early 1980s saw an incredible mushrooming of private television and radio stations throughout the country. The new stations broadcast everything from porn to propaganda. No wonder television was dubbed 'The New Wild West'. Berlusconi's defiance was particularly spectacular. Not content with a local station here and there, he deliberately chose to take on RAI's national networks. Since 1975, a supreme court ruling had restricted local stations to local coverage and given the government concern RAI the monopoly on national news broadcasting.

Acting on what he saw as a flaw in the legal wording, Berlusconi devised a simple means to get round the anti-commercial network provision. He arranged for taped copies of the same programme to be bicycled round the various local stations – literally delivered separately by couriers – in his embryo network. The tapes were then played out at the same time. The effect was just the same as if the programmes were being transmitted on a live network.

Years of legal challenge and counter-challenge dragged by while Berlusconi continued to build up his television empire. In the absence of any broadcasting law, media control was by decree and actions in the courts. On Tuesday 16 October 1984, Berlusconi stations in Piedmont, Rome and Aquila were taken off the air after rulings in local courts that he was breaking the law against networking. In response, Berlusconi ordered the blacked-out stations to carry messages which read: 'This station is temporarily off the air for political reasons.' It was now time to cash in on some of the valuable political contacts formed from his early days in the construction and development business.

Berlusconi put out a series of local interviews with hundreds of residents of the three areas affected, all in his support. 'This is worse than Russia,' said one. Berlusconi himself appeared on screen talking of the threat to jobs and the local economies. By the weekend, the protests against the blackout had shown no sign of abating. Now Berlusconi played his trump card. The Socialist Prime Minister, Bettino Craxi, was a close ally of Berlusconi from the entrepreneur's days as a developer. Craxi's daughter Stefania worked as a journalist at Berlusconi's Canale 5. Acting in response to what was claimed to be an unprecedented public outcry, Craxi issued an emergency decree giving Berlusconi's private networks the right to continue broadcasting for another year. As a quid pro quo, Craxi announced that the government would be preparing draft legislation that would finally regulate the TV sector.

It was to be another six years before that law was passed by the Italian parliament, in October 1990. By that time, Silvio Berlusconi – the man from Milan – had made himself undisputed king of Italy's new TV frontier.

By the early 1980s, the three state RAI networks were already on the ropes, heavily defeated in the ratings by Berlusconi's three competing channels. Berlusconi's target was a bloated, complacent state corporation that even today is regarded by its own top officials as heavily overstaffed.

At first, Berlusconi scored easily in the ratings against RAI through his strategy of buying US soaps and film packages. RAI fought back uncertainly. In 1981, the network cancelled *Dallas* after just thirteen episodes. It was gleefully snapped up by Berlusconi. After seeing the soap rise to head the ratings, RAI went on the offensive with imported series and massive movie packages. Exploiting its position as a system funded partly by licence and partly by advertising, RAI upped the ante by running up to eighteen minutes an hour of commercials in peaktime. The audience was not impressed. Gradually, however, under the influence of a new Director General Biagio Agnes, appointed in 1982, RAI changed direction. Agnes, a RAI professional of thirty-two years' standing, saw that playing Berlusconi at his own programming game was not the answer.

Guided by Agnes, RAI began to fall back on its traditional strengths of production values and home-grown programming. Agnes introduced an innovative strategy of prestigious international co-productions, notably the *Octopus* Mafia series. RAI also exploited its advantages in sport and its monopoly of live news. Under Agnes, and some able lieutenants, its pride and ratings were somewhat restored.

But the war with Berlusconi had cost RAI dear. By the end of 1989 its deficit stood at over 300 million dollars. At the same time Berlusconi's tactic of poaching top RAI stars such as Rafaella Carra and Pippo Bando had not improved the early success he scored against RAI. But Berlusconi was a powerful enemy. When RAI beat Berlusconi to buy a large film package through distributors Cecchi Gori, Berlusconi complained that RAI had paid way over the market price.

Berlusconi had also complained about RAI's manipulation of advertising rates. Each year, a forty-member parliamentary commission meets to determine RAI's annual budget. It is invariably late. In what was seen as a deliberate ploy to force changes at RAI, in 1989 the commission would not agree RAI's advertising ceiling.

Under Agnes's leadership, RAI had not only fought back against the onslaught of commercial television *alla Berlusconi* but had established a convincing lead in the battle for audience share. But Agnes became a victim of his own success. As the all-powerful figure at the helm of RAI for the last four years, he had led the battle to restore the organisation's fortunes. RAI, having been the disregarded butt of the media in the 1970s, had once more asserted itself as the nation's premier broadcaster. Its lead in the ratings meant that Italy's politicians were keener than ever to influence the appointment of its top executives. In an unholy alliance, Berlusconi sought to limit RAI's effectiveness as a commercial competitor.

Like snow melting on the Apennines, Agnes mysteriously began to lose the patronage of the politicians. While the Christian Democrats under the moderate influence of Ciriaco De Mita had always supported Agnes, the new CD leadership under Prime Minister Giulio Andreotti and Party Secretary Arnaldo Forlani made no secret of their preference for a more right-wing future.

For some time Berlusconi had been overtly courting Andreotti – a clear indication that he understood his alliance with the socialist Bettino Craxi was not enough to give him the conditions of live broadcasting and favourable legislation he needed for the future.

Frustrated by maladministration, deserted by his former political allies, Agnes took the honourable way and resigned. Said Forlani dismissively: 'If I took notice of all the attacks I get in the papers I would resign every day. I don't know why Agnes felt he had to resign.' Elsewhere, Agnes's resignation was seen as an heroic attempt to force some final and long-lasting decision-making about RAI's future and its financial resources. The move shocked the political powers and brought into sharper focus the need for legislation on the question of mass media ownership.

RAI was hurriedly given a new budget. The following summer Italy was due to host the World Cup and with the eyes of the world upon it RAI needed a cash injection of around 200 billion lire to supply coverage.

Twelve years after it was first mooted, a broadcasting bill to regulate the 'Wild West' was still to appear. The bill, now widely known as 'The Berlusconi Bill' because it was expected to reduce the Milanese entrepreneur's domination of commercial television, was no longer to be put off. Just what its results for Berlusconi turned out to be we shall see.

VIII

The Boy from Brazil: Marinho

It is said there are four forces that drive Brazil – the Army, the Church, the Communist Party and Globo Television. But, the saying goes, 'the greatest of all is Globo'.

Roberto Marinho was clearly thrilled to be in Banff to receive the festival's award for 'Outstanding Achievement'. This diminutive, elegant 87-year-old has been described – not without reason – as the most powerful man in South America. His stature belies the power he wields through his Brazilian Globo broadcast and publishing empire. He has been credited with toppling presidents and military juntas alike. Marinho is widely agreed to have been the most important influence in ending the 'rule of the generals' which led to the fragile flowering of democracy under first Sarney and then Collor.

With trim moustache, silvering hair and military bearing, the elder Marinho is a man of charm and genuine old world courtesy. In Banff, Marinho was at ease. Whether striding the corridors of the Banff Park Lodge Hotel where the event was held, surrounded by a phalanx of Globo staff men, or square dancing at the festival barbecue for two hours with the young millionairess, Lily de Cavalho, who was later that year to become his second wife, he was unusually approachable. Holding court in a suite at the Banff Lodge, and speaking in heavily accented French, he described how in 1925 he went to work for his father at the Rio de Janeiro newspaper he had only recently started.

It turned out to be a traumatic introduction to what Rupert Murdoch calls 'the art of newspapering' for the nineteen-year-old. 'My father died only three weeks after founding *O Globo*,' he recalls, glancing out of the window at the snowy vistas so alien

69

from his native Brazil. 'There had been just twenty-three issues and then my father was taken ill and the next day he died.'

Marinho was cast in at the deep end of a business about which he knew nothing. Had this affected his subsequent career, we wondered? 'I think it formed his personality,' one of his most trusted aides told us. 'He was very young and the newspaper small and he understood at that time that he was not able to direct the newspaper and he learnt to trust in talent. He started at twenty years of age hiring good professionals to run the newspaper. It helped him because he was young. . . . Many people used to say at the time that he was a crazy man, Murdoch the same, Azcárraga . . . these people who build big companies.'

In 1931 he assumed control of the family business. It was the same year that Keith Murdoch's son was christened Keith Rupert, and the BBC announced a new Empire-wide radio service from Daventry, while His Master's Voice merged with Columbia as Electrical and Musical Industries (EMI).

In 1944 Marinho moved into radio. 'We bought a little radio station which was operating from a private house, but I knew the station had a licence for Chile,' Marinho recalled. 'I was very friendly with the Chilean president, who had been ambassador in Brazil. I was able to use the same licence. Then I went into TV, as well as a printing press and a magazine. I think I was the first in two hundred years to control a magazine with the printing press and the sales as well. Then came the opportunity to found TV Globo.'

The Brazilian dictator Gertulio Vargas, who had started out as a reforming president in 1930, ruled uninterrupted apart from a military junta from 1945–51. In 1954, Vargas resigned amid allegations of corruption and committed suicide. In 1957, Globo started the country's first TV channel and the important licence of the new capital of Brasilia was granted to Marinho by President Joao Goulart in 1963. Marinho quarrelled with Goulart by his own admission – 'we fought afterwards and did not have any liaison with him' – and threw the weight of his organisation behind the rapidly growing opposition of the middle classes and landowners to Goulart's plans for radical reform. With the backing of the United States, Goulart was ousted in April 1964 and the army seized power, beginning a junta that was to last for over two decades.

'His [Marinho's] warm ties with the military regime . . . helped Globo TV expand its presence across the country,' commented the *New York Times* in a profile. In 1965, Marinho set about building TV Globo into a national force and entered into a joint venture with the large American combine Time-Life. But new laws introduced in the 1970s made it illegal for a foreign company to own a Brazilian TV station, forcing Marinho to try to buy back the Time-Life share. 'To do so he mortgaged everything; his house; his art; his stocks; even the company buildings. Today Marinho owns it all.'[1]

Some forty-eight television stations scattered across Brazil form Rede Globo, the TV network he founded in the 1960s. Rede Globo gains around 70–80 per cent of the available audience – and this it must be remembered in a country where over half of its estimated 155 million inhabitants are illiterate and perhaps no more than one-sixth of the population is reached by the written word in any form. Rede Globo jostles with Rupert Murdoch's ever-increasing Fox Television for the position of the largest television network in the world, after the three main US networks, ABC, CBS and NBC. Rede Globo's weekday evening half-hour news at 7.55 pm, sandwiched between the two main soap operas of the day, has a regular audience of at least 50 million Brazilians.

The soap operas, known there as 'telenovelas', bring most Brazilian adults under the sway of TV Globo. Their export to other parts of the world beyond South America, including Europe, mean that they are doing for Brazil what Hollywood once did for America – providing a picture, albeit distorted, of the country. The series *Isaura the Slavegirl* attained ratings of 90 per cent at home and has been seen as far apart as Britain, Poland and China.

The Globo Productions Centre in Rio employs some 1,350

[1] *Forbes*, 5 October 1987.

permanent staff, of whom 480 are actors. The centre produces simultaneously three serials, various mini-series, four weekly shows, two special musicals a month, a daily children's programme and also a monthly programme for teenagers. In its Globo Journalism Centre, TV Globo produces over twenty-one hours a week of news and current affairs.

Like Hollywood, it is a profitable business. In the nine years from 1977–86, according to *TV World* (November 1986), international sales of TV Globo's programmes rose from $300,000 to $8 million.

Globo's TV division comprises seven fully owned stations, including those in Rio de Janeiro, São Paulo, Recife, Belo Horizonte and Brasilia. There are six partly owned stations, and some thirty-six affiliated stations, in all bringing in an estimated annual income of $500 million. Globo's thirty or so radio stations reach 85 million listeners. Together, radio and television reach about 90 million Brazilians, literate and illiterate, and of all social classes. *O Globo* is Brazil's largest daily. With the magazines and television programme sales to ninety countries, including mainland China, the business brings in an estimated annual revenue of perhaps $1,000 million.[2]

It is almost impossible to estimate accurately the personal Marinho family wealth (he has three sons), not least in view of their secrecy. Most guesses put it at least at one billion dollars. Marinho's family empire also owns finance companies, cattle ranches, shopping centres, records, video sales, advertising, merchandising, agriculture, real estate, mining and telecommunications. The Marinhos have one of the largest collections of art in South America, in a country which has lopped twelve noughts from the value of its money since the end of the Second World War.

A diminutive figure, Marinho was a devoted horseman and loved to be pictured riding his favourite white stallion. One of Marinho's prized possessions is his large aviary at his country house near Rio, an interest he shares with Jose Sarney, who at the

---

[2] *Forbes*, 5 October 1987.

time of our interview in June 1989 was the first civilian president in over twenty years – thanks in large part to Marinho's influence.

'I am very friendly with him,' Marinho told us, 'but I have no political links with Mr Sarney. The other day I phoned him – I know he has some birds from the North Amazon – and I said I would like some and we talked on the phone about birds, not about the grave problems of Brazil. He said, "I will send you some birds," and I thanked him and three days later he phoned and said he had a lot of pleasure in talking about birds with me. I never asked the government for things for Globo or myself, for newspapers and TV are not meant for extracting favours from the President and the military. So the only gift I have ever received from President Sarney is a cockatoo.'

Roberto Marinho went out of his way in Banff to discount the charge that Globo owes its position today to the unprecedented growth it enjoyed under the twenty-one years of military dictatorship.

'I take this opportunity now to tell you about a German newspaper which recently had a very good article about us. It said some very nice things about me but it also said that Globo, in return for supporting the generals, received many advantages. I wrote to the newspaper telling them this was absolutely wrong. TV Globo did not have a single concession from the military. General Castello-Branco [head of government, 1964–7] was the greatest of all the military of the revolution. It is a pity he was killed in an accident which you will remember, a plane crash. We had no concessions from him and I never asked anything from the military,' Marinho said emphatically.

Then, as if correcting an old man's memory, Marinho added: ' "Never" is not true, for there was one occasion when I asked General Castello-Branco for something. It was the case of Mr Leonel Brizola, to whom I had sold a Globo concession. He was a very intelligent man, very strong, you have heard of him, an amazing man. He began to use his talent and the power he had over the population for bad objectives, and I started to fight him. He was the Governor of Rio de Janeiro. He started to persecute TV Globo. . . . There was a programme at 5 pm for children with a marine officer and his pipe and beard . . . and he started to put out this programme at 8 pm when the children were going to bed.

'I asked Castello-Branco if he could do something because it was the beginning of the persecution of TV Globo. He said he would censure the Governor's power over the TV. This is the only time I asked for help from the government.'

Marinho's opposition in 1986 led Brizola to attribute his loss in the elections to the 'electronic shock' applied to voters by the network's campaign against his government.

Brazil is the size of the continental United States and occupies half of the South American land mass. It is the eighth largest economy in the Western world. The huge distances and extremely hostile territory, including the Amazon region, kept the country separated from itself for hundreds of years. Until very recently, Stone Age tribes existed which had never seen a white man. Remnants of the last of these untouched cultures may still be clinging precariously to life in some of the remoter jungle, in the face of the wholesale depredations of miners, ranchers and settlers.

These distances and divisions were bridged for the first time by television. 'When Globo brought the suffering of Brazil's drought-stricken north-east into the sitting rooms of the urban south last year . . . a problem dating back generations was suddenly discovered,' reported the *New York Times*. 'Television is also beginning to blur regional identities by slowly homogenizing the slang, fashions and buying habits of Brazilians thousands of miles apart,' it added.

In April 1988, TV Globo decided to re-edit the series *O Pagador de Promesas*, based on a Dias Gomes book which in a film version directed by Anselmo Duarte won the Palme d'Or at Cannes in 1962. Gomes himself was contracted to write the screenplay. After the second episode had been screened, the director Tizuka Yamasaki was instructed to re-edit the series and cut four episodes. She refused. The suggestion was that scenes shot by Yamasaki covering disputes over landownership between peasant farmers and big landowners may have been a little too near the knuckle in relation to what is actually happening in Brazil today. Even Globo is willing to admit that parts of the cuts were demanded by the station's owner, Roberto Marinho, who found the series went against his personal wishes.

Marinho, who has survived the often hair-raising vicissitudes of Brazilian politics, is deceptively straightforward about his role. 'We give all necessary information, but our opinions are in one way or another dependent on my character, my convictions or my patriotism. I assume responsibility for everything I run,' he had told the *New York Times*. 'We would like to have the power to fix everything that doesn't work in Brazil. We dedicate all our power to this. If power is used to disrupt a country, to destroy its customs, then it's not good. . . . But if it's used to improve things, as we do, it's good. I don't think this will much occupy the attention of the Constituent Assembly.'

In 1984, a large demonstration in São Paulo against the junta coincided with the date of São Paulo's founding. Globo, it is reported, covered the event straightfaced as celebration of the anniversary.

In January 1985, Tancreido de Almeida Neves was elected as Brazil's first civilian president in twenty-one years. He died on 21 April, the eve of his inauguration, after undergoing six operations, the last a tracheotomy to relieve breathing difficulties. The last few days of Neves were played out as a real-life soap opera by Globo TV, amid rumours that Neves had been shot. 'From boardroom to slum bar,' reported *The Financial Times*, 'televisions have been left on permanently since the presidential drama began. . . . Normal business activity has been almost impossible because so many key figures have been glued to the box, waiting for the next flash from the hospital. . . . The strong-willed wife of the president-elect and their ambitious, 25-year-old grandson make the decisions over his treatment, virtually ignoring the constitutional authority represented by the acting president. In the background, the shadowy figure of the National Intelligence Service chief personally supervises the news bulletins to be fed to an anxious public.'

Amid this three-ring circus, stand-up rows broke out periodically between the rival medical teams treating Neves – all this brought blow-by-blow courtesy of Globo as part of their unstated but no less obvious decision to support Neves against his military-backed rival. What reinforced the idea that it was Globo and not Vice-President Sarney who was running the country during the crisis was the fact that the new presidential spokesman, Antonio Brito, was himself a former Globo journalist. His was now the task to issue medical bulletins approved by the intelligence chief, General Ivan Souza Mendes, who had installed himself in the São Paulo hospital. 'The ailing leader's aides know the importance of TV Globo in easing the country through these difficult days just as much as their military predecessors did,' commented *The Financial Times* reporter.

In throwing his weight at a crucial time behind the civilian politicians, Marinho had effectively brought to an end the military junta. When we tackled him about this in Banff, he was at first polite but evasive.

'TV Globo does not have theories, it does not push one strong opinion. I think we have the best newspapers and the best TV in Brazil. We have very good reporting of facts, but we do not push opinions.'

Was it not the case that Marinho's influence had been decisive in changing the government of General Joao Figueireda in 1985, when Globo had backed Neves, we asked?

'No, that's not true.' Clearly unused to such direct questioning, for a moment the autocrat peeped out as Marinho broke into Portuguese in a rapid exchange with his ever-present aides before resuming in French.

'The general was my friend when he was a lieutenant. He got married – I did too, before him, because I was older. He had an interest in politics, and you'll understand that as a lieutenant he couldn't go very far. We have been friends all our lives. He liked horse-riding and competing. I did too, only I was luckier because I was champion for six years – he was mad about horse-riding but he wasn't very successful in competition. We are still friends. He was always very brilliant and cultivated and I supported Figueireda more than the other military chiefs at the time. Now we see Brazil in rather a chaotic situation, but we are not remorseful about having, on occasion, supported the military. Some are very good but there were some who were violent.

'President Figueireda and his wife were friends of me and my wife. He had an operation when he was already President of the Republic and he was not very well after the operation and came to my house for five days to convalesce. We were good friends until he went to Cleveland for heart treatment. In Cleveland he had a centre where he got news from home. There were good reports and bad reports and I think he had bad reports of me in Cleveland. But I do not have a bad conscience about having done anything against him.'

Nevertheless, we asked, is it not true that whoever controls the press and the TV at the same time has a lot of power? 'Yes,' he answered shortly.

'You have three sons each of whom controls a part of Globo?'

'Yes,' replied Marinho, 'and all three follow the same path as I do.'

At the end of 1989, for the first time in three decades, Brazil voted freely for a new president on a universal ballot. There was little discussion in the campaign of Brazil's pressing problems such as debt rescheduling or saving the Amazon rain forest. Perhaps lacking practice, Brazilians tend not to take elections over seriously, on one famous occasion electing a rhinoceros to Congress. In the November 1989 elections there were forty candidates. Leading the polls until a week or so before the ballot was Silvio Santos, a former clown and now a television chat show host on a rival television network.

Santos had started his career selling counterfeit Parker pens across the Guanabara bay from Rio. Within a few years Santos, the child of poor Greek-Jewish immigrants, had made a multi-million dollar fortune and controlled Brazil's second largest TV network, SBT, where he hosted what has been described as 'one of the world's most vulgar variety shows'. This apparently gave him a platform to contest the election, his only statement of policy being: 'The people know me and they trust me. Let them decide.'

The veteran socialist candidate, Leonel Brizola, was none other than the Rio governor whom Marinho had crossed swords with to

Brizola's cost in 1986. Brizola was well-known but widely distrusted and ill-equipped to conduct a campaign in an election which had become a game show, with the presidency as the star prize beckoning the toothy gagman, Silvio Santos. His relatively unknown main opponent was Fernando Collor de Mello, a forty-year-old black-belt karate expert, behind whom Globo now began to throw its considerable weight.

In its first poll, Gallup put Santos in first place, with 29 per cent of Brazil's population apparently prepared to vote for him. 'The fact that Silvio is making Brazil an international laughing-stock does not contradict the fact that his candidacy is no laughing matter,' one world-weary political commentator stated.

Just a few days before Brazil went to the polls in the expectation that the country would elect a former clown to the highest office in the land, Santos was disqualified from the contest. The little-known grounds were that he owned a television station, which ownership he should have apparently given up three months before polling day to legitimise his run for office. The disqualification left the way open for the dark horse.

In the event, Sarney was succeeded as president in December 1989 by Fernando Collor, ostensibly a radical reformer but suspected by many as another scion of the oligarchy which has dominated Brazilian politics for several decades. It will come as no surprise to learn that Collor's family runs an affiliate of the Globo TV network.

IX

The Electronic Chancellor: Azcárraga

The Mariachi, strolling musicians in maroon and silver suits and star-spangled cartwheel hats, serenaded with a Trio Los Panchos medley from the 1950s at the foot of the marble stairs leading down to the terrace of the Villa Arabesca. The villa had been carved out of the cliffs facing west across Acapulco Bay. The mirror surface of the sea seemed to flow out from the terrace-level pool along the trail of the setting Pacific sun. There was a pause in the music and tequila cocktails and conversation lapsed as three figures descended the wide spiral staircase. The statuesque Baroness Sandra di Portanova held the left arm of a small man wearing impeccable 'Etiqueta Acapulqueña' – dress shirt serving as a jacket worn outside black dress trousers that is traditional evening wear for tropical Acapulco. It might have been a scene from *Dynasty*, an impression encouraged by the figure on the man's right arm. This was not Alexis Colby, but rather her alter ego Joan Collins: star guest of the twelfth Acapulco Reseña de Reseñas (Festival of Festivals).

Baroness Sandra di Portanova is one of the world's leading socialites, Miss Collins one of its great film icons. The man escorting them was Miguel Alemán Velasco – a name practically unheard of in Europe but one to conjure with in Mexico. There is hardly a town in the country without one of its principal streets bearing the name Alemán in honour of his father, President of Mexico from 1946 to 1952.

It was Miguel Alemán Velasco's grandfather who first brought the name into Mexico's history books. General Miguel Alemán was a storekeeper turned revolutionary general who died opposing the assumption of power by Alvaro Obregón for a second term in 1928. Obregón himself was assassinated shortly afterwards.

The general's son, Miguel Alemán Valdés, became President in spite of restrictions on his education because of his father's politics. He is widely considered to be the architect of modern Mexico. His son, now chatting with Joan Collins and surrounded by attendant stars, starlets and journalists, was at the time (November 1987) President of the Televisa commercial broadcasting empire.

Like Roberto Marinho, Miguel Alemán Junior is physically slight, dapper rather than elegant. One of the first things that you notice are his prominent ears, which give him the air of a pixie or leprechaun. Like Marinho, he too is a man of great charm and in his time as president of Televisa did his best to open it up to public scrutiny and improve its programming.

Televisa's four channels have a near monopoly of television viewers in Mexico and regularly achieve a 90 per cent share of the audience. The Televisa group is the largest and most powerful media conglomerate in the Spanish-speaking world. In addition to its television interests, the company also owns a cable network, ten radio stations, Mexico City's biggest bullring, a soccer stadium and two soccer teams.

Alemán moved easily among the guests including Cantinflas, John Phillip Law, Michael York, Jane Seymour, Hugh O'Brian and Motion Picture Association of America chief Jack Valenti. Apparently oblivious of the camera flashes and the looks and comments as he passed, Licenciado Miguel Alemán Velasco is equally at home with film stars, politicians, pressmen and the cream of Acapulco society. Not least Teddy Stauffer – Mr Acapulco – one-time husband of 1930s leading lady Hedy Lamarr. Stauffer was born in Switzerland in 1909. He arrived in Acapulco in 1949 in Errol Flynn's yacht *Zaca* and, as the saying goes, has stayed ever since.

Under the Spanish, Acapulco was the staging post for traffic from the Philippines to be transported across Mexico by mule to Vera Cruz for onward shipment to Spain. As a tourist resort, Acapulco was largely the creation of Miguel Alemán's father when he was in charge of tourism. It owes its present prosperity and the tourist infrastructure of hotels, airlines and services to the former President and the main bayside strip – the Costera Miguel Alemán, Acapulco's equivalent of Cannes's La Croisette – is named in his honour.

Acapulco today boasts some three hundred hotels, including Teddy Staufer's world renowned Villa Vera and the luxurious 'Las Brisas' hotel high on a hill overlooking Acapulco Bay, boasting one of the most beautiful panoramic views in the world. Close to Miguel Alemán's own villa is the Villa del Rio, the former home of film star Dolores del Rio in the 1940s.

Miguel Alemán, as in so many other things, has followed his father's footsteps into the promotion of tourism. He once likened Mexico to a passenger liner, whose captain was the President, the citizens of Mexico the crew and the passengers the tourists. More importantly, for Mexico tourism is a vital source of revenue, the country's second greatest resource after oil.

As Hiram Garcia Borja, director general of the Acapulco Festival and former head of the National Bank of Cinematography, told us: 'Tourism in itself is a form of international communication. The Reseña wants to put Acapulco in the world headlines. Joan Collins in Acapulco – that is good value for money.' Others agreed – Televisa's co-sponsors of the event were Bacardi, Domecq and AeroMexico.

A little way along the Costera Miguel Alemán stand the twin fifteen-storey towers of the Ritz Hotel, conceived by Emilio Azcárraga Vidauretta in 1962. Like that of Alemán, the name Azcárraga is a household word in Mexico. It is also a name that has been associated with broadcasting in Mexico since the very beginnings.

Mexico has always been a land of barons or 'Caciques' since the days of Montezuma II's Aztec Empire in the sixteenth century. The Caciques were recruited from the old Aztec ruling classes to help in the collection of taxes and the organisation of labour. In exchange for their services, which included the maintenance of order and the supervision of the distribution of land, food and water, the Caciques were allowed to own land and pass it on to their children and to engage in trade. The word comes from the Caribbean Arawak word 'kassiquan' meaning to own or maintain a house and was imported by the Spaniards to apply to the Mexican Indians they co-opted to exercise authority on their behalf.

Today Caciques can be found at every level of society. At one level there are men like Rafael Gutierrez Moreno – Cacique of the 'pepenadores', poor scavengers who live and work in Mexico City's refuse dumps.

> Local bosses like Gutierrez emerge in newly developing
> neighbourhoods by wangling essential government services
> for the poor – water, electricity – and making sure
> everyone knows whom to thank. After such a boss, known
> as a Cacique, has established himself as a neighbourhood
> leader, he reaches an understanding with the government:
> the Cacique delivers the vote for the PRI and in return
> receives free rein to run the community for his personal
> economic profit.[1]

When Mexico gained its independence from Spain in 1821, the loss of the minimal protection offered by the Spanish Crown led to new injustices. Large landholdings or 'latifundias' taken from formerly communal land were created and a new breed of landowning Caciques came into being. The Caciques, who were invariably also generals, owed formal allegiance to central government. In practice, they ran their territories with considerable autonomy.

Today 'Caciquismo' lives on, from the rubbish tips of Mexico City to the financial and industrial groups of Monterrey in the north. Emilio Azcárraga Milmo, the current president of the giant Televisa communications empire, is often described as a 'Cacique of Communication'. But his domain runs far beyond the frontiers of Mexico.

Certainly, it seemed unbelievable when, on 11 August 1986, the chairman of the board of Televisa, Rómulo O'Farrill, confirmed that Azcárraga was to relinquish the reins of Televisa in

[1] *Wall Street Journal*, 1 July 1988.

Mexico after fourteen years to take up responsibility for its international operations – principally in the United States. Was this the end of the extraordinary relationship between three families – the Alemáns, the Azcárragas and the O'Farrills – that had spanned half a century and created one of the world's most powerful communications empires?

Televisa's roots go back to the upheavals in Mexican society dating from the nineteenth-century war with the US and resulting in the Mexican Revolution of 1910–17. In 1792 an Irishman named Lewis O'Farrill from County Longford emigrated to Mexico and adapted his Christian name to the Spanish form. Luis O'Farrill's son Stephan fought with the semi-mercenary St Patrick's Battalion commanded by General O'Leary against the invading United States troops in 1847. On 20 August he was gravely wounded at the battle of Churubusco and left for dead. Hidden by local inhabitants, he escaped the fate of many of his colleagues who were shot or hanged by the Americans.

The O'Farrill family had won its spurs and future generations were to give much to their adopted country. The family settled in Puebla and the second half of the nineteenth century saw several doctors, among whom Dr Gustavo O'Farrill Seoane discovered a medicine for the treatment of anaemia. The family also founded the first sanatorium in Mexico for the treatment of alcohol and drug addiction. Federico Jimenez O'Farrill founded the Bank of Mexico under President Calles and was later his country's ambassador in London.

Many O'Farrill women have also made their mark. The poetess Maria Adriana O'Farrill de Camarena was from 1940 to 1958 the presenter of a cultural programme on Mexican radio, *Amenidad y Progreso* ('Leisure and Progress'). Maria Adriana read all the commercials herself – in verse. Each year crowds packed the streets of her home town of Puebla as she distributed gifts to children on which she spent all her earnings from the programmes. Margarita O'Farrill, a model, was also the presenter in the sixties of a radio programme for Spanish-speaking women in the United States. She received the freedom of Los Angeles from Ronald Reagan, then Governor of California, for her work on behalf of Latin women in the US. Carolina O'Farrill is a member of the House of Representatives in Mexico City.

In January 1992, the O'Farrill family celebrated the 200th anniversary of the arrival of their dynasty's founder in Mexico. To mark the event his descendant Martha O'Farrill de Barrientos, writer and founder of the Irish College in Mexico City, organised a convention to reunite all living members of the family. Present were the widows of Gustavo and Federico Jimenez O'Farrill as well as Eduardo, Carmen and Teresa – the first representatives of the fifth generation of Mexican O'Farrills.

Rómulo O'Farrill Silva was born in Puebla in 1894. A keen motor rally driver in the 1920s, he gained his pilot's licence in 1942 and by 1987 had clocked 7,260 flying hours. He set up the first motor car factory in Mexico for Packard and in 1950 he introduced television to Mexico. His son, Rómulo junior, worked with his father on all his enterprises. Born on 15 December 1917, he was educated in Puebla and studied business in Detroit, the automobile capital of the United States, followed by a qualification in journalism in New York.

The fate of the O'Farrills and Alemáns became entwined in 1944 when Miguel Alemán Valdés needed the support of a newspaper in his bid to win the presidential nomination. He secured the departure of the former owners of the *Novedades* newspaper and placed in control his son Miguel and Rómulo O'Farrill Silva, who was later succeeded by Rómulo junior. Today Miguel Alemán and Rómulo are joint presidents of *Novedades* and of the English language Mexico City *News*. Rómulo O'Farrill is also honorary consul for Ireland in Mexico.

In 1922, Raúl Azcárraga Vidauretta was the owner of the Alameda Garage in Mexico City. The Ford Motor Company's famous Model T – 'in any colour as long as it's black' – was sweeping the United States and had begun to invade Mexico along with massive investments by US corporations who were stepping into the shoes of the European companies which had financed Mexico before the Revolution of 1910–17. The advertising potential of Mexican newspapers and above all the infant radio was vital to them. At the same time, the new medium offered a home for what was left of the fortunes of pre-Revolutionary Mexican bankers and industrialists.

The sales agent for Henry Ford at the time was an ex-US army colonel, Sandal S. Hodges. The Colonel persuaded Raúl Azcárraga of the importance of radio and its commercial potential. As a result, the young garage proprietor travelled to Texas and underwent a course in wireless technology at the Sam Houston military base. On his return he founded the Casa del Radio (Radio House), which soon linked up with the *El Universal* newspaper.

El Universal had supported the Allies during the First World War, not least because its directors included an Englishman, a Frenchman and a Belgian. As a result it lost some of its investors and the United States had stepped willingly into the breach. La Casa del Radio was founded precisely at the moment when President Obregón was negotiating with the United States for recognition of his new government.

Mexican broadcasting was founded on the basis of foreign capital and commercial influences imported from the United States, with the Mexican government taking a secondary role. Relations between the Azcárragas and the United States had remained close ever since Raúl went to Texas in 1922. Raúl's brother, Emilio Azcárraga Vidauretta, himself attended college in Austin, Texas.

At the outbreak of the Second World War in 1939, the Azcárraga radio station XEW was known as the 'Voice of Latin America from Mexico'. The respected *Time* magazine described XEW as 'the most powerful station in the Western Hemisphere'. *Time* pointed out that the maximum power permitted for a radio station in the United States at the time was 50 kilowatts. XEW operated on 100 kilowatts and was authorised to go as high as 200 kilowatts. In addition, Azcárraga's company had been awarded a prize for 'administrative excellence' by *Variety*.

Azcárraga, XEW and the United States government were to become deeply embroiled in a propaganda war, of which little is known in the English-speaking world. The results might have been disastrous both for Azcárraga and the US.

At the end of 1940, the US was still an uncommitted bystander in the war with Hitler's Germany. William Paley, the founder and Spanish-speaking president of the CBS network, set off on a tour of Latin America seeking to sign up radio stations as affiliates. He returned with sixty-four contracts in his pocket. Each five-year contract stipulated that the station would transmit a minimum of one hour per day of CBS programming. 'It will,' said Paley, 'give us a dominant position in comparison with any other nation. The Germans, naturally, have bought time on radio but we will still have the dominant position thanks to these arrangements.'

In July 1948, John Royal, Vice-President of NBC, carried out a similar journey with even more spectacular results. These included the signing of an exclusive deal with Azcárraga's XEW which was the biggest network in Mexico to join NBC's 'Cadena Panamericana' (Pan-American Chain). Azcárraga also made a deal with CBS, by which his station XEQ formed part of that network's 'Cadena de las Americas'. The link between Azcárraga and the two largest radio networks in the world was to be of enormous significance in the future.

Nelson Rockefeller had been appointed late in 1940 by President Roosevelt as head of the Office for Interamerican Affairs. One of the tasks of the Office was to establish a blacklist under which Latin American companies would be rated as hostile, pro-Nazi or opposed to United States policies. The ratings depended in large degree on the perceptions of US companies which had relations with such foreign concerns. Needless to say, the criteria were open to abuse by unscrupulous commercial rivals.

Between 6 April 1941 and the middle of 1942, both Emilio Azcárraga Vidaurreta personally and his radio network came under the close scrutiny of the FBI and the State Department following reports from secret agents suggesting that Azcárraga was pro-Nazi and anti-American. Allegations had been made that XEW – 'The Voice of Latin America' – was transmitting coded messages to be picked up, recorded and deciphered in Berlin. The secret messages, it was claimed, were being inserted in normal announcements between musical numbers and commercials. The code was supposedly a simple one based on a sequence of selected letters chosen at random from within given words.

Given the power and influence of XEW within Mexico, and its links with CBS and NBC, the reports were given top priority. The US Intelligence Services reported:

> Azcárraga is a Mexican with strong anti North American feelings and pro Nazi sympathies. He is at the moment pressing the Associated Press agencies to obtain exclusive rights for the transmission of North American news. There are trustworthy reports that Azcárraga receives approximately 20,000 pesos per month in revenue for North American advertisements.[2]

Specific allegations were made that Othón Vélez, manager of XEW, was the spymaster and that he had in his home a powerful radio receiver on which he received and recorded messages from Berlin to pass to the German Legation in Mexico. In addition it was alleged that the deputy manager, the artistic director and the engineering supervisor of XEW as well as most of the staff of XEQ were all pro-Nazi.

The source of these allegations was one H. J. Corson, representative in Mexico of the American Association of Advertising Agencies and 'Observer' for the Export Information Office. In fact Corson was an American spy. He claimed that Azcárraga's pro-German sympathies were well known to the British and French business communities in Mexico.

Meanwhile, messages from the US Embassy in Mexico were giving a different picture. A confidential letter dated 26 May 1942 from the Embassy to the Secretary of State stated:

> Subject: Repeated accusations that Emilio Azcárraga and Radio Station XEW at Mexico City are pro-Nazi Considered [sic] by the Embassy to be Without Foundation,

[2] National Archives Washington, War Department, 13 September 1941, 59,862,20210/4.

The Honorable
The Secretary of State
Washington

Sir,

I have the honor to refer to the Department's strictly
confidential airmail instruction No. 670 of May 21, 1942,
and to repeat that the name of the person in question is
Emilio Azcárraga, and to the Embassy's despatch No. 14959
of January 14, 1942, and to repeat that a thorough
investigation of Sr. Azcárraga fails to reveal any evidence
that he is pro-Nazi.

    Sr. Azcárraga is known to practically all the American
businessmen in Mexico City who have been here for any
length of time. At a meeting of the Coordination Committee
for Mexico at which approximately twenty leading American
businessmen were present, Azcárraga was discussed at
considerable length and it was the unanimous opinion of
these men that Emilio Azcárraga is really pro-American.

On 30 July a similar message from the Embassy to the State
Department reported that 'after a lengthy and careful investigation
of station XEW' the suggestion that it was being 'operated by a pro-
Nazi and suspected of being used to transmit messages to Nazi
agents' were without foundation. Among those who testified to the
Embassy was John Royal, NBC Vice President, who said he had
known Emilio for nearly ten years and that 'he could not imagine
anything more absurd than the suggestion that [Azcárraga] might be
anti-American or pro-German'. The message ended:

The chain of radio stations controlled by Emilio Azcárraga
is by far the most extensive and powerful advertising
medium that exists at present in Mexico. Unfavourable
treatment toward this chain or toward its members could
produce almost unlimited damage to our cause. The
Embassy can only urge most strongly that the records in
Washington be corrected as soon as possible . . .

Televisa is led today by Emilio Azcárraga Milmo, the son and heir of Emilio Azcárraga Vidauretta. Milmo, in a unique example of cultural imperialism in reverse, has spent and continues to spend considerable time and effort in wooing the growing Hispanic population of the United States. His efforts have extended beyond broadcasting to organising a system by which Mexicans working in the States can remit money to their families in Mexico.

Emilio Azcárraga Milmo – 'El Tigre' ('The Tiger') – once boasted: 'My only boss is the President of the Republic.' He had little formal education and unlike most of his peers in the Mexican business world has no university degree. While his father was alive, Emilio Junior was restricted to only relatively minor positions within Televisa. His father – the Czar of Mexican Television – was domineering in both his public and private life. Critics of Azcárraga claim that he has inherited this trait.

At the end of one lunch which he gave for the Secretary of State at which senior executives and Televisa's top newscaster Jacobo Zabludovsky were present, the Secretary rose to thank Azcárraga for the meal and Zabludovsky and the executives for their work in television. Azcárraga interrupted: 'Why are you thanking them? They are only here to serve.'

His arrival at Televisa is presidential, as he steps from his blue Mercedes with a distinctive white streak in his carefully coiffured hair. As a result of his enormous wealth and power, Azcárraga inspires both fear and respect within Televisa. When his return from the United States was announced after the crisis that hit Televisa in the late 1980s, one headline ran: 'Panic in Televisa at Azcárraga's return.' He once claimed that he never gave press interviews, though he was more accessible during his recent campaign to sell Televisa stock in the United States.

Azcárraga has challenged the power of the state on more than one occasion. Two incidents in 1986 which undoubtedly contributed to Azcárraga's brief 'exile' in the United States seemed to indicate an intention on the part of Televisa to run directly counter to Mexico's foreign policy.

In 1986, the declared policy of Mexico towards the Sandinista regime in Nicaragua was one of strict non-intervention. Televisa's anti-Castro and anti-Sandinista sympathies were well known. In March 1986, an interview by Televisa's Washington reporter Yolande Sanchez with the American Secretary of State George Schultz was given star billing on the main *24 Hours* news programme. Schultz used the opportunity to defend United States intervention in Nicaragua and to criticise the peacemaking efforts of the Contadora Group. It was described by one Mexican journalist as 'a little masterpiece of disinformation'.

A second, apparently more trivial incident was to create even greater waves. During the recording of his weekly show at a beauty contest in Villahermosa, the Televisa presenter Raúl Velasco stopped the appearance of the young 'Miss Nicaragua', Diana Traebecke, on the grounds that the presence of a representative from Sandinista Nicaragua might 'offend' Televisa's audience in Miami. The incident hit the headlines across Mexico.

The Tabasco politician Cesar Raúl Ojeda deplored the discourtesy to the young beauty queen saying 'Televisa does not set Mexico's foreign policy.' Others described it as 'flagrant ideological discrimination'. The matter was eventually raised in the Mexican Chamber of Deputies by the government deputy Santiago Onate Laborde: 'No consortium, however powerful it be, however powerful it aspires to be, can justifiably represent the national interest nor parade as temporary chancellor, as parallel chancellor or as an electronic chancellor.' Onate went on to deplore the apparent interference of Televisa in Mexico's foreign policy in such matters as the recognition of foreign governments and its invariable observance of the right of self-determination. 'For our party, for the Institutional Revolutionary Party [the PRI],' declared Onate, 'it is not admissible through the chance concession of an electronic oligarchy and much less through the medium of television to place in doubt the foreign policy of our country.'

There were other events. One was a highly public row with the artist Rufino Tamayo over Televisa's management of his major collection of contemporary art valued at over $10 million and housed in a building constructed by Televisa and the Alfa Group on land donated by the government. The collection was to be a gift to the nation but the museum was used by Televisa for its own purposes as if it owned the collection. Tamayo was so incensed at the lack of response to his protests that in 1985 he had threatened to go on hunger strike. 'Mr Azcárraga has no right to think he owns anything,' complained the artist. 'He has improperly and impudently taken over the museum without any right whatsoever.' A public outcry in favour of Tamayo led to government intervention. The President of Mexico, Miguel de la Madrid, called for the museum to be opened to the public 'rapidly and permanently'. Two weeks later Televisa announced that it would withdraw from the running of the museum and hand it over to the nation.

Tamayo and public opinion had managed to defeat Azcárraga but, queried PRI deputy Edmundo Gonzalez Llaca: 'How many artists, scriptwriters, composers and musicians without the international renown of Tamayo have had their work stolen or boycotted by the television monopoly?' Others claimed that it was yet another example of Televisa trying to impose its own, strictly commercial concept of art and culture on Mexico.

The 1986 World Cup soccer competition held in Mexico brought Azcárraga into another conflict of international dimensions that once again was to involve the President of Mexico. Twenty years earlier, in 1965, the Azcárragas had built the giant Aztec Stadium in the south of the city close by the Autonomous National University of Mexico. Football, with its enormous popular following in Mexico and throughout Latin America, was rightly seen as a potentially lucrative investment.

In 1985 the Brazilian Joao Havelange became a partner with Televisa in an attempt to acquire the Record television chain in Brazil, following the opposition of Roberto Marinho's Globo network to Azcárraga's ambitions to extend his empire to that country. Azcárraga was later to deny categorically that he was interested in acquiring stations anywhere outside Mexico. 'I could have gotten into Brazilian broadcasting in the days of Aziz Chateaubriand, when he ran Rede Tupi in São Paulo, but wasn't interested in doing so. Our main interest at present is buying satellite transponders to distribute our programmes.' Commenting later on the enforced sale of part of his United States interests in 1987, which we shall examine more closely, he continued during a rare press conference: 'I'm not interested in owning stations in the US. I strongly believe nations should own stations of their own countries and have always been opposed to NBC and CBS owning stations in Latin America.'

Havelange was re-elected as President of the International Football Federation (FIFA) shortly before the World Cup. The West German sports equipment manufacturer Adidas, headed by Havelange's friend Horst Dassler, was to be one of the sixteen multinational companies that invested in the event. The Vice-President of FIFA and Chairman of the organising committee for the Cup was Guillermo Cañedo, who also happened to work for Televisa as Vice-President for legal affairs.

A 75 per cent Televisa-owned subsidiary, Telemexico, was charged with commercialisation and distribution of the pictures. The tariff Telemexico proposed charging for the television signal and for office space in Televisa's luxurious specially constructed transmission centre in the San Angel quarter of Mexico City raised howls of protest from broadcasters world-wide and the threat of a boycott from the members of the European Broadcasting Union. Worse was to come. The opening ceremony reached twenty-three countries by satellite without sound. Canada received the German commentary, Germany received the French commentary and there were frequent breakdowns in the satellite feed.

It was, said John Bromley, at the time head of sports for the United Kingdom's Independent Television (ITV) network, 'one of the greatest transmission disasters in the history of sport'. The representative of France's Antenne 2 was more direct. 'FIFA and the organisers of the World Cup are more interested in their bank accounts than in our technical problems.' Jack Anderson wrote in *The Washington Post* that the hopes of the government of Mexico to improve the image of the country through its hosting of the World Cup had not counted 'with the Mexican television executives to whom they entrusted this mission'. Subsequent signals from the Presidential Office led rapidly to the appointment of a new executive director of Telemexico.

In spite of all this, the 1986 World Cup was good business for Televisa. It is calculated that domestic advertising sales alone brought in $20 million without counting gains from the sale of the signal overseas. In addition, the technical equipment bought for the event was used to decentralise Televisa's studios. The main loser had been the good name of Mexico.

In March 1986, Televisa had set up an office in Los Angeles. It was headed by Emilio Azcárraga's daughter Sandra with the title of International Programming Coordinator.

On 11 August 1986, the following terse announcement was issued by Rómulo O'Farrill, the Presidente del Consejo (Chairman) of Televisa: 'In consideration of the growing importance of the Televisa Group's activities in the international field, we have asked Mr Emilio Azcárraga, president of Televisa, to take over the very important responsibility for these activities, which he has accepted with particular interest.' Azcárraga packed his bags to join his daughter in the United States, together with his news lieutenant Jacobo Zabludovsky. Within ten months he was back. One commentator, Raúl Trejo Delarbre, later dubbed that interlude of ten months 'La Primavera de Televisa' – the spring of Televisa. The phrase 'particular interest' was a masterpiece of understatement.

Various theories were produced for Azcárraga's sudden flight to Los Angeles: the state of his health, weariness with fighting the government, his intention to go to the States to defend his own personal interests, which appeared threatened by the American government. Whatever the reason the announcement was greeted with some relief, not least among the employees of the Televisa group and those outside who were concerned that Televisa under Azcárraga's control was becoming a threat not only to Mexico's cultural values but even to the traditional balance of the country's political system.

The fact was that Azcárraga's United States empire was under siege. Federal Communications Commission judge John H.

Conlin concluded on 8 January that although the Azcárragas owned only 20 per cent of stock in the Spanish satellite SICC network beamed into the United States – the maximum foreign holding permitted by the FCC – the outlets' other partners were in fact agents of the Azcárraga family. Conlin recommended that the FCC revoke the licences. In spite of efforts to work out an acceptable corporate restructuring with the FCC Mass Media Bureau, Azcárraga was finally forced to sell.

The sale was to Hallmark Cards Inc./First Chicago Venture Capital and the reported price $301 million. *Forbes* magazine reckoned that the company with partner First Chicago 'have spent more than $500 million to buy Univision, the largest Spanish-language network, and ten TV stations previously owned by Spanish International Communications Corp'. It was said at the time that 'Spanish broadcasting caters to a fast growing, brand oriented population'.

Azcárraga's short-lived exile was over. In the intervening ten months he had presided over the sale of Televisa's television stations in the United States. It was a sale forced by the US authorities, but left Azcárraga and the consortium not only with a substantial sum to re-invest but also with its power and earnings potential in the USA very little diminished. As a result of a complex series of financial manoeuvres a new organisation, Univisa, was formed to run production, sales and distribution of television and other media in the United States.

Azcárraga himself returned with greater power than when he left. On 25 May 1987, the creation of an executive committee responsible for the running of all the activities of Televisa and Univisa was announced. Its chairman was – of course – Emilio Azcárraga.

The public image of 'El Tigre' is an abrasive one. It contrasts sharply with the softer and more 'simpatico' style of Miguel Alemán, the man who took over Televisa's Mexican operations during Azcárraga's absence in the States. Azcárraga's roots are in the modern Mexican industrial 'Caciquismo', Alemán's in Mexico's political elite. Alemán is a politician and a diplomat, while Azcárraga is a businessman. Their relations with the press offer a sharp contrast. While Alemán talks freely and easily, Azcárraga cannot abide the trade of journalism.

In 1952, Emilio Azcárraga's father, Vidauretta, met a young former actor from Massachussetts. The actor, Rene Anselmo, was trying to sell American television series dubbed into Spanish to the new Mexican television stations. It was the start of a long association between the Azcárraga family and Anselmo.

Azcárraga Senior had subsequently appointed Anselmo as head of Televisa's United States affiliated SIN network and during the 1960s he built it into the most important Spanish language network in the US. In 1980, SIN wanted to install an antenna on top of New York's World Trade Centre for its New York station. Anselmo responded to objections to the project by going on a week's hunger strike.

When Emilio Azcárraga Junior (Milmo) was forced in 1987 to sell his interest in the Spanish language SIN satellite network in the US by the Federal Communications Commission, Anselmo put his share of the $301 million received from the sale behind a project to launch PanAmSat – the first ever privately owned international communications satellite system. Rather than leasing time, Anselmo's project was to sell individual transponders on his 'condominium' satellite. Anselmo was reported as saying at the time: 'This is my new holy war. Don't be surprised if you see another hunger strike.'

It wasn't necessary. Anselmo's company, Alpha Lyracom, launched its first PanAmSat satellite in 1990. Within two years, all eight transponders had been sold out and there was a waiting list for Anselmo's condominium in the sky. Alpha Lyracom was examining ways of squeezing six more channels on its first satellite and was announcing plans to launch three more Hughes satellites in 1994.

In 1992, while the United States and Europe were in the grip of a long-lasting recession, the economies of Latin American countries were showing clear signs of economic recovery after years of crippling inflation. In spite of the ever-present danger of a military coup threatening newly founded democracies, investments started pouring into the region from the United States,

Japan and Europe. Talks between Canada, Mexico and the United States gave an added boost to interest in the region.

The changing political and above all economic climate in the region, with its promise of new audiences and markets, led to considerable activity in the field of satellite and cable television. American, Japanese and European interests started to move in. Sales by companies within the American Film Market Association almost doubled from $44 million in 1990 to $83 million in 1991 and early in 1992 Warner Bros. TV acquired a 50 per cent interest in Marte TV, a leading producer of 'telenovelas' in Venezuela.

Roberto Marinho's Brazilian Globo TV, Azcárraga's Televisa and Cisnero's Venevision in Venezuela are responding to the threat by expanding both within and beyond their own frontiers.

Venevision's sales to Spain in 1991 represented a quarter of all sales and those to the United States almost 20 per cent. The company was planning a new Spanish language cable network in the United States to be launched at the end of 1992 and was involved in co-production projects with Berlusconi's Tele-5 in Spain.

In Brazil, where Marinho's Rede Globo continued to claim 60 per cent of the advertising market in 1992, the Brazilian Sky Baron launched a satellite and cable network – Globosat – at the end of 1991 and was planning to build a major new studio complex called Projac in the Barra de Tijuca area outside Rio de Janeiro. Globo's steadily increasing foreign sales totalled $20 million in 1991. Globo also owns 15 per cent of Portugal's first private TV network, SIC, scheduled to start broadcasting at the end of 1992.

In December 1991, Mexico's Azcárraga bought 49 per cent of Megavision (Channel 9) in Chile. The company's general manager said: 'Our 1992 programmes will be approximately 32 per cent Televisa, 30 per cent Chilean, 15 per cent from the US and the remainder [23 per cent] from Brazil and Europe. This does not imply that the station will become Mexicanised, but less elitist and more massive, by which I do not mean coarse.' Azcárraga was also reported to be in discussion with ATC (Channel 7) in Argentina.

In December 1991, Mexico's Stock Exchange, the Bolsa, was valued at $93 billion – nearly seventeen times its value five years earlier at the end of 1986. In the same month, Emilio Azcárraga offered for sale 22 per cent (69 million shares) in his Televisa Group at a target price of up to $11.50 a share, valuing the company at nearly forty times predicted 1991 earnings. When the sale took place on 10 December, the shares immediately jumped to $12.50, valuing the company at $3.9 billion, on estimated 1991 revenues of $760 million. Some nine million shares were sold to public investors on the Mexican Bolsa and 60 million (some 87 per cent) in private placements in the US, Japan and Europe, raising a total of $754 million, or 2.26 trillion pesos.

It was a surprising move for this most private of private companies, which for the first time had to open its books and its affairs to public scrutiny. The usually secretive Azcárraga stomped the United States with a 'road show' selling the shares. He forecast after-tax profits of $100 million in 1991 (32 cents a share) and claimed that earnings would double in 1992. Televisa had $1.08 billion in assets at the end of August 1991, but it posted losses of $168 million in 1990.

Some analysts say that taking account of inflation, the company is still losing money. 'Whether Televisa is worth almost forty times earnings and five times revenue is very much open to question,' observed Joel Milman.[3]

About half the money raised from the sale (nearly $400 million) will be used to cover the buyout of Miguel Alemán and Rómulo O'Farrill's 41 per cent share of the group in August and the remainder on paying off some of Televisa's short and long term debt of $740 million. Today Azcárraga, his son, nephew and sister together own 64.5 per cent of Grupo Televisa's shares.

There is a threat from the Salinas government plan to privatise its own TV channels, which would breach Televisa's monopoly of commercial television for the first time. No date has yet been set for the sale nor have the ground rules been announced by the finance ministry which oversees privatisations and has been busy

[3] *Forbes*, 6 January 1992.

selling off various of Mexico's nationalised banks. Azcárraga recognised the possibility of competition for revenues in his prospectus offering stock in the group.

Meanwhile, Mexico is actively pursuing with the US and Canada the creation of a free-trade area throughout the North American continent. This may create conditions in which US entrepreneurs such as Ted Turner, who already provides a Spanish language service in the United States, may apply for the new licences. Miami-based Univision, which also targets US Hispanics and was once owned by Azcárraga, is also known to be interested. A 1973 law allows only Mexicans to invest in TV and certain other fields, but a waiver was given recently when Teléfonos de Mexico was sold in part to US and French companies. It is rumoured that Silvio Berlusconi may well look across the Atlantic to Mexico when his European ambitions are fulfilled.

On 30 April 1992, the day the World Fair 'Expo '92' opened its gates in Sevilla, eighteen Latin American countries together with Spain's national network RTVE launched 'The Channel of the Americas' – 'Cadena de las Americas'. Twenty hours a week of programming provided by the participants were put together and transmitted via satellite by Televisa. The service was seen as an experiment for the duration of the Expo which was to end in October 1992 but if it is successful and attracts viewers in sufficient numbers it will continue and become the largest regularly scheduled multinational television service in the world. The name of the Channel is the same as that of the radio network, created by CBS in 1938 to counter Nazi propaganda, of which Azcárraga's father's radio station XEQ was a member.

X

The Sleeping Giant:
Bertelsmann

Pastures speckled with black and white Friesland cows, isolated redbrick and half-timbered farmhouses, meandering streams, ancient oaks, rows of beeches and pine woods mounting gentle sandy slopes. These provide the setting for the sleepy district capital of Gütersloh.

The first Stone Age inhabitants of Gütersloh, according to local historians, settled at some time between 10,000 and 4,000 BC along what is today known as Carl-Bertelsmann Strasse. Later, around the time of the birth of Christ, there were to be some bloody confrontations between the resident Germanic tribe of the Brukterer and the troops of the Roman Empire.

Gütersloh faded back into its pastoral surroundings for most of the next eighteen hundred years. But in 1825 the village with its three hundred private houses and some two and a half thousand inhabitants (2,126 Protestants, 196 Catholics and 82 Jews) was designated a town by the Prussian government so that it could be eligible to elect representatives to Parliament.

The distillation of spirits was well established in North Germany by the beginning of the sixteenth century. The protein-rich residues of the distilling process provided invaluable supplementary fodder for the livestock eking out a meagre existence on the sandy Westphalian soil. Most of the farmers had two things in common. They all spoke the local 'Platt' dialect and they all operated stills to produce spirit from Juniper berries. One farmer in Steinhagen, today under the administrative control of Gütersloh, produced a distinctive version of this 'korn' or 'schnapps', now marketed world-wide under the name of 'Steinhager'.

Carl Bertelsmann was a bookbinder by trade. He was a devout Protestant – his father a Lutheran pastor. Unable to earn sufficient money for his needs from his trade, he took on a second job as a local tax collector. In 1822, he became town treasurer of Gütersloh. That same year he married and his fortunes began to change. Two years later, he set up a lithographic engraving business in spite of having no formal training in the trade.

On 1 July 1835, Carl Bertelsmann established the firm which bears his name to this day. He expanded his bookbinding and engraving concerns to include publishing and set up shop in a half-timbered house at No. 3 Kirschstrasse in Gütersloh. The firm Carl founded began life publishing hymn books in collaboration with Johann Heinrich Volkening, a member of the Minden-Ravensburg Evangelical Movement. Bertelsmann's first big success was the publication of 'The Little Mission Harp' ('Kleine Missionsharfe'), which was eventually to sell over two million copies and run through seventy-eight editions – a bestseller by any standards.

Today Carl Bertelsmann's business is still run from the sleepy town of Gütersloh (pop. 80,000) in the heart of the ancient Leutoburger Forest in what is today North-Rhine Westphalia in the Federal Republic of Germany. The roar of juggernauts leaving its vast industrial complex to the west of the town carry its publications and records to the four corners of the world. Occasionally the noise is drowned by the activities of low-flying jets from the nearby RAF base or a helicopter leaving the executive pad opposite its headquarters. Soon, the jets will go along with the redundant British and American presence in the newly re-united Germany.

The firm remained in the family, eventually passing at the end of the war to the son of Carl's granddaughter – Reinhard Mohn. Mohn was a captain in the Wehrmacht when he was captured by Allied troops while fighting with Rommel's forces in Tunisia and spent the rest of the war in a prisoner-of-war camp in Concordia, Kansas, in the United States. He spent the long empty hours of his confinement reading voraciously to improve his English. When he was released in 1945 he was to bring back with him two lessons from his reading. The first was the idea of the Book of the Month Club and the second the theory of strictly controlled decentralisation practised by Alfred P. Sloan, the legendary head of General Motors. Sloan was the pioneer of a system of separate integral units each with its own management structure but all working together in a coordinated effort. Mohn read Sloan's *Adventures of a White Collar Man*, published in 1941, from cover to cover. He was fascinated by the contrast between America's open society and the patriarchal management and social tradition he knew at home. The company, wrote Sloan, was a machine whose moving parts were human and whose lubricant was merit:

> Think of the corporation as a pyramid of opportunities
> from top to bottom with thousands of chances for
> advancement. Only capacity limited any worker's chance
> to grow, to develop his ability to make a greater
> contribution to the whole and improve his position as
> well. . . . Any plan that involved too great a concentration
> of power upon a limited number of executives would limit
> initiative . . . and would reduce efficiency and
> development. Further it would mean an autocracy, which
> is just as dangerous in great industrial organisations as in a
> government.[1]

Another man influenced by Alfred P. Sloan's philosophy was Lee Iacocca, who after being fired from the Ford Motor Company had a dream of a vast corporation – 'Global Motors'. It was to be a consortium of European, Japanese and US companies that would challenge the might of General Motors. 'I envisaged myself as the new Alfred P. Sloan,' he said later. When investment bankers told him his dream would shatter on the US anti-trust laws, he settled for the top job at Chrysler. Reinhard Mohn has realised Iacocca's dream in the world of communications.

On his return to Gütersloh, Mohn found the town devastated by the war, the Bertelsmann printing presses destroyed and his two

---

[1] Alfred P. Sloan, *Adventures of a White Collar Man*.

brothers missing. Like so many entrepreneurs in postwar Germany, Mohn relied on barter to get one press working and secured a contract to print and supply labels for one of the many local distillers of korn schnapps in exchange for cases of spirit. The spirits he exchanged for bricks to rebuild the shattered printing works.

Today the Bertelsmann headquarters on Carl-Bertelsmann Strasse are housed in a massive modernistic and luxurious office building in landscaped gardens. It has its own helicopter pad where busy executives depart and arrive on their world-wide travels. A copy of the first book the founder printed is preserved in a glass case in the entrance atrium.

Remembering Alfred P. Sloan's theories, Reinhard Mohn turned his back on traditional Teutonic hierarchical management structures and adopted a decentralised approach with separate operating groups encouraging individual entrepreneurial aggressiveness. He kept the business firmly focussed on publishing apart from brief forays into chicken farms and a chain of cinemas in the 1960s.

It was early in the sixties that Mohn put into practice the idea he had brought back from the United States: the book club. The book club had one great advantage over other publishing ventures: you got the money up front. By 1987, Bertelsmann's book and record clubs had over 16 million members in nineteen countries around the world.

In the late 1960s Mohn moved into magazine publishing through the purchase of a stake in Gruner & Jahr, publishers of Germany's most influential magazine, *Der Spiegel*, and of *Stern*, which earned world-wide notoriety in 1984 when it published the bogus Hitler diaries.

Following his rigid rule for all Bertelsmann staff, Mohn retired in 1981 at the age of sixty. He and his family own 90 per cent of the company estimated in 1987 to be worth $2.5 billion. Reinhard Mohn still keeps a close watch on the enterprise and has a hand in its business strategy.

It has been said of Reinhard Mohn that he is the sort of man from whom you could buy a used car with confidence. But, as those who tell you this add, he will probably persuade you to buy two new cars instead. Mohn lives simply, hates talking about himself and used frequently to take lunch with office staff in the canteen. There is nothing flashy about the style of Mohn's modest home life with his wife and three daughters. For relaxation, he chops wood on the estate.

The special strengths of Bertelsmann have always been those of a family business. Mohn has sought to ensure that after his death the family firm will not be subject to battles over ownership, either within the family or outside. The family shares will go to Bertelsmann Stiftung, a charitable foundation he set up twelve years ago. The foundation supports library, research and teaching work.

He turned Bertelsmann into an Aktiengesellschaft (joint stock company), apparently preparing for the day when Bertelsmann might go public. The company's *Genussscheine* (profit-sharing certificates) are traded on the over-the-counter market, but that is still a far cry from an official stock-exchange listing. The 10 per cent of the stock not in the hands of the Mohn family are held by the Hamburg publisher, Dr Gerd Bucerius.

By decentralising decision-making and motivating employees from boardroom to factory-floor level, and by introducing semi-autonomous 'profit centres' Mohn encouraged a spirit of competition within the group. He also introduced a company charter with generous social benefits and a profit-sharing scheme. He was convinced that the better employees were treated, the more they were kept informed and given responsibility, the more efficient – and profitable – the company would be.

The foundations Mohn laid with his bartered bricks in the ruins of Gütersloh after the war have turned his maternal grandfather's firm into a global publishing corporation. In 1986 it was the world's richest publishing house with sales of $5.1 billion and interests in books, music, magazines and TV. The same year saw cash-rich Bertelsmann on a massive American shopping spree with the purchase of the RCA/Ariola record company for $330 million and only two weeks later the Doubleday publishing house for a further $475 million. Bertelsmann is known locally in

Gütersloh as 'The Sleeping Giant'. After these purchases, the giant settled down to digest its acquisitions.

'It doesn't matter to us whether we are number one, two or three in the market,' said Bertelsmann aide Helmuth Runde, the suave and respected public face of the corporation, in 1987. 'Our plans are to consolidate our operations until the middle of 1990 and we are sticking to it. We are not making any major acquisitions until after then, no matter what is offered,' he added.

By 1992 Bertelsmann AG had become the third largest media group in the world after Time-Warner and Rupert Murdoch's News Corporation, according to a report by brokers James Capel.[2]

There is a paradox between the inward and outward face of the sleeping giant created by Reinhard Mohn. His great grandfather, Carl Bertelsmann's father – the Lutheran pastor of Gütersloh in the early 1800s – would no doubt approve of the caring measures introduced by Mohn for staff welfare and profit sharing. He would probably endorse the policy Mohn first learnt during his enforced residence in the United States from Alfred P. Sloan and General Motors, designed to encourage enterprise and initiative through controlled diversification within the company. On the other hand he might feel concerned at some of the aggressive 'foot in the door' practices of Bertelsmann's book club salesmen, which contributed to the company's dynamic growth in the fifties and sixties. He certainly might raise an eyebrow at some of the erotic films shown on Bertelsmann's national commercial pay-TV television channel RTL-Plus and he might have been amazed at the company's massive expansion in Europe and the United States.

To the outside world, Bertelsmann has at times presented a Mr Hyde aspect that contrasts starkly with the good Dr Jekyll image of its internal organisation. The dynamic growth of the book clubs brought a reputation for 'ugly' salesmanship which Bertelsmann has found hard to shake off.

In 1988, Bertelsmann announced a new issue of *Genussscheine* to raise DM231 million to top up the war chest into which its

[2] *The James Capel Media Book*, 1992.

steadily growing profits were pouring. The issue consisted of 1.32 million new notes at 175 per cent of their DM100 nominal value. The notes entitled their holders to a dividend in the second half of the year to June 1989 and were offered in a ratio of three old notes for each new note by a banking consortium co-led by Deutsche Bank and Commerzbank.

Mohn has transferred a majority of the family's share capital to his son Johannes, the sixth generation, and the remainder to his wife and five other children. Reinhard Mohn himself retains a DM500 million share with all the voting power.[3]

Mark Woessner, Bertelsmann's Chief Executive, saw the Time-Warner merger that pushed Bertelsmann from its position as the world's largest communications company as a defensive measure against outside takeover attempts and foreign competition. 'Two scared rabbits have decided to get together because they think they are less likely to get shot that way,' was the comment of one US investment banker. By 1992, Bertelsmann was talking business with Time-Warner about cooperation on a new German TV news channel, Westschienenkanal.

Bertelsmann's declared editorial policy is one of strict impartiality, although it is generally considered to be Christian Democrat in its outlook. Impartiality was not a consideration for Axel Springer. His intelligence and his overwhelming charm convinced the British press control officers to grant him two licences in 1946. The first was for the Hamburg newspaper *Hamburg Abendblatt* and the second for Germany's first postwar radio listings magazine, *Hör Zu* – which continues to be the best-selling TV magazine in Germany. In 1953, Springer purchased at a bargain price *Die Welt*, a newspaper set up by the British after the war. It was to become his favourite paper. Although it was never a commercial success, Springer used it relentlessly as a platform for his own opinions.

By contrast he built the lurid tabloid *Bild Zeitung* into Europe's biggest-selling newspaper, with sales of five million copies a day

[3] *Forbes*, 24 July 1989.

and over 80 per cent of the West Berlin market alone. Published in eight cities across Germany, one in four Germans read it. *Bild* unashamedly mixes news, comment and 'entertainment'. It is said that news vendors used to warn buyers of the paper 'to make sure to shake the blood out' before they read it. Much as Rupert Murdoch, Springer relished having both a serious, prestigious paper in his stable as well as a determinedly downmarket tabloid.

In Hamburg, special legislation – the 'Lex Springer' – allowed the group to own 33 per cent of Radio Hamburg in spite of its control of the daily newspaper market. The only restriction was that Springer could not have more than 25 per cent of the votes in the company.

Axel Springer became the biggest newspaper publisher in Germany. From the mid-1960s he used his newspapers to support the political parties of the right – at times the far right – and to promote reactionary causes which earned him an undeserved reputation as a political extremist. Neil Ascherson, one-time correspondent in Germany for the *Observer* newspaper in the United Kingdom, observed that Springer was 'demagogic, very right-wing, but fascist he was not'.

This did not prevent violent reaction to Axel Springer's views among the left, which came to a head during the student demonstrations of the late 1960s. In fact, Springer had supported the SPD in the 1950s and early 1960s. In the deepest days of the Cold War he backed the policies and philosophy of Willi Brandt, the mayor of Berlin. But as detente began, Springer switched his allegiance to the conservative CDU. Springer was not a party politician in the accepted sense. He saw political parties as the servants of the state and believed that politics should be based on the moral principles of the Christian religion. He adopted as his motto: 'If God is driven out of the State then it is doomed.'

Four basic principles underlay Axel Springer's political philosophy – and the editorial policy of his newspapers. The first was the re-unification of Germany, which he did not live to see. In the 1960s he moved his headquarters to Berlin, right next to the infamous Wall. Now the imposing 22-storey building stands at the very centre of unified Berlin. The second principle was reconciliation between German and Jew. Axel Springer's newspapers not only supported the State of Israel but Springer, who was not a Jew himself, made financial contributions to it. The third principle was a complete rejection of dictatorship and the fourth, unwavering support for the market economy. Springer personally selected his editors on the basis of these four principles and any journalist who stepped out of line would never again work for his newspapers.

Alex Springer's father had been the publisher of a small newspaper in a Hamburg suburb which had been closed by the Nazis before the war. Axel escaped conscription because of his bad health and spent the war working at the Waterloo cinema in Hamburg. He had Danish as well as German blood and many who knew him commented that he was not at all a 'typical' German although he believed passionately in Germany as a nation. Debonair and possessed of a ready wit, he was a far cry from the image of the typical Prussian or Bavarian. Springer was always one jump ahead of the game and had an intuitive sixth sense and an instinctive knowledge of the mentality of the man in the street. He read perfectly the mood of postwar Germany and used his newspapers to promote the kind of consumer society the Germans yearned for.

One of the richest men in Europe, Springer spent his last years ill, disappointed and depressed. One of his sons had committed suicide for no apparent reason and his other son suffered from cancer. Before Axel Springer died in 1983, he turned his personal empire into a public company. After his death there ensued a long and bitter battle for control, eventually won by Springer's widow and heirs.

The Kirch Group had attempted to form a powerful alliance of print and audiovisual media with Springer. What amounted to an attempt at a hostile takeover failed when Kirch's former allies the Burda family sold their stake in Springer back to his widow and heirs, allowing the family to retain control of the company. Springer's widow Friede holds 52 per cent through the Axel Springer Gesellschaft für Publizistik. Leo Kirch and partners own 10 per cent and Kirch is said to control a further 15 per cent through trustees. The UK merchant bank Morgan Grenfell holds 2 per cent.

Axel Springer Verlag controls seven book publishing companies and has interests in printing and marketing concerns in addition to its predominant position in the newspaper field. Internationally, the Group has launched special interest magazines in the United Kingdom, France, Spain and Italy and is moving into Eastern European markets.

Axel Springer Verlag joined forces with the Stuttgart property tycoon and film impresario Rolf Deyhle and the film production and distribution company Bodo Scriba to form Capitol Film & TV. The aim was to acquire feature films for German language television services – a market almost exclusively controlled by Kirch at the time. Springer put up 60 per cent of the capital.

On the broadcasting front, Springer has a 15 per cent share in the burgeoning satellite/cable TV channel SAT-1 and interests in four commercial radio stations in northern Germany and Berlin.

Our third German Sky Baron, Dr Leo Kirch, is almost a legend in Germany for his secretiveness and reclusiveness. Kirch was born in Wurzburg in 1926, the son of a Bavarian vineyard owner. After studying business administration, he moved into the film industry.

Kirch is the dominant partner in the Kirch and Springer owned SAT-1 pay-TV network. The highly politicised nature of Germany's media is reflected by the fact that SAT-1 has tended to receive the best broadcasting frequencies in the states ruled by the conservative CDU, while its arch-rival RTL-Plus, mainly owned by Bertelsmann and the Luxembourg group CLT, has tended to flourish in the states dominated by the social democratic SPD. The SAT-1 headquarters are in the capital of the CDU-ruled Rhineland Palatinate, while RTL-Plus is based at Cologne, in the SPD stronghold of North-Rhine Westphalia.

The Kirch Group has had a near monopoly in supplying feature films to SAT-1. It also owns 51 per cent of PKS, SAT-1's leading programme supplier and had virtually cornered the market in filmed material for television, owning some 15,000 TV features alone.

Leo Kirch's remarkable career in the media began in 1954 when he bought the film and television rights to Fellini's classic, *La Strada*. In 1959 he purchased a $6 million package of films from Warner Brothers and United Artists. It was to be a profitable deal. He paid only $3,000 for the rights to *Casablanca*, which he sold thirty years later for a reported $150,000.

Kirch is the outright owner of two major film companies, Beta and Taurus, in addition to his interests in SAT-1. Through a holding company (PKS), he controls 40 per cent of the channel and through his holding in Springer has an interest in a further 15 per cent. Kirch is also involved with his son and principal heir Thomas in a movie channel, Pro-7, together with two video companies (Taurus Film Video and Videobox) and a new pay-TV channel Premiere (25 per cent) in partnership with Bertelsmann's UFA film subsidiary (37.5 per cent) and the French Canal Plus (37.5 per cent).

The Kirch Group is closely involved with the Deutsche Genossenschaftsbank (DG Bank). It has recently begun to expand abroad and owns companies in Rome and Paris. Kirch has launched a joint venture with the Tribune Broadcasting Corporation in the US to produce TV films and mini-series.

The fact remains that Kirch has a virtual monopoly in Germany of what Hollywood likes to call 'A-product'. From his original investment in *La Strada* Kirch has built up a collection of television fare ranging from feature films to documentaries, children's programmes and operas that is unrivalled in Europe. They are stored away in an air-conditioned vault underneath the Kirch headquarters in the Munich suburb of Unterforing. The collection – over 80,000 hours of television, enough to fill a 24-hour TV channel continuously for eight years – is worth close to $2 billion. To give an idea of the size of this hoard, it has been estimated that on average some 4,000 new feature films are made each year world-wide and less than half of those are suitable for television. This was one of the reasons why Kirch, like other Sky Barons, moved into the film production business. 'New productions are so rare and so expensive,' Kirch says, 'that even we, who produce more than others, are dependent on cooperation on a

European scale.' Kirch's co-production ventures have involved Berlusconi, the French entrepreneur Jérôme Seydoux and Robert Maxwell, as well as the Tribune Entertainment Company.

Kirch, a Catholic, is politically conservative. He is a devoted family man, and believes his private life is of no public interest. Like Silvio Berlusconi, he has a taste for works of art. The walls of Kirch's homes in Munich and St Moritz, between which he commutes using his aptly named Mystère jet, are lined with masterpieces. He has groomed his son Thomas to take over his empire. Thomas has already established himself in his own right in television as 49 per cent shareholder in the private Pro-7 channel.

Leo Kirch is less reluctant to talk about his business which he describes as 'simply fun'. Joachim Theye, Kirch's consultant and friend, describes him as a businessman of genius: 'Communication and media ask for imagination and economic bigness. Kirch has both.'

XI

Out of the Ruins:
Maxwell and Berlin

On 6 July 1945, the Fifth Battalion of the Queen's Royal Regiment marched proudly down Berlin's Charlottenburger Chausee, bayonets fixed and colours flying. Among their number was a young lieutenant who was something of a hero. Two months earlier, General Montgomery had personally pinned the Military Cross on his chest.

Lt Ian Robert Maxwell MC had begun his tour of duty in Berlin as a field security officer responsible for interrogating German prisoners-of-war in the devastated capital. His war record, his energy and his fluency in eight languages were soon to bring him to the attention of the Control Commission in the British Sector responsible to the Foreign Office but staffed by military officers.

The Public Relations and Information Services Control Section (PRISC) of the Commission acted as a licensing agency for Germans who wanted to operate cinemas or theatres or publish books or newspapers. In fulfilling their task, PRISC's objectives were to ensure that no trace of the Nazi philosophy filtered into the cultural life of postwar Germany and that democratic foundations were established for the new generation of plays, films, books and newspapers.

Robert Maxwell was appointed Temporary Officer Grade III, Information Services Control Branch and promoted to the rank of Captain – a title of which he was to become inordinately fond.

Maxwell's job was effectively that of censor. Later he was to boast to *Daily Mirror* staff: 'At twenty-one I was editor of *Der Telegraaf* in Berlin.' His main duty was the vetting of every article published in the newspaper, founded by Arno Scholtz, an independent socialist who had been arrested soon after Hitler came to power and, although later released, was forbidden to work through most of the war. Although Maxwell later denied it, it seems likely that he was instrumental in securing the licence for Scholtz to launch his newspaper.

Maxwell and Scholtz struck up a strong friendship. Scholtz provided Maxwell with introductions to important figures in postwar Berlin and Maxwell provided Scholtz with stories from officials in the military government and, more importantly and miraculously, supplies of newsprint and ink, both of which were in desperately short supply. With unaccustomed modesty Maxwell said later: 'If a publisher came along and said he was short of paper, say for an election campaign, I would make a few telephone calls.' Scholtz and Nicholas Huijsman, Maxwell's superior at PRISC, were both godfathers to Maxwell's first son Michael.

Der Telegraaf was a success. The eight-page tabloid sold a quarter of a million copies six days a week and within two months took over its competitor *Der Berliner*.

It was Arno Scholtz who set Maxwell on the path to publishing fame when he first sowed in the mind of the recently demobbed army captain in search of a peacetime career the potential of the hidden goldmine of German scientific publishing. According to Vernon Baxter, who worked for Maxwell after the war: 'Scholtz told him, if you help re-establish the trade, the trade will kiss your feet.'[1] It was an idea Maxwell could not resist.

But there was another German publisher who had cause to be grateful to Robert Maxwell in the immediate postwar years and to whom in turn Maxwell owed the rise and fall of his empire. In 1842, seven years after Carl Bertelsmann set up his bible printing shop in Gütersloh, Julius Springer (no connection with the Axel Springer newspaper group) was opening a small bookshop in Berlin. The shop stayed in the family and passed to Julius's grandson Ferdinand in 1907.

A scientific and technological revolution was poised to sweep the world. Henry Ford was perfecting the blueprints for his

[1] Tom Bower, *Maxwell: The Outsider*.

Model T; telegraphy, sound recording, radio and moving pictures were all poised for rapid development. Ferdinand Springer approached a number of selected German scientists and engineers and offered to publish their works. His authors included a number of Nobel Prize winners and he published the first works of such pioneers as Paul Ehrlich, Karl von Frisch, Max Born, Max Planck and Albert Einstein.

In addition to publishing single books, Ferdinand Springer produced series of volumes edited by panels of eminent experts on subjects ranging from chemistry and medicine to engineering, psychology and mathematics. These – the Beilstein series – were required purchases for every serious library in the world.

It was a lucrative business as the series and the journals were sold on subscription and paid for in advance. In addition, a demand grew up for back copies for newly established libraries. To capitalise on an ever growing demand, Springer speculatively printed far more copies than he could immediately sell. By the end of 1932 Springer was the biggest scientific publisher in the world.

In January 1933, the German President, von Hindenburg, appointed Hitler Chancellor of Germany. Springer's world changed overnight. Under the Nazis' race laws he was deemed a half-Jew and his cousin Julius – a partner in the firm – three-quarters Jewish. In addition, an immediate ban was placed on sharing Germany's scientific secrets with the rest of the world. The Springers gained a temporary reprieve on the grounds of the world-wide prestige of their operation, but after the enactment of the infamous Nuremberg Decrees in 1935 Julius, as three-quarters Jewish, was forced to sell his shares. Laws already existed forbidding marriage or extra-marital relations between Jews and Aryans. The Nuremberg Decrees deprived Jews of their German nationality, barred them from employment in public services and from teaching, journalism, farming, radio, the theatre and films. Julius Springer's shares were bought by the firm's manager Tonjes Lange, with whom a secret arrangement was made that should they both survive the Third Reich Julius could re-purchase his shares. In 1942, Ferdinand too, was forced to sell his own shares. The same agreement was made with Lange.

In November 1943, Sir Arthur Harris, chief of RAF Bomber Command, promised to bomb Berlin 'until the heart of Nazi Germany ceases to beat'. With Ferdinand's agreement, Lange made arrangements to transport out of Berlin 63,000 books and tens of thousands of handbooks, series, journals and manuscripts worth some £6 million in prewar prices. The stock was split to spread the risk. Some went to the Springer branch in Vienna but the bulk of the stock was stored in a warehouse in Lausitz, south of the capital.

It was a prudent move. By the end of the war, Springer's Berlin warehouses had been devastated in the Allied Blitzkrieg. The headquarters in Linkstrasse on the border between the British and Soviet Zones survived but Lange watched helplessly as the million pounds worth of books still there were plundered through the back door by the Soviets and spirited away to Moscow. The teams of Allied specialists fanning out across Germany to seek out German scientific secrets were too late.

Later in 1945 Julius, who had survived the Oranienburg concentration camp, Ferdinand who had been captured by the Soviet forces but later released and Tonjes Lange were reunited. The firm of Ferdinand Springer was back in business.

In October 1945 they were awarded a licence by PRISC. Orders were beginning to arrive from libraries all over the world anxious to fill the gaps between 1933 and 1945. Springer began negotiations with the Soviet authorities for the release of the stock in the warehouse in Lausitz in the Russian Zone. At the same time he decided to move the firm to Heidelberg to avoid the problems caused by Berlin's isolation deep within Soviet-occupied Germany.

In the course of his duties at PRISC, Maxwell struck up a friendship with Springer and Lange. Two years later the former army captain returned to Berlin. Allied restrictions were preventing Springer Verlag and other publishers from exporting individual copies of books and journals to their customers. Maxwell offered to act as Springer's representative outside Germany.

Over the following nine years their joint business was worth

DM20 million. 'Never will the Springer Publishing House forget the help Captain Maxwell gave us . . . the drastic and successful methods invented by the British Captain [with an MC] produced unimaginably successful solutions to overcome these conditions so we could start exporting again.'[2]

Germany's recovery from the war provided the basis for the new media empires of Bertelsmann, Kirch and the Springers. It also gave a start to Robert Maxwell, the archetypal postwar entrepreneur whose black market background ultimately corrupted his vision. Of the three great German media empires, only that built by Axel Springer is based in Berlin. Springer sited his company's towering new headquarters as close to the Berlin Wall as he could get it in a gesture of defiance at Communism.

On the edge of the city's western suburbs, there stands a greying building of unremarkable appearance. On entering through the chrome and glass-plated doors one is transported back in time to the 1930s. It is not just the Art Deco style of the interior. To one side of the entrance, a continuous wooden lift circulates almost inaudibly, collecting and disgorging its passengers like a contraption from some modern adaptation of *Das Rheingold*.

It is the same lift that Paul Joseph Goebbels took to the radio studio from which he poured forth to the German nation the propaganda that sustained the rationale – such as it was – of the Third Reich. Today, the building houses the friendly and efficient staff of the German regional public broadcaster Sender Freies Berlin. If the SFB building has ghosts, they are almost certainly kept in a tidy file with a lapel badge and a photograph so that they can be greeted cheerily by first name.

In the spring of 1987, SFB was hosting an event known as the Prix Futura Berlin. Held every two years, the Prix Futura is different from other broadcasting festivals in a number of respects. Its screenings and playbacks, and the ensuing critiques and credos, are held in almost Billy Graham-like sessions of public self-criticism. Meanwhile the valued awards are settled in

[2] Tom Bower, *Maxwell: The Outsider*.

smoky private sessions of horsetrading and downright gerry-mandering. The Prix Futura is also distinguished, as its name implies, by focussing on programmes that have significance for the future of mankind.

At the 1987 Prix Futura sessions held in the then still divided city of Berlin, it was not just the programmes that had significance for the future. The spring of revolution was in the air. While some of the productions from the broadcasters of the Eastern bloc still betrayed the dull plod of state funding and propaganda, others – from Hungary, Poland and Czechoslovakia in particular – bore irreverent if not downright hostile critiques of the Communist system. Outside, in the bustling streets and bars of Berlin, life went on as normal, overshadowed by the menacing Berlin Wall. Inside, the *sans-culottes* of the Fourth Estate were already dismantling it from within.

It is a mark of the immense role that broadcasting and broadcasters played in the ending of the old Communist tyrannies that the gap between the informed and the public view should have been so wide. On one evening, at a local bar near the SRF building, a group of Prix Futura delegates became enmeshed with a family party celebrating the twenty-first birthday party of the son of a Berlin city councillor. The beer, as it will in Germany, flowed freely. So did the schnapps and champagne. When one of the delegates said almost casually that the hated Berlin Wall would probably be dismantled by the time of the next event, two years hence, the native Berliners were openly incredulous. 'Impossible,' they declared. In the ensuing debate the delegates, including senior broadcasters and journalists from both East and West in some cases on first-name terms with the leaders of their countries, were adamant. Under Gorbachev, the Wall would fall.

In the event, it took a little longer than two years for the Berlin Wall to come down. But nobody among the company that April evening in 1987 would have believed that not only the Wall but the entire Soviet system would be demolished within the space of just four short years.

Germany has always had a taste for revolution. In the middle of the fifteenth century, about sixty years before Martin Luther nailed his theses to the church door in Wittenberg, a Rhenish goldsmith called Johannes Gutenberg successfully developed a new means of volume printing using individual movable type. The invention caught on. Over five hundred years later, reunited Germany is a land awash with print. A thousand newspapers and over three hundred magazines ply for readership – and for advertising. The flood of newspaper titles produces a total newspaper circulation of around 150 million copies; for magazines, even more.

From those early Mainz printing presses onwards, to the most recent developments in telemetry and broadband cable, Germany has been at the forefront of technological change in communications. German scientists such as Werner von Braun were the prime movers in the space satellite programmes of the USA and the former USSR. Shortly before re-unification in 1991, the Federal Republic became the second European state to launch and operate a high-power direct broadcast satellite system (DBS). Satellite television, with its ability to cross boundaries, is central to Germany's new identity and ambitions. In January 1992, the Director of Germany's external broadcasting system called for satellite broadcasting to lead 'a cultural offensive for the German language and culture' in the newly liberated territories of Eastern Europe that were once part of the Prussian and Austro-Hungarian empires.

Already there are seven satellite-delivered channels in Germany. By the year 2000 it is estimated that DBS will serve 23 million households in Germany. There is a much larger total of over 100 million German speakers within its 'footprint' – the area within which the satellite's television signals can be received.

As in most democracies in Western Europe, the development of the press and of broadcasting in Germany has been dictated in part by the hundred years of history that preceded the 1939–45 war and in part by the constitution it was left with at the war's end.

At the end of the First World War, the Director General of the giant steel and armaments concern Krupp AG, Alfred Hugenberg, had built a secret media empire designed to further the interests of heavy industry and of nationalist politicians.

Alfred Krupp was later to face the Nuremburg War Crimes Tribunal and served a term in Spandau.

Hugenberg's group included national and local newspapers, news agencies and the UFA film production company, now part of the Bertelsmann group. His publications consistently attacked the fledgling Weimar Republic and supported the Nazi party of Adolf Hitler. Hugenberg was to become minister of economy, food and agriculture in Hitler's first cabinet in 1933.

At the end of the Second World War, the Allies were determined to create press and broadcasting structures that would ensure there could never be another Hugenberg. There was a strict licensing system designed to ensure that a plurality of opinions and political views found expression in the press.

The caution was hardly surprising. Josef Goebbels, the arch priest of Nazism, had used radio as a tool of mass propaganda. It seemed to the military control authorities and those of its senior officers such as Hugh Greene, later to become Director General of the BBC in its most daring era, that the safest bet to keeping conquered Germany in check was to divide it up. In the postwar settlement in West Germany, broadcasting was organised in such a way as to vest control in separate regional authorities based on the regional states or *Länder*. Never again, vowed the Allies, would German broadcasting be under a single central control.

It was in the 1960s that the West German President, Dr Konrad Adenauer, first attempted to break the postwar mould of German broadcasting. Adenauer felt that the prevailing orthodoxy of close control after the war had outlived its usefulness. By the so-called *Proporz* system, an appropriate political spread was supposed to be maintained within the state broadcasting network. Appointments to senior positions within the regional broadcasting corporations were, however, subject to local political approval. Adenauer's Christian Democratic Union party had believed for a long time that these arrangements tended towards a prevailing liberal socialism. A national commercial television network, argued the CDU, would help to redress the balance.

In the event, Adenauer's attempt to introduce a federal broadcasting network was rebuffed by judges of the Constitu-

1 Rupert Murdoch (*left*), with trusted lieutenant Andrew Neil, took on the British television establishment.

2 (*below*) Roberto Marinho at Banff: 'the most powerful man in South America' (p. 69).

3 & 4 (*left*) Ted Turner
aboard the *Courageous*:
'the sea and a sense of
adventure were to be
formative influences'
(p. 45); (*below*) Turner
at his desk at CNN.

5 & **6** (*right*) Silvio Berlusconi with Jérôme Seydoux, his partner in French TV channel La Cinq; (*below*) Berlusconi in a studio at La Cinq.

7 & 8 Key players on the Australian scene: Kerry Packer (*left*) at Smith's Lawn, Windsor and Alan Bond (*below*), celebrating victory in the America's Cup.

AUSTRALIA II

9 Conrad Black (*above*) looks set to follow
his newspaper career with a TV empire.

10 Bruce Gyngell (*below*): 'perhaps the only person
ever to have received an apology from Mrs Thatcher'.

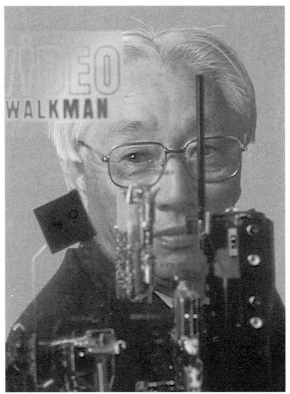

11 Akio Morita (*left*) started with a two-man repair shop and created Sony: 'from my childhood I have loved the products' (p. 127).

12 A youthful Reinhard Mohn (*below*), still in soldier's greatcoat, addresses the Bertelsmann staff in 1947.

13 & 14 (*left*)
Emilio Azcárraga
Milmo (*in the
foreground*), owner
of the Televisa
empire, with
Rómulo O'Farrill;
(*below*) Miguel
Alemán (*centre*),
flanked by Placido
Domingo and
comedian
Cantinflas, tried to
democratise
Televisa.

15 (*left*) MGM's Leo the Lion tamed Giancarlo Parretti.

16 (*below*) Robert Maxwell's last big throw was the purchase in March 1991 of the New York *Daily News*.

tional court in 1961. Only the *Länder*, they said, were empowered to regulate broadcasting. The federal role was to be confined to transmission engineering aspects under the auspices of the German Bundespost and its telecommunications subsidiary. The judgment had far-reaching consequences. Not until 1983 did the first private radio stations begin to appear on the scene, followed by television.

Rebuffed by the courts in their attempts to introduce competitive broadcast services, the German Federal Government eventually found a way to create a limited network through cable and satellite. SAT-1, launched by Chancellor Kohl and backed by the Springer publishing giant, was the first of these systems.

The revival of German cinema in the 1970s and 1980s was a different and subsequent phenomenon to the general revival of European cinema in the 1960s, which petered out because of its lack of any real relationship with television. Film makers such as Rainer Werner Fassbinder, Volker Schlöndorff and Margarethe von Trotta worked closely with German television, particularly with the second channel, Zweites Deutsches Fernsehen (ZDF). Among the key factors are the annual promotion agreements between ARD, ZDF and the German film industry, which in the last few years have made over £30 million in annual grants available for television cooperation with the cinema. ZDF's Director General, Dieter Stolte, said that 'thanks to the impact of television, the German cinema film has become rich in the substance of social experience and the perception of reality'. Certainly these qualities have been marked in productions such as the widely acclaimed social history *Heimat* or in Fassbinder's epic fourteen-part *Berlin Alexanderplatz*, which was made both for TV and cinema release.

Berlin is now bidding to become the film and television centre of Europe. As part of the unshackling of the old Communist *dirigiste* state enterprises, the Federal Government set up the Treuhand Anstalt with the task of selling off former East German state enterprises. One of the supposed jewels in the Treuhand's crown is the historic DEFA studios at Babelsberg in Potsdam, just outside Berlin.

After the fall of Berlin in 1945, Dr Gerd Bucerius, 10 per cent shareholder in and for some time chairman of the Bertelsmann board, was authorised to set up the *Die Zeit* weekly newspaper, whose chief editor is now the former West German Chancellor, Helmut Schmidt. Bucerius had been briefly a conservative MP in the CDU but later left the party. In his autobiographical book, *Der angeklagte Verlager* ('The Publisher Accused', Munich, 1974), Bucerius borrowed the words of Lord Thomson of Fleet to describe the licence he received from the British Control Commission after the war as 'indeed virtually a permit to print money'.

Like Rupert Murdoch, Leo Kirch sees himself at the head of a crusade against the state having any role in broadcasting. 'With the joint power of printing presses, data-banks, television, film and video, we will break the predominance of public television.'[3] Kirch believes that media markets need to be redefined, that they have long outgrown the barriers of language and culture. To compete on an international scale it is essential, he argues, to seek new dimensions. Hence his interest in Springer.

'There are enough examples of logical cooperation between the monoculture print and the monoculture television,' he points out. 'What are Murdoch, Berlusconi or Hersant [the French press baron and former main shareholder in the La Cinq TV channel] doing? By combining print and TV in their countries they have outplayed state television and at the same time been unbelievably successful with newspapers and magazines. Why? Because both media are backing and promoting each other. Put together they are more than just their sum.' Unlike Robert Maxwell, who had similarly set out in the ruined postwar landscape of the Third Reich to build a media empire, Kirch never overreached himself. One wonders whether he or Reinhard Mohn, the former Wehrmacht officer who applied American business principles to create the media giant Bertelsmann, ever ponder the strange contrast of their respective fates with that of Maxwell.

In September 1946, Robert Maxwell had bought shares in a

[3] *Wirtschaftswoche*, 22 April 1988.

company set up a year earlier by a Czechoslovak living in London and became a director. Arnos Lobel's company, Low-Bell, was engaged in the manufacture and sale of fancy goods and kitchen utensils. According to Joe Haines in his biography of Maxwell it 'dealt in anything and everything, including caustic soda, cement, dyes, eucalyptus oil and peppermint, leather cider taps, Turkish carpets, coal, cinnamon, vanilla, feather dressers, boots and shoes, furniture, neon signs, pencils, deer skins and dried peas'. Everything had its price in the world of barter that had grown up after the war. Low-Bell was to become the foundation stone of Maxwell's empire. It still existed as Maxwell Scientific International (Distribution Services Ltd) when he died.

Maxwell the merchant was looking for something to sell. In the words of Peter Thompson and Anthony Delano in their biography of Maxwell: 'Out there in the world were a host of greedy consumers in pursuit of a cornered market. Information, it seemed, was just as much of a commodity as newsprint or penicillin. All that needed to be done was to match the supply to the demand. And set the price.'[4]

In 1947 Maxwell set up a second company operating out of the same Trafalgar Square office as Low-Bell with the grandiose title European Periodicals Publicity and Advertising Corporation or EPPAC. 'There were two desks,' write Thompson and Delano, 'at one of which Betty [Maxwell's wife], not yet pregnant with her second child, Anne, sat at the only typewriter. At the other sat Maxwell the merchant beneath a huge picture of Montgomery the field marshal pinning the MC on Maxwell the captain.'

The ostensible principal activity of EPPAC was to distribute German language newspapers to German prisoners-of-war in Britain. In Berlin, Maxwell told friends that it was to sell scientific literature in Britain and the United States. He negotiated the sale of some Julius Springer documents with His Majesty's Stationery Office and the Bodleian Library in Oxford. It was a good deal for Maxwell. He paid Springer £12,000 for the documents and sold them for £20,000.

[4] Peter Thompson and Anthony Delano, *Maxwell: A Portrait of Power.*

Julius Springer and Robert Maxwell prospered on the sale of the publisher's extensive backlist of scientific publications. But the real crock of gold was a cache of wartime and prewar journals that had been salted away in the warehouses in Lausitz and in Austria. There were seven railway wagons full of documents, which Maxwell parked beside an old pickle factory in Newington Butts, East London.

Maxwell first arranged for the transportation of the contents of the Lausitz warehouse and secured the necessary export licence. Some 150 tons of books and another 150 tons of journals worth over £500,000 at today's rate of exchange had been secured by Maxwell for the equivalent of less than £50,000.

Maxwell then set about getting his hands on the books and journals in Austria. Commercial contacts between Germany and Austria were a criminal offence under Allied regulations. An arrangement was made for Maxwell to purchase the stock for pounds sterling. The value of the stock in 1945 prices was around £100,000. Had the true value of the documents been known, their export would have almost certainly been banned. Springer decided to undervalue the stock and the invoiced price to EPPAC was £4,000 – later increased to £12,000.

Maxwell was to carry two other legacies from his Berlin days to the grave on Jerusalem's Mount of Olives. The first was the name he was to bestow to one of his key companies, Pergamon. The Greek town of Pergamon was famous for its altar dedicated to the goddess Athena and for its library. It was also the name of Berlin's great museum, then in the Soviet Zone. The Pergamon company motto may well have come from those black marketeering days, too. It is 'Invenimus viam aut faciemus' ('We shall find a way or we shall make one').

The second legacy was a dental bridge made of platinum and vanadium fitted by Dr Eibisch – Hitler's own dental surgeon.

XII

The Japanese Experience: Morita

At noon on 15 August 1945, a young naval officer stood stiffly to attention in his ancestral home in the village of Kosugaya. He wore full dress uniform complete with sword. With his father and mother and sisters, he listened in silence to a thin, reedy voice speaking in Court Japanese through the static on the radio.

> The war situation has developed not necessarily to our advantage. . . . We have ordered our government to communicate to the governments of the United States, Great Britain, China and the Soviet Union that our empire accepts the provisions of their joint declaration. . . . Let the entire nation continue as one family from generation to generation, ever firm in its faith in the imperishability of its sacred land, and ever mindful of its heavy responsibilities and of the long road ahead. Unite your total strength and devote it to rebuilding for your future. Cultivate the ways of rectitude; foster nobility of spirit; and work with resolution so that you may enhance the innate glory of the Imperial State and keep pace with the progress of the world.

It was unconditional surrender.

The voice was that of the Emperor Hirohito, never before heard by the Japanese people. Until the previous evening, when he had made the recording in a makeshift studio in the Imperial Palace, only the emperor's closest advisers had ever looked on his face. When he travelled outside the palace, people along the route were ordered to turn away.

Japan was and still is an essentially feudal society in its social relationships and attitude to authority. That this society should have produced the most advanced high-technology economy in the world is one of the facets that Western commentators never cease to point out.

Unquestioning obedience is one of the roots of Japanese society. Before that historic first broadcast by the Emperor Hirohito, the announcer in the state broadcasting service NHK's Studio 8 instructed the Japanese people, kneeling on a hot summer's day at home before their radios and in the streets in front of loudspeakers, thus: 'A broadcast of the greatest importance is about to commence. All listeners will please rise.' The young naval officer who obeyed the instruction along with millions of his countrymen was Akio Morita. He had been born twenty-four years earlier, on 26 January 1921, in Nagoya, the busy industrial capital of Aichi Prefecture.

Fourteen generations of the Morita family had brewed one of the finest brands of 'sake' – Japanese rice wine – in the nearby village of Kosugaya. The brand name 'Nenchimatsu' symbolised longevity and happiness. 'The atomies of sake,' wrote Kenichi Yoshida in *Japan is a Circle*, 'seep into one's system carrying with them their message of stars and visions and fountains playing in the shade in marble basins and thrones of gold and chalcedony.' Akio Morita was to become an elder statesman of Japanese industry and his Sony Corporation the owners of that symbol of Americanism, Columbia Pictures, with its star-spangled statue of Liberty.

Columbia had been founded by Harry Cohn, the son of a German tailor and a Russian mother, in 1920, with the name CBC. Its low-budget two-reel comedies earned it the nickname 'Corned Beef and Cabbage'. Columbia and Universal were regarded as 'the little two' of the seven main Hollywood studios. The 'big five' were originally MGM, RKO, Paramount, Warner Brothers and Twentieth-Century Fox. After Howard Hughes acquired most of RKO in 1948, the company steadily ran into the ground and today it is replaced in any 'big five' by the Walt Disney Corporation.

Cohn became well-known for what he called his 'foolproof' device for judging a picture's quality: 'If my ass squirms,' he once said, 'it's bad. If my ass don't squirm, it's good. It's as simple as that.' For all that, when Cohn died in 1958, Columbia's stock was at a high point. Its credits included some of the most successful international co-productions, including *Lawrence of Arabia*, *A Man For All Seasons* and *The Bridge on the River Kwai*. What Columbia's new owners really think of this pretty factual account of the Japanese treatment of prisoners-of-war would make for an interesting discussion. An even more interesting conjecture might be whether a Columbia under Japanese control would ever make such a picture again.

Akio Morita's tastes are ostensibly more sophisticated than the founder of the studio that his company, Sony, now owns. Led by his mother's love for classical music and her collection of early gramophone records, he retained not only a taste for music but also a fascination with the technique of sound reproduction. He studied physics at the University of Osaka and became an electronic engineer.

In 1944, Morita enlisted in the navy as a technical officer under a programme that would allow him to continue his studies. He worked with a team of scientists and engineers on thermal-guidance weapons and night-vision gunsights. Morita had seen at first hand the effects of the fire-bombing of Tokyo on the night of 9 March 1945, when the fire storm created by the incendiaries dropped by American B29s left one hundred thousand dead. He had seen the devastation of Japan's industrial centres, including his birthplace, Nagoya, the home of the Zero fighter. He had heard the news of the annihilation of Hiroshima by 'a new kind of weapon that flashed and shone' and as a physicist knew what kind of device it was. He knew then that the war was lost. 'The news of Hiroshima was truly incredible to me,' he wrote later. 'The technology gap it represented was tremendous.'

It is interesting to speculate how many of Morita's fellow countrymen drew just that same conclusion from the evidence of the overwhelmingly superior technology that had ended Japan's role in the Second World War. What we do know is that as Morita listened to Hirohito's surrender speech he had realised that 'Japan would need all the talent it could save for the future.' He determined that he had a role to play in that future.

In 1946, together with his partner Masaru Ibuka, an engineer, Morita founded the Tokyo Tsushin Kogyo. The company was later renamed Sony, from the Latin 'sonus' ('sound'). In a workshop inside a large store in the area known as the Ginza, which had been devastated by the war, the partners repaired radios and gramophones. More importantly, they developed a copy of a German tape recorder. The machine weighed fifty kilos. It was not an immediate success.

From that two-man repair shop grew what is today the world's largest electronics and communications concern, a company valued in 1989 at $16 billion and with an investment of $1.3 billion annually on research and development. Particularly interesting to the present-day situation is the character and ideology that have informed the steady and unrelenting growth of the Japanese leviathan.

Morita himself did not travel outside Japan until 1953, when he was thirty-two years old and made his first visit to Europe. One of his appointments was at the BBC, where he saw a recording being made on a prewar vintage machine with a needle moving across a heavy master disk. When he asked why the world's leading broadcasting organisation did not use tape recorders, he was told that the unions would not allow them. Already feeling slighted at being considered 'just a transistor salesman', he must have marvelled at this block to the progress in which he so fervently believed.

Morita remains Chairman of Sony and was its Chief Executive until he handed that post to Norio Ohga in 1989. He lives in one of the most beautiful houses in Tokyo. He also has apartments in New York and Paris and spends his holidays in Hawaii and Salzburg. His circle of friends has included George Schultz, Henry Kissinger, Herbert von Karajan, Leonard Bernstein and Zubin Mehta.

Morita is a familiar figure on golf courses around the world. He recalls a game with an American friend in the New York City suburbs. 'As I stood on the tee I took out my [US made] MacGregor driver. My friend, who likes to tell me that Japan is appalling and how unfair that is, pulled out a [Japanese made] Yonex. I chided him for using these clubs. He replied that his Yonex clubs gave him better purchase on the ball. So we set off on our round, safe in the understanding that using Japanese clubs was a necessary evil.' Morita continued, 'After the round he invited me back to his home and showed me around while his wife prepared an evening meal. In the garage were a snowmobile, a motorboat and a four-wheel drive vehicle – all Japanese. In the house he had a Sony television and stereo. In fact, there were Japanese products everywhere. So I asked him frankly: "Time and again you have angrily claimed that Japan doesn't buy American products, but if you yourself use only Japanese made things, what do you suggest we can buy from you?"[1]

'From my childhood I have loved the products,' he says. 'That's why I became an industrialist. Every week, I take a new product to my home to use – to play with, just like a layman. That's how I find what we should improve. I read the instruction manuals. Sometimes I cannot understand how to use the machine! The product should be *loved* by the customers. That's how we can enrich their lives.'[2]

Morita was once considered something of a maverick among Japanese businessmen but today he is respected as a corporate statesman. But he and the company he founded have lost none of the combativeness that made Sony the most famous Japanese consumer electronics company in the world.

Morita's choice of successor perhaps owed much to his love for classical music and his dedication to the perfection of the reproduction of sound. Nine years younger than Morita, Norio Ohga trained as a concert musician at Tokyo's National University of Fine Arts and Music. He then became an opera singer. In 1953, he began working part time as a consultant for Sony and eventually joined full time. Morita groomed him to

[1] *Fortune*, 27 September 1989.
[2] *Newsweek*, 9 October 1989.

become a leader. Ohga was made president of the company in 1982 and has been at the forefront of the company's global diversification strategy.

In March 1989, Morita and Ohga shared the Keizakai Businessman of the Year Award a few days after the start of Japan's new Heisei Era. The citation referred in particular to Sony's bold acquisition of CBS Records as a major step in the transformation of Sony into a fully integrated, multinational corporation. The move set 'a milestone for the rest of Japanese industry in efforts to further internationalise their operations.'[3]

Morita is unusual among Japanese businessmen in being almost as well known abroad as in his own country. He is certainly no stranger to controversy. In 1989 Morita co-authored a book that became a bestseller in the United States as well as in Japan. *The Japan That Can Say No* took its title from the prevalent Western belief that it is impossible to do business with the Japanese other than on their terms because of their habit of never actually turning down a proposal directly. The co-author of the book was one Shintaro Ishihara, a senior Liberal Democratic Party politician who was a candidate for Prime Minister in August 1989. Ishihara attacked America as racist. 'It is my firm conviction that the roots of the US–Japan friction lie in the soil of racial prejudice,' he wrote. 'American racial prejudice is based upon the cultural belief that the modern era is the creation of the white race, including Americans.' Clearly no pourer of oil on the troubled waters of international relations, Ishihara went further. 'At times it appears to me that the Americans behave more like mad dogs instead of watch dogs. . . . Americans force other cultures to give up their traditional values and impose the American culture upon them. And they do not even recognise this is an atrocity – a barbaric act.'

Ishihara's views are considered extreme even in Tokyo. Significantly, Morita had his name removed from the English translation. His contributions to their book are less inflammatory. He is critical of his own countrymen. 'Perhaps as a result of

---

[3] *Business Tokyo*, March

Confucian influences, we Japanese find it very difficult to say a clear "no" in inter-personal relationships. Large numbers of Japanese feel that even if they remain silent, they will be understood.'

As we shall see later, Ishihara's complaint has parallels in the present-day outcries of large sections of the European film industry about the dominance of 'American product' on the big screen. Was the Sony acquisition of CBS Records and Columbia Pictures – both first of their kind – inspired to some extent by motives that were more mixed than we give credit for? And are the parallel lamentations of the US entertainment industry as it is remorselessly swallowed by the Japanese leviathan entirely to be dismissed as not much more than the crocodile tears of an industry that had already priced itself out of a job?

While the jury may still be out on the success or otherwise of the Japanese moves into entertainment 'software', two comments are worth making. The first is that Sony and the other companies that have so far followed suit – Matsushita, Fujisankei, Toshiba and C. Itoh – have for the most part extremely limited experience in the intensely idiosyncratic fields of film and music entertainment, with their own lore of studios and stars, artistes and repertoire. The second point is that companies like Sony for the most part have grown through product development rather than acquisitions. Takeovers – particularly on such a lavish and world-wide scale – are not their usual modus operandi.

There is a even a school of thought which suggests that those cautious Japanese may have been at least partly afflicted by that peculiar disease known as 'the lure of Hollywood'. When Sony sanctioned the spending of $65 million on Columbia's *Hook* by Stephen Spielberg it was also signing up for a deal that included a box-office rake-off for Spielberg calculated to be almost a third of the picture's cost.

If it is to take on Hollywood, Sony will face problems more formidable and more extreme than those confronted by Rupert Murdoch with the British press or Bruce Gyngell at TV-am. It is of course one thing to take on the might of trade unions and quite another to suggest that Dustin Hoffman might like a smaller fee.

In any case, Sony will no doubt be more systematic in its attempted rationalisations at Columbia than the British producer David Puttnam, whose crusade to reform Hollywood ended in heroic failure.

Certainly, Akio Morita is critical of many aspects of American and Western business strategies. 'Real business,' he writes, 'entails adding value to things, by adding knowledge to them, but America is steadily forgetting this. That terrifies me. America no longer makes things, it only takes pleasure in making profits from moving money around. . . . There has been a lot of hot air about America gradually transforming itself into a post-industrial society. But now the country is facing the question of what happens if manufacturing ceases to exist. In fact, even now America is not producing for itself the things that it uses.'[4] Morita recalls a conversation with a money trader in New York. 'I enquired how far ahead he looks. One week? "No, no," came the reply. "Ten minutes." If Americans think only in terms of ten-minute action, while we Japanese think in ten-year terms, America assuredly faces gradual decline.

'The main reason why Japan's industrial might has become so strong is not that it borrows basic technologies – though, to be sure, many have been brought in from abroad – but that it leads the world in devising ways of creating products derived from those basic technologies. America is by no means lacking in technology. But it does lack the creativity to apply new technologies commercially. This, I believe, is America's biggest problem. On the other hand, it is Japan's strongest point.'

Morita tells the story of when his firm first tried to break into Western markets with their new transistor radio. A large American firm with an extensive distribution network offered to sell them in the United States – provided that the name Sony was replaced by that of the distributor. Morita refused. The company remonstrated that no one in America knew the name of Sony whereas they had been in the market for more than fifty years. Morita insisted, saying: 'Fifty years ago, who had heard of your name?'

[4] *Fortune*, 25 September 1989.

He is also critical of what he sees as a lack of energy in Europe. In 1988, he visited an exhibition in Japan marking the visit of Philip Franz von Siebold, a Dutchman who came by ship in the early 1800s when Japan was a closed country to foreigners. Von Siebold stayed for several years to teach medicine. Interviewed in 1988, Morita said: 'I admire the European pioneering spirit. Europeans used to come to the Far East in wooden ships around Capetown. It took a long time. Now you can come by plane in twelve hours. But they don't come.'[5] In the same interview Morita sounded what may be seen as a warning to Europeans against complacency: 'Japanese are not fools. We have four years until 1992. Japanese managers know what they should do during those four years. Japanese industry will move technology into Europe.'

As 1992 began, this threat had itself been overshadowed by a marked deterioration in relations between the United States and Japan over trade imbalances. What role the Japanese involvement in American communications companies will have to play in key areas such high-definition television looks to be subsidiary to a larger argument as to which of the two powers will dominate the new 'Pacific Rim' economies. The former militaristic, closed nation that is now the world's leading industrial leviathan; or the once mighty industrial power whose technology bombed Japan into submission in 1945, but whose most famous cultural products it surrendered without a struggle?

[5] *The Financial Times*, 8 August 1988.

XIII

Hollywood Nights

The film industry – and Hollywood in particular – has long exercised a special fascination for dreamers. From all walks of life, men and women have been bitten by the bug of the cinema and the lure of overnight success. Yet the founders of Hollywood were for the most part men from distinctly hard-headed business backgrounds. Marcus Loew, the first of the MGM founders, and Adolph Zukor, who started Paramount Pictures, both began in the clothing trade. So too did Carl Laemmle, the creator of Universal Pictures. So too did the Warner Brothers – Harry, Albert, Jack and Samuel – real name Eichelbaum. So too did Samuel Goldwyn, and so too did William Fox, founder of Twentieth-Century Fox. They were nearly all Jewish émigrés and refugees from Europe, men who had a reason to fight for something new. They were perhaps the kind of men who today might be called 'chancers', seeing an opportunity here, following a trend there. Many of them came to the film business via the operation of gaming machines in penny arcades, which became the venues for the nickelodeons – the first cinema houses. It is striking how in the popular mind those classic studio names have remained unchanged – albeit their ownership, their business and character have been transformed beyond recognition.

Perhaps the most famous of all the Hollywood studios was Metro-Goldwyn-Mayer, the original dream factory. MGM's fortunes and fate are intimately bound up with our story.

Like many of the movie pioneers, Marcus Loew had been a nickelodeon operator and music hall impresario. Loew's National was typical of the theatres combining vaudeville and pictures, but at 2,800 seats it was the biggest in New York. At that time, in

1909, the operators were hamstrung by the restrictions placed upon them by the Motion Picture Patents Company, which had been set up by the inventor Thomas Edison to try to control motion picture production by licensing the technical equipment and limiting films to the length of one reel – about ten minutes. Ducking and weaving to escape the Patents Company, many of the early independent film producers such as Carl Laemmle moved further and further west, until they reached Los Angeles and there was no further to go.

Marcus Loew saw that in order to supply his theatres and compete with the likes of Zukor and Fox he needed production capacity. In 1919 he bought Metro Pictures. Even this was not enough to supply the quality films – at least one new production a week – needed to keep the theatres going. In 1924, Loew bought Goldwyn Pictures, the company originally set up by Samuel Goldwyn who had since given up studio ownership and become an independent producer.

Loew, who stood just over five feet tall, was known as 'Little Napoleon'. What he lacked in stature, however, he made up for in determination. 'You must want a big success and then beat it into submission. You must be as ravenous to reach it as the wolf who licks his teeth behind a fleeing rabbit; you must be as mad to win as the man who, with one hand growing cold on the revolver in his pocket, with the other hand pushes his last gold piece on the "Double-O" at Monte Carlo.'[1]

One of the major attractions of the Goldwyn Pictures company to the New York based Loew was its production base at Culver City, Los Angeles, complete with its logo over the entrance of a lion and the motto: 'Ars Gratia Artis' ('Art for Art's Sake').

It quickly became apparent to Loew and his right-hand man Nicholas Schenck that both the Metro and the Goldwyn companies were spending lavishly on stars and other overheads, while there was little production control. One of the few around who combined a sense of business discipline with first-hand experience of studio production was a barrel-chested man who had been

---

[1] Quoted in Peter Hay, *MGM – When the Lion Roars.*

Metro's company secretary and left to set up his own production company.

Louis B. Mayer was a former scrap metal dealer who had caught the show business bug around 1907, after turning an old burlesque house in Haverhill, Massachusetts, into a theatre. In Mayer, the family-oriented and respectable Loew found a soul mate. 'L. B. Mayer was my father, my father confessor, the best friend I ever had,' the actress Joan Crawford was to say in later years. 'I worship good women, honourable men and saintly mothers,' said Mayer, who once punched Erich von Stroheim in the face after the great director had ventured the opinion that 'all women are whores'.

To Mayer, the movies were much more than a business, however. 'Each picture should teach a lesson, should have a reason for existence,' he once said. 'My unchanging policy will be great star, great director, great play, great cast. Spare nothing, neither expense, time, nor effort. Results only are what I am after.'

Under Mayer and Schenck, Loew's theatres, showing MGM's pictures, became synonymous with quality and reliability. In the golden thirty years or so from 1924, MGM's mighty production line rolled out a stream of successes that ranged from the first *Ben Hur* (1924), through to *Mutiny on the Bounty* (1935), *Gone With The Wind* and *The Wizard of Oz* (1939), *Easter Parade* (1948), *Singin' in the Rain* (1952), *Gigi* (1958) and the remake of *Ben Hur* (1959).

There were the stars – Greta Garbo, Clark Gable, Jean Harlow, Spencer Tracy, James Stewart, Judy Garland, Cary Grant, Katharine Hepburn, Fred Astaire, James Cagney, Grace Kelly and many more. And there were the directors and producers – King Vidor, Eric von Stroheim, David O. Selznick, Fritz Lang, Vincente Minnelli, Busby Berkeley, John Huston and George Cukor. As for writers, MGM tried the big names – Scott Fitzgerald, Ernest Hemingway, William Faulkner – but soon learned that deadline chasers like Hecht and MacArthur or experienced screenwriters like Frances Marion and Anita Loos fitted into the MGM production line better.

At MGM none were bigger – or rather none were allowed to get bigger – than the studio itself. The studio system reached its height of perfection at MGM. Dubbed 'the film factory', in its heyday MGM also consistently made larger profits than the other studios. MGM's reputation as a studio and its vast library of films were to make it a prime target when, like the other Hollywood studios, it fell on hard times. So too was the large amount of real estate which MGM occupied at Culver City.

Marcus Loew had died in 1927, but his creation was carried on under the guidance of Louis B. Mayer and Nicholas Schenck. When Mayer was ousted by Schenck in 1951, it was, in retrospect, the beginning of the end. Mayer *was* MGM, spanning nearly thirty years of its golden age and supervising the release of some 800 pictures.

As part of the deal under which Mayer left MGM, he agreed to sell his rights to future profits from those films for a lump sum of £2.6 million. It was a lot of money, but a pittance compared with the profits that would be engendered in the future by rights from TV, video, cable and satellite, none of which could have been foreseen, except perhaps for television, in 1951.

To take one illustration, in 1990, the singer Peggy Lee successfully sued the Walt Disney Corporation for a share of the profits made from the video rights of *The Lady and the Tramp*, released in 1955. In her autobiography, *Miss Peggy Lee*, the singer recalls how she was paid just $3,500 for her extensive voicework and other contributions to the production over a three-year period. *The Lady and the Tramp* went on to be reissued again and again, becoming the top-selling video cassette in 1988. In the court case brought against Disney, Miss Lee was awarded some $1.5 million in compensation.

Film libraries were to become a vital weapon in the armoury of today's Sky Barons. The Walt Disney Corporation has the world's outstanding collection of animated features. Disney also has an almost legendary reputation for guarding its own products. Its executives once walked out of the Oscar ceremonies and threatened to sue the Academy of Motion Pictures for using its characters in its tribute to Disney in the presentation awards ceremony. Just how Disney manages to lay claim to copyright on the Brothers Grimm legend of Snow White, for example, is a conundrum that has exercised more than one commentator.

For the most part, the Hollywood moguls and the press barons had pursued different paths, each content to be kings in their own separate spheres. William Randolph Hearst was something of an exception among the press barons in developing a yen for Hollywood.

The reclusive tycoon Howard Hughes had bought himself into Hollywood with his father's money and produced some hits in the 1930s – notably *The Front Page* (1930) and *Scarface* (1931). His purchase of RKO in 1948 however spelled the end for the studio, which ceased independent production a few years later. Hughes also became obsessed with owning a TV network and went as far as purchasing KLAS-TV, a local CBS affiliate in his Las Vegas retreat. He spent hours in front of the screen issuing detailed programming instructions.

Not only did Hollywood and the press pursue their separate paths. Radio, which had spawned its own generation of musical and theatrical stars, offered no threat to the movie houses and the great golden age of radio ran exactly parallel with that of the movies throughout the 1930s and 1940s.

What changed everything was television. In the United States, television sets had begun to be manufactured in significant quantities just after the Second World War. By 1951, an estimated 10 million homes in the US had sets. The network companies which had come to the fore during the golden age of radio – RCA/NBC, CBS and ABC – were the ones that were to dominate television.

Hollywood's attitude to television was at first supercilious, particularly at MGM. After all, the cinema was art. 'So far, television hasn't hurt the box-office,' pronounced MGM's Nicholas Schenck in 1949. By 1955, however, movie attendances had more than halved from the 1945 figure of 80 million to just 35 million. Deprived of a ready-made source of programming via the film libraries, the TV companies instead looked to their own resources, drawing upon the supply of talent from radio and show business. In response, the film companies came up with an ever more desperate parade of technical wheezes designed to stimulate the eye and stun the brain. Experiments with 3-D and 'stereoscope' were followed by Cinerama, CinemaScope and eventually Panavision. None of them succeeded in drawing the moviegoers back.

The uniform hostility of the Hollywood studios to TV was breached in 1954 when Walt Disney launched a weekly *Disneyland* to promote his new California theme park of the same name. MGM made a deal with ABC for a weekly *MGM Parade* and in 1956 licensed a package of nine films including *The Wizard of Oz* to CBS for $1.7 million.

But it was not just television that troubled Hollywood in the 1950s. The Communist witch hunts of Senator Joseph McCarthy had seriously demoralised film makers, leading to the infamous blacklisting of several top directors and writers. A number of its top directors began to look elsewhere to make the kind of films they wanted to make. It was Europe, increasingly, to which they turned. By the end of the 1950s, the New Wave was rolling through England, France and Italy. European directors like Resnais, Fellini, Truffaut, Antonioni, Godard, Richardson and Visconti were joined by Hollywood exiles such as Stanley Kubrick, Carl Foreman and Sam Spiegel.

For the latter part of the 1950s, most of the Hollywood studios had been deliberately making 'B' category pictures to run second-on-the-bill to the main picture. It was an obvious ruse to keep up attendances at the theatres. Films based in the everyday realities of police procedure, low-budget westerns and comedies were, ironically, in many cases ideally suited to the new medium of television. It soon dawned on the Hollywood studios that the appetite of the TV networks for their back catalogue was an opportunity not to be missed. Nor was it very long before the studios realised that the production-line methods they had evolved over the years made them ideally suited to supply this relentless demand. Producers like Aaron Spelling and studios such as Universal started to make such films specifically for the TV networks. Stars who thought their acting days were over suddenly found a new lease of life in the 'made-for-TV' films and series, many of them spawned from original feature films. *The Invisible Man*, *Peyton Place*, *The Munsters*, *Dr Kildare*, *Rin Tin Tin*, *Batman*, *MASH*, *Perry Mason* and *Lassie* were but a few among the many series offshoots that were to achieve for their principals if not immortality then in some cases a longevity that outlasted their own earthly span.

Of all the studios, MGM was the slowest to respond to the challenge of TV. The release of the remade *Ben Hur* by MGM in 1959, successful and spectacular as it was, was a temporary stay of execution for the once-proud studio. Although other successes such as *Doctor Zhivago* (1965) were to follow, MGM continued to stake its future on blockbusters. By the end of the 1960s, MGM was in real trouble.

MGM's executioner was an unknown financier who had once been a handyman around the film lots. Kirk Kerkorian, the son of Armenian immigrants, was now to dismantle the studios where he had once moved scenery. Kerkorian had made his money in the travel business. With the proceeds, he gradually built up a controlling interest in MGM stock. Under Kerkorian's influence, MGM sold off the Culver City backlots to developers, closed its London studios and sold off its foreign cinema houses. Tens of thousands of props and costumes were auctioned off in 1970 as Kerkorian and his henchman, James Aubrey, decided to concentrate the business on gaming and real estate.

By this time, production had shrunk to a handful of films a year, and in 1981 MGM absorbed United Artists. In 1985 Kerkorian brought in Alan Ladd Junior, the son of the film star, to run MGM/UA. Ladd was respected and liked in the film business. It is doubtful he would have taken on the role if he had known what was in store for him at the dream factory.

In fact, Kerkorian was already negotiating the sale of MGM/UA. By far the keenest would-be purchaser was a cable TV entrepreneur from the Deep South who had recently failed in an audacious and some would say probably only half-serious attempt to purchase CBS. It was time for the Ted Turner show to roll again.

XIV

Hollywood Nightmares

Jilted by CBS, Ted Turner was on the rebound. Compared with the $5.4 billion he had offered for CBS, the asking price for MGM/UA looked to be easily within his reach. In a complex deal, Turner agreed to pay $1.5 billion for the company whilst at the same time assuming another $500 million in outstanding MGM/UA debt.

It was still a staggering sum. But as Turner's intentions became clearer, the transaction began to acquire more rationale. Whether or not Turner knew he could not afford to pay the price, we do know that the deal was saved by a face-to-face meeting between Turner and Kerkorian at which the latter agreed to buy back UA and other assets, including the famous lion trademark, for a combined sum of about $780 million. At the same time Turner moved quickly to sell the remnants of the Culver City lot to the production company Lorimar.

Turner had entered the market in the nick of time, as Rupert Murdoch appreciated when he quickly followed suit by buying the assets of Twentieth-Century Fox. Unlike Murdoch, who wanted both the Fox library and its television interests, Turner had a different strategy. In June 1986 he sold MGM's TV operations to Kerkorian.

As recounted in a recent book published by Turner's own company, 'the deal left Turner with what he had always wanted – the richest film library in the world, including its crown jewel, *Gone With The Wind.*' As the book also recounts, Turner was told repeatedly by journalists and others that he had paid far too much for old movies. Replied Turner: 'How can you go broke, buying the Rembrandts of the programming business when you are a programmer?'[1]

It must surely rank as one of the greatest show business deals of all time. In view of Turner's shrewd stripping away of the (to him) non-essential parts of MGM/UA, the price he eventually paid for outright ownership of eighty years of MGM movie history, excluding the debt, was a sum estimated at perhaps less than $500 million in cash. Turner has gone on adding to the collection. The Turner Entertainment Company subsequently acquired most of the pre-1950 Warner Brothers films as well as the rights to RKO pictures in the US. With the acquisition in 1992 of the famous Hanna-Barbera cartoon picture stable, Turner has added hundreds of animated titles as well.

By 1989, the stock market fever for takeovers and mergers was running at its height. Nowhere was the atmosphere more perfervid than in the media. The Hollywood press corps was awash with rumours as Sony announced its successful bid for Columbia Pictures, to be followed shortly by rival Matsushita's acquisition of MCA/Universal.

Meanwhile, what was left of MGM/UA was back in the hands of Kirk Kerkorian. Under Alan Ladd Jr, the studio had scored some notable successes – including John Cleese's *A Fish Called Wanda* and *Rain Man* with Dustin Hoffman and Tom Cruise. But in truth, Kerkorian's mind was on another deal. He had sold MGM once. Why not sell it again?

In the summer of 1990 there was an Odyssean list of suitors for MGM. None however could match the astonishing dowry of $1.3 billion now being offered by a relatively little-known Italian businessman called Giancarlo Parretti. If Ted Turner's attempt to take over CBS had been the guppy trying to swallow the whale, what sort of fish was this Italian entrepreneur who was trying to buy the legendary MGM studios?

Giancarlo Parretti had made his money in the dark and undisclosed business dealings of the Italian south. In 1982 he was

---

[1] Peter Hay, *MGM – When the Lion Roars.*

arrested in connection with the failure of a finance house, the Cassa Rurale, and on 30 March 1990 was convicted by a Naples criminal court on a charge of fraudulent bankruptcy and sentenced to a 46-month prison term in connection with the financial collapse, in 1981, of a chain of Naples newspapers (*Il Diario*). His appeal is still outstanding. He has consistently maintained that all the charges against him have been trumped up.

Parretti had first come to the attention of the world's media watchers when he stepped in to rescue the ailing Cannon Pictures group. Over the next few years, the world's trade and financial press faithfully recorded Parretti's dealings without questioning the increasingly suspect financial juggling which sustained them.

In 1962, two cousins from the Galilee port city of Tiberias in the Israeli-occupied West Bank formed a small film production company called, appropriately enough, Noah Pictures. Menahem Golan and Yoram Globus went on to produce the first of several exploitation movies for the Cannon Group, a small US independent producer and distributor known for such fare.

Golan and Globus had tried to set up shop around 1973 in Los Angeles as Ameri-Euro Productions. They produced several unsuccessful US films, including *Lepke* with Tony Curtis, before returning to Israel. Undeterred in their efforts to make it in Hollywood, the cousins returned to America to buy out the nearly bankrupt Cannon, whose prior output had been mainly sex-exploitation films.

Over the next few years, Cannon expanded rapidly across all the spheres of production, distribution and exhibition. The films produced were a strange mixture of exploitation pictures starring the likes of Chuck Norris, Charles Bronson and Jean-Claude Van Damme and more challenging material such as Robert Altman's *Fool For Love* and the Meryl Streep vehicle *A Cry in the Dark*. Cannon also launched itself enthusiastically into the home video market. In 1985 it announced a $50 million home video rights deal with Media Home Entertainment, followed by a second agreement in 1986. In the UK, Cannon had acquired the Classic cinema chain in 1982, to be followed later by the Star and ABC groups, making it the largest exhibition chain with about 400 screens. In the Netherlands, it likewise became the major exhibitor by aquiring about seventy screens.

In May 1986, *TV World* reported that Cannon Television had unveiled ambitious plans to develop and produce programming for network, syndication and pay-TV, to be revealed at the MIP-TV fair in Cannes. On 7 May, the trade magazine *Variety* reported that 'the momentum of pan-European commercial broadcasting is being watched, studied and encouraged by heads of state, high-finance, publishing interests, international advertisers and the entertainment community.' *Variety* also cited an unpublicised meeting held a week earlier between Golan and Globus and Silvio Berlusconi, ostensibly on possible co-production projects. Elsewhere, the president of the Italian directors association, Carmine Cianfarani, predicted that Europe's burgeoning TV channels would require some 125,000 hours a year of TV programming.

A few days later, under the banner '*Takeover*', the film weekly *Screen International* reported that 'after three days of intense and secret negotiations in London,' the Cannon Group had agreed terms of £175 million with Alan Bond for the purchase of his Screen Entertainment arm. 'The deal completely changes the structure of the film industry in Britain and gives the combined company assets in excess of $1 billion,' *Screen International* reporter Terry Ilott confidently asserted.

The purchase came just one week after Bond himself had bought Screen Entertainment from Thorn EMI for a reported £125 million. The £175 million paid by Cannon for the same package – not quite what Sony's Akio Morita meant by 'added value' – gave it Screen Entertainment's 287 screens in the UK, the Elstree Studios, a video distribution company and Screen Entertainment's 2,400-title library.

When Thorn EMI had put Screen Entertainment up for sale just twelve months earlier, there had been an outcry at the prospect of the UK's leading film company falling under foreign control. Bond had acquired the company by default of a failed management buyout. 'Because of difficulties with the buyout, the only way for us to complete the purchase was to take 100 per cent of the company,' said Bond.

In May 1987, it was announced that 'the financier Giancarlo Parretti' had joined the board of Cannon. In October of that year, it was revealed that Cannon was to sell its British cinemas and the Elstree studios for about £183 million ($300 million) in a complicated sale and leaseback deal with Renta Immobileria, a listed Spanish property company controlled by Interpart SA of Luxembourg. In so doing it had been forced to cancel an agreement with Warner Communications for an undisclosed penalty. Warner had had an option to pay $50 million for half of Cannon's cinemas in Europe. It was a panic deal, enabling Cannon to meet nearly £15 million in interest payments due immediately to shareholders. The hand of Parretti was strongly suspected in the arrangement.

Cannon had by this time come under the gaze of the US Securities and Exchange Commission. Wall Street was reported by the Press as unimpressed with the disclosure that some $11.6 million in stock had been paid to a company called Intercorporation, itself controlled by Interpart SA (formerly Comfinance), whose directors included Parreti, Golan and Globus.

By March 1988, Comfinance/Interpart was letting it be known to the press that it might try to gain control of Cannon. In April, Cannon, already projecting losses for 1987 would 'substantially exceed' the previous year's $60 million deficit, said in a Securities and Exchange Commission filing that it had started the 'initial phase' to settle all federal securities class actions pending against it. These actions included one brought by its own auditors, Mann Judd Landau.

None of this was to prevent Cannon the same month from stepping in to buy for an undisclosed sum another dubious asset, a defunct East Coast production company called 21st Century. By this time *Variety* (6 April 1988) was beginning to wonder aloud: 'Why would financially beleaguered Cannon, which several months ago sold its valuable 1,000-title Screen Entertainment Ltd library to Weintraub Entertainment Group, want to buy the shell of a bankrupt New York Indie?'

A week later *The Financial Times* reported that Globus and Golan had agreed to a 'complex' $100 million financial rescue.

Under the terms of the deal, the *FT* reported with a straight face: 'Control of Cannon will pass to Mr Giancarlo Parretti, an Italian financier who controls Melia Group, a travel services company quoted in Amsterdam, and Renta Immobileria, a property company quoted in Madrid. Mr Parretti owns these companies through a Luxembourg based group called Interpart, whose directors include Mr Golan and Mr Globus as well as Mr Parretti.'

In its own report, *Variety* quoted Golan as likening the deal to Coca-Cola's friendly takeover of Columbia. Under the agreement with Parretti, Golan and Globus would become – with seven-year employment agreements – respectively Chairman/Head of Creative Affairs and President/Chief Executive Officer of Cannon Entertainment. As with other Parretti agreements, the value of this pact was soon to be called into question. More significantly, Parretti became President and Chief Executive Officer of the controlling company, Cannon Group Inc., whose new chairman, Florio Fiorini, was managing director of the Swiss based investment group Sasea. With Parretti's promises ringing in their ears, if not their pockets, Globus and Golan set out for the Cannes Film Festival. The duo were pictured in apparently expansive mood on the Croisette in *Variety* (4 May), along with reports that the Cannon studio would now have access to a $100-million credit line for film production for the next year – this on top of a promised cash injection of $100 million from the deal with Parretti.

A less remarked upon aspect of the deal was Cannon's sale of its theatrical, distribution and production interests in Italy. Silvio Berlusconi, who had supped with a long spoon at the Cannon table, bought the Italia Cannon screens for a reported $12.8 million, bringing his nascent Cinema 5 chain to just under 300 theatres – the largest exhibitor in Italy.

It did not take long for the Cannon horror story to begin to unfold. On 1 June 1988, *Variety* reported that the Cannon group had suffered a 'staggering loss' of $98.3 million for the previous year. The 'disastrous' results widely exceeded the previous year's deficit of $60.4 million. Contained in the figures was a 65 per cent increase in 'selling, general and administrative expenses' to $86.6

million. Interest charges alone amounted to some $50.5 million. Cannon's net worth at the time was estimated at just $37.5 million. The report included a note that the company's Chief Financial Officer, Frederic Scheer, had tendered his resignation.

The ten sound stages at Elstree Studios, north of London, were fully occupied at the end of June 1988. Stephen Spielberg, wunderkind of the 1980s Hollywood revival, was completing his latest Harrison Ford epic, *Indiana Jones and the Last Crusade*. On Wednesday 29 June, the Cannon Group's UK managing director Barry Jenkins turned up with fellow directors in the middle of film-making to announce that the 28-acre studios had been sold to a UK based property company – later revealed to be Brent Walker. Film production, said Jenkins, would end on 28 October, with the loss of twenty-eight jobs.

It was widely agreed that the Cannon Group's pressing need for cash was the main factor in the sale. Within a few days *Variety* was reporting that 'fancy footwork has helped the Cannon group close out the first quarter of 1988 with its financial health much improved'. According to the report, asset sales and debt payments had combined to help turn an operating loss of $13.9 million into a net profit of $10.5 million. The sale of the US and Italian theatres had contributed $28 million.

That same day (6 July), a Paris business court approved the buyout of the troubled GTC-CTM film laboratories and surrounding real estate by Cannon France, which had announced plans 'for a horizontal, state-of-the-art film production and post-production centre' (*Variety*, 13 July 1988). Cannon had been a surprise outsider in the race to grab GTC when the management lease ran out earlier in the year.

It was not the only surprise. Early in September, it was announced that Parretti and Fiorini had made a 'friendly' takeover bid for Pathé Cinema's 157-screen cinema chain, one of France's three major exhibitors. In partnership with the Swiss merchant bank Sasea, Parretti had apparently purchased between 38 and 40 per cent of the outstanding shares of Rivaud, a financial holding company owning 51 per cent of Pathé, for a reported $190 million.

By now, some of the more sceptical of the film press corps were beginning to phrase publicly the questions about Cannon which had been circulating for some time within the industry. *The Hollywood Reporter* on 13 September noted: 'The Pathé deal in many ways mirrors the Parretti/Sasea strategy in disposing of Cannon's Elstree Studios in the United Kingdom. In both instances, an outside company takes control of a national film industry icon – in France, the Pathé circuit and its name; in Britain, the long established Elstree studios – then threatens to shut it down. The outcry generally produces a rescue bid, allowing Parretti/Sasea to sell at a substantial profit.'

In an accompanying article, the paper's reporter Paul Mungo noted that the strategy behind the Cannon Group's moves remained unclear. 'In the United Kingdom,' after the sale of Screen Entertainment's back catalogue and the Elstree studios, 'Cannon is left with, basically, a cinema chain,' Mungo observed. 'And though Cannon promised "to develop British national films of quality" when it bought Screen Entertainment, its UK production activities have been moribund for at least a year. Cannon's other promise "to develop British first-time directors and allocate a budget to produce their first films" has also come to little.' As to why Cannon would invest in production facilities in France while simultaneously unloading Elstree, Mungo could find no unsatisfactory response from Cannon.

An advertorial in *Variety* in October 1988, paid for by Cannon, admitted that the group 'while asset-rich, was faced with a mounting debt which threatened its very existence.' It went on to proclaim that: 'Once again, Golan and Globus assayed [*sic*] the situation practically and pragmatically to effect a method of refinancing Cannon without destroying the ongoing elements which had accounted for its vitality.' This had been achieved, the *Variety* blurb continued, 'through the involvement of Intercorporation SA and its director Giancarlo Parretti.'

It was only twelve months before the scenario sketched out in *The Hollywood Reporter* news story on the Parretti takeover of Pathé came to pass. At first it seemed like the perfect alliance of interests. Jérôme Seydoux, powerful and wealthy head of the French holding concern Chargeurs SA, had bought France's second largest film company Pathé Cinema back for the nation from Italian entrepreneur Giancarlo Parretti earlier in 1990, as Mungo had predicted. It was known that the ambitious and shrewd Seydoux was eager to extend his network of cinemas outside France and tap into a large chunk of the 700 million market of moviegoers in Europe. Not for the first time, Parretti was in a hurry to sell. The so-called financier needed to sell off his movie theatres in Europe to bankroll part of his audacious $1.3 billion bid for MGM/UA, which was due for payment on the key date of 23 October.

By September of 1990, Chargeurs executives were letting it be known to the media that they were 'carefully evaluating' the Pathé cinema network in the UK and the Netherlands but were not yet ready to make an offer. 'Unattributable' sources within Chargeurs claimed that so far there had been 'no serious negotiations' with the Parretti group.

By contrast, Florio Fiorini, the Pathé Communications chairman, was telling journalists that negotiations were under way for the sale of the Pathé cinemas in Britain and Holland. 'That could be a bit of wishful thinking on the part of Mr Fiorini,' noted one of the unattributable Chargeurs sources.

What was bothering Chargeurs was the actual value of the British and Dutch movie theatres. Cinemas, especially those of the older chains, had long been recognised by property speculators as underdeveloped real estate. They usually occupied large sites in prime High Street locations with car parks and their buildings were often in decay.

In their contacts with Chargeurs and others, the Parretti-owned Pathé had put a price of $700 million on their 450-plus theatres in the UK and 67 screens in Holland. Some doubt existed about precisely what was being sold – did it or did it not include the real estate attached to the cinemas?

The mystery deepened as some in the Parretti camp tried to claim that Pathé had agreed earlier in the year to sell its Dutch and

British theatres to a Dutch concern called Cinema 5. The deal had not been completed, they said, 'because of technical problems'. The Pathé sources could give no details of who or what Cinema 5 was. An executive at the Geneva based investment group Sasea, which was run by the Pathé chairman Fiorini, stated to reporters that 'the deal with Cinema 5 would be cancelled if Chargeurs decided to take up the offer'. None of which did much to allay Chargeurs' suspicions.

Parretti was by this time having something of a credibility problem in the US in his attempt to purchase MGM/UA. Deadlines to come up with the first tranche of his purchase of the studio from the financier Kerkorian had been missed. The deadline of deadlines – 23 October 1990 – was also the day on which a number of other pieces in the Italian jigsaw puzzle were falling into place. Parretti was also having problems in his native Italy. Odeon TV, the ailing television network acquired at the end of 1989 by Parretti and Fiorini, was reported as having amassed $30 million in debt, with over 1,200 creditors. Three of its subsidiaries had already ceased trading. The 23 October deadline for Parretti to stump up the money for MGM was also the date by which Odeon TV must find a buyer if it was to be a saleable asset. After that date, according to the new television law passed by the Italian parliament in August, any networks which had not applied for a licence of simultaneous broadcasting over the national territory would be considered a local network, allowed to operate only within a very limited area. To apply for a national licence, however, the three Odeon companies which had ceased trading would have to be rescued from bankruptcy.

As in the case of Chargeurs, Parretti said it had a buyer. Luigi Franco, the Odeon TV trustee, admitted they had not received any offer but were in discussions with Italiana Produzioni, owned by Stefania Craxi, the daughter of the Italian Socialist Party leader. Prompt came the reply from Ms Craxi: 'We do not intend to buy Odeon TV. We were interested in their film library but we could not agree on the price.'

Meanwhile, back in France, the plan of Jérôme Seydoux and

Chargeurs to buy Pathé Cinema was running into opposition. To put matters in context, Jérôme's brother Nicolas was also the chairman of Gaumont, France's third largest film production and distribution company. The French Association of Film Producers was claiming that the Seydoux brothers were planning to merge Pathé with Gaumont and then buy out UGC, the country's second largest film company. Analysts noted that there was a perfect concordance of interest in this plan. Pathé, with its famous crowing cockerel, had a library of cinema newsreel footage dating back to the 1930s and 1940s estimated to be worth up to $60 million, but had no production facility. Gaumont, for its part, had a smaller library but was a very active producer.

In spite of the doubts and difficulties in Europe, Parretti was plunging on with his MGM takeover. Not the least of the questions occurring to those who knew about his problems in Italy was how could Parretti, whose Odeon TV network was technically bankrupt, afford the $1.3 billion asking price for MGM?

Parretti was now playing lukewarm in Europe. He was said to be 'less in a hurry' to sell the Dutch cinemas and had announced that the UK chain was no longer up for sale. 'We don't consider this latest declaration as definitive,' said a Chargeurs spokesman, adding that Parretti still needed to find the bulk of financing for the MGM deal. Chargeurs still believed Parretti was asking too much, whether for the cinemas as a whole or for the Dutch network only.

To the astonishment of Wall Street and the media watchers, on 23 October 1990 – the final, much extended deadline to close the purchase – the newspapers were reporting that Parretti's Pathé Communications had delivered bank cheques necessary to complete its $1.3 billion purchase of MGM/UA. This despite the missed deadlines to complete the purchase and the little reported collapse of a $600-million licensing deal with Time-Warner.

Where, then, had the money come from?

On the same day in late November 1990 that Chargeurs reported it was still interested in buying the Pathé cinema chain,

French deputy François d'Aubert tabled a motion asking for an investigation into the role played by the Dutch subsidiary of the Crédit Lyonnais bank in financing Parretti. It would be hard to imagine stranger bedfellows. Crédit Lyonnais, the sleepy, conservative, state-controlled bank that had grown up on advances to French industrialists. Parretti, the one-time waiter from Orvieto, whose March 1990 criminal conviction for fraud under appeal would seem to have debarred him from any banking favour.

Just how Parretti came to persuade Crédit Lyonnais to part with the $1.3 billion to enable him to purchase the legendary MGM is a story still to be told, given the secretive nature of French commercial life. What is beyond doubt is that the bank's Dutch subsidiary, Crédit Lyonnais Bank Netherlands, did see fit to advance massive credit lines to Parretti in order to purchase MGM/UA Communications Co. – despite his record.

Parretti was in trouble at MGM from the start. At the time of the purchase, a typically complex transaction depending on the 'retirement' of large amounts of MGM/UA debt through the junk bond market, analysts noted that apart from the purchase price Parretti would need about $500 million just to finance ongoing production.

It was only a matter of time before the ship started to leak again. On 19 February 1991, *The Hollywood Reporter* bannered a story on its front page that MGM-Pathé had removed the John Candy comedy *Delirious* from its spring release date because it was unable to come up with the $7 million opening commitment for publicity and advertising. In the weeks and months that followed a stream of similar stories flowed from MGM. It was in litigation over its supposed deal with Time-Warner.

By June, it was clear that even Crédit Lyonnas had finally had enough, asking a Delaware court for control of the MGM studio and to confirm the effective removal of Parretti. The case was in court through October and November of 1991, with the judge not expected to deliver his verdict before Christmas.

When Parretti's nemesis came, it came with the suddenness of a Mafia hit.

On 27 December 1991, Parretti – still in name the president of MGM, most famous of all the great Hollywood studios – was arrested by Sicilian police whilst waiting to board a plane at Ciampino airport in Rome for an undisclosed destination in North Africa – variously reported as either Tunisia or Egypt. He was put into solitary confinement in a Sicilian gaol, pending charges of criminal association, tax evasion, falsifying accounts and destroying financial records.

Giancarlo Parretti, the former Dorchester Hotel waiter, had successively taken over Cannon, Pathé and MGM. In his schemes, he had received considerable help from banks, politicians and officials whose duty it was to ensure that men like Parretti could never acquire control of public companies. As in the case of Maxwell, in the headlong rush to get into the media, these organisations and individuals had apparently suspended their normal standards of judgment.

In a bizarre coincidence, the officer who had arrested Parretti ten years previously on similar charges, Major Gaetano Rabuazzo, was the same officer who arrested him in Rome in December 1991.

For Parretti, worse was to come. Only three days after his Rome arrest, on Monday 30 December, the judge in the Delaware court broke his silence after weeks of deliberation on the battle between Parretti and his former bankers Crédit Lyonnais over control of MGM. In a ruling that ran to eighty-nine pages, Judge Allen unequivocally ruled that Crédit Lyonnais had acted properly in removing Parretti from control of MGM for violating a corporate governance agreement. In delivering his judgment, Allen said that from the moment Parretti signed the two-page corporate governance agreement he 'barely masked his efforts to dominate and control management of MGM.' Apart from the legion of financial and administrative misdemeanours, the court had heard evidence of how Parretti had continued to defy the agreement with Crédit Lyonnais and meddle in the running of MGM.

MGM's almost legendary trademark of Leo the lion – two short snarls and a longer growl – has been shamelessly imitated by lesser concerns. Its motto of 'Ars Gratia Artis' was an exaggeration even in the studio's heyday. However, Leo had never before suffered the indignities heaped upon him under the reign of Giancarlo Parretti.

As always, though, Leo had got his revenge. Like the treasures of the Egyptian Pharaohs, the famous snarling lion trademark has been plundered in modern times by other media corporations. Like the Pharaoh's Curse, it has not been lucky for its imitators. Robert Maxwell shamelessly hijacked the MGM logo for his Mirror Group Newspapers. Mary Tyler Moore, the former comedy actress, built up a fine TV production company responsible for such groundbreaking series as *Hill Street Blues*. Her company, which she called MTM, 'borrowed' the MGM logo but for a lion wrily substituted a kitten. MTM was subsequently sold by Moore to the British ITV contractor, TVS, a purchase which put TVS under severe financial pressure and led indirectly to the loss of its franchise in the revolution taking place in the British broadcasting scene.

XV

Best of British

In 1987, at the prestigious Prix Futura conference in Berlin, broadcasters gathered as usual to vote for the best of their peers' work. A delegate from Poland, at that time beginning to dip its toe in the waters of freedom though still under Communist rule, made a telling observation.

The delegate was one of those now fast-disappearing older generation Poles whose elegant manners hark back to the Francophone court of the Duchy of Warsaw. He was astonished to learn that the British government was considering changing the dual system of BBC and ITV that had dominated the major awards at international festivals and competitions over the years. 'This must not happen,' he said, gesticulating with his ever-present cigarette in its holder, 'you already have the finest broadcasting system in the world.' Then, after a moment's reflection, he added thoughtfully: 'But maybe we Poles now will have a chance.'

It is sometimes said that Britain has, if not the best, then the least worst television system in the world. That may at least have been true until the introduction of the 1990 Broadcasting Act, now acknowledged by even its supporters and proponents to have been a disaster.

What drew the admiration of foreign observers was the way in which Britain had evolved first of all the best-known and probably most respected broadcasting organisation in the form of the BBC. This was then added to with the introduction of a commercial system of ITV which generally accepted the broad public service remit established by the BBC. ITV also added new forms of programming, particularly fresh and less obeisant approaches to news and current affairs. To its admirers, this system was 'balanced and complementary'. To its critics, who, as we have seen, were numerous by the mid-1980s, it was 'a cosy duopoly'.

The Conservative government re-elected for a third term in June 1987 had started to turn its attention to broadcasting. For some time, Mrs Thatcher and senior ministers like Norman Tebbit had developed a view of both the BBC and ITV establishment as inherently anti-government and disloyal. Traditional Conservative mistrust of the BBC harked back to the independent line the Corporation had taken over the 1954 Suez Crisis. Memories of Suez were rekindled during the Falklands War in 1982 when Conservative backbenchers openly accused the BBC of treachery.

In 1986, when the BBC's Chairman Stuart Young, the brother of senior minister Lord Young, developed a leukemia that was to prove swiftly fatal, Mrs Thatcher appointed Marmaduke Hussey as the new Chairman. One of 'Duke' Hussey's most significant qualifications was that he was an old *Times* hand. A distinguished Second World War veteran, Hussey was managing director of Times Newspapers during Rupert Murdoch's purge of the unions.

Hussey inherited as Director General Alasdair Milne. A distinguished programme maker and old-style defender of the BBC's divine right, Milne brushed aside the criticisms. As crisis followed crisis the problems facing Milne became overwhelming. After 87 days of testimony, a libel suit against *That's Life* was settled out of court at a cost to the BBC of nearly £1 million.

The simmering row over a 1984 *Panorama* programme called 'Maggie's Militant Tendency' also boiled over in 1986 when two Conservative MPs involved decided to take the matter to court. The BBC's film had, on the flimsiest of evidence, purported to show that some Conservative backbenchers were neo-fascists. Having stood by the programme, Milne had been prepared to face a huge and damaging court action. Under pressure from Hussey and the BBC's board of governors, the BBC climbed down and settled out of court.

Shortly afterwards Milne was summoned abruptly before a board of governors lunch, and informed by Hussey and deputy Joel Barnett of his dismissal. It was an act unprecedented in the annals of the BBC.

A short period of speculation about the next DG followed, including a bizarre interview during which Channel 4 chief Jeremy Isaacs was beadily quizzed by one of the governors as to whether he could take orders. In the end, Deputy Director General Michael Checkland, an accountant by training, was confirmed as the new DG. The sigh of satisfaction from Downing Street was almost audible. The BBC was now in safe hands. . . .

The Peacock Committee had been appointed to examine ways of financing the BBC other than the licence fee. Resisting strong pressure from the government to force advertising on BBC Television – 'just a minute or so round the nine o'clock news' Mrs Thatcher had suggested – Peacock instead put up a massive smokescreen. The committee tuned into the prevailing economic arguments of the time by suggesting that broadcasting should become a kind of electronic marketplace. Viewers, urged Peacock, should be free to choose amongst an array of television channels much as they could browse among the titles in a bookshop.

The argument bore no relationship to the economic realities of television. Individual television programmes may be like the books in a shop, but the channels are more like the large bookstore chains themselves. But Peacock had succeeded in turning the guns away from the BBC, levelling them instead at commercial television. ITV was a sitting duck. The commercial system had become fat, overstaffed and complacent in its long years of monopoly. Prompted by the right-wing press, ministers from Mrs Thatcher down publicly condemned the waste in ITV. Camera crews from commercial television would turn up with a dozen or more staff to conduct interviews with ministers and other politicians. With the new lightweight technology, such filming could be carried out by three people.

Rupert Murdoch and Andrew Neil had fought through the new technology in the British newspaper industry in a bitter and sometimes bloody confrontation with the print unions. The staff at the News International headquarters in Wapping were those who had joined the exodus from Fleet Street and its 'old Spanish customs', as the restrictive practices were known. The *Sunday Times* especially saw the fat cats of ITV and its union leaders as ensconced in a cosy collusion only possible because of the ITV monopoly. It was like the old relationship between Fleet Street proprietors and the print unions.

It would be wrong to suggest that News International's view was governed only by commercial considerations. Murdoch and Neil have a genuine dislike for the cosy and closeted British approach to information, contrasted with America's freedom of information acts. Week after week in the *Sunday Times*, Neil and his staff detailed the iniquities that were rife in ITV. *Sunday Times* reporters found examples of people paid thousand of pounds in ITV for doing nothing, of gross overstaffing and pusillanimous management. They were aided from within. Frustrated ITV managers and producers besieged them with calls about the corruptions endemic in the industry.

News International and its subsidiary Sky Television disliked the ITV-dominated British Satellite Broadcasting even more than the BBC. They saw BSB as a doomed attempt by the old guard of British commercial television to impose itself on the new satellite TV industry. Moreover, BSB was Sky's main competitor in the satellite race.

Clearly it was in Sky Television's interest to weaken the all-powerful grip of ITV on UK commercial television. It was also clear that there was not enough room for both Sky and BSB. It would be a fight to the death. When Murdoch appointed *Sunday Times* editor Neil to the chairmanship of Sky, it was widely taken as a sign that the gloves were off.

The shape of the new regulatory framework for ITV after the 1991 licence round, and the collapse of BSB, proved that Sky achieved its two aims. In doing so it had to survive a financial crisis that threatened to sink News International itself. But in doing so it could hardly have hoped to have been so blessed with the incompetence of British television bureaucracy and BSB's own management.

In the 1991 ITV franchise round conducted under the new

system of cash bidding, three large ITV companies – Thames, TV-am and TVS – lost their franchises, together with the smaller TSW company in the south-west of England. The 1991 franchises were notable for another reason. They introduced to Britain for the first time a major foreign international media company, Walt Disney Corporation, as one of the main owners of an important UK television station. This was the direct result of the highest bid legislation. With the moratorium on takeovers of ITV companies due to be lifted in 1993, concerns such as Time-Warner, CLT, Fininvest of Italy and others were expected to follow Disney's lead.

Others went further. Thay claimed that the hostility shown to 'Death on the Rock' by Murdoch's newspapers was part of a determined effort to discredit and weaken ITV at a time when both it and its governing body the IBA were under close scrutiny by the government.

It is worth examining these issues in more detail. The 'Death on the Rock' programme was a *This Week* special on the shooting by Special Air Service regiment undercover soldiers in March 1988 of three IRA terrorists who were planning to plant a bomb on Gibraltar. It was transmitted in April after the IBA rejected an appeal by the Foreign Secretary of the time, Sir Geoffrey Howe, to reconsider whether the programme should go ahead.

Thames Television's *This Week* had a record of tackling thorny problems under its editor, Roger Bolton. Bolton had been a programme maker and *Panorama* editor at the BBC in the *après-moi-le-déluge* years of Alasdair Milne. In some respects, Bolton lives up to the romantic sixties notion of the journalist battling against all the odds to tell the truth. In his book '*Death on the Rock' and Other Stories*, he admits to 'this familiar feeling of sickness and excitement as I stood in the dark' when faced with the howls of outrage about the programme.

The government had learned of 'Death on the Rock' through press reports and Thames's own advance publicity. This seemed to make it clear that in the view of *This Week*, at least, the British authorities had a case to answer over the fact that the three IRA terrorists, who turned out to be unarmed, were shot down rather than arrested.

This Week and its reporter, Julian Manyon, had found eyewitnesses who said that they heard no warnings given by the soldiers before the three were shot. The allegations were made more sensitive by the 'shoot-to-kill' controversies which had surfaced from time to time in relation to the policy of the security forces in Northern Ireland and which had led to the resignation of John Stalker.

In terms of public sympathy, the broadcasters were on to a loser. The SAS had been popular media heroes ever since the television news had brought their startling techniques into viewers' living rooms when units intervened to stop the killing of hostages in the Iranian embassy siege. The stories of men like Captain John Hamilton, who had fought single-handed to the finish when surrounded by Argentinians in the Falklands, or of Captain Robert Nairac, who refused to break under IRA torture, had left regimental folklore and entered the popular consciousness through best-selling accounts. The popular reaction to the news that the SAS had foiled an overt IRA bomb attempt, which would have killed dozens of onlookers as well as soldiers, was an immense sigh of relief. That Thames, and those who took the decision to show the programme at the IBA, were thought by the government and the popular press to be out of tune with this feeling was deeply significant.

'Death on the Rock' showed beyond much doubt that there were at least conflicting accounts as to how the three IRA members met their end. Beyond this, however, the programme seemed to its critics to be taking sides with those newspapers, notably the *Observer*, which were not only casting doubt on the official statements about the incident but had gone on to suggest that the IRA had somehow been lured into a trap. Fleet Street had divided more or less along party lines over the shooting, with the *Sunday Times* and the *Sun* in particular tending to support the government's view as read out in the House of Commons statement by the Foreign Secretary.

Under the law governing commercial television (then and now), and also appended to the BBC Charter, broadcasters in the UK are obliged to display 'due impartiality' in matters of controversy or current public policy. In practice, this obligation is exercised by the programme makers, with the broadcasting authority keeping a look-out for particular problems. At the IBA it was standard practice for one senior officer to maintain regular contact with the producers of topical documentary/current affairs strands, particularly *World in Action* and *This Week*. Again, in practice, the editors or producers would tend to refer any programmes where there might be difficulties to the IBA. The system at the IBA, like that at the BBC, is essentially one of 'upward referral'. That is to say that if problems could not be sorted out at the senior officer level, they would be referred to the Director of Television or his deputy. The next level up was Director General and the next the Chairman.

Because of the press furore surrounding the shootings, 'Death on the Rock' had quickly reached the level of the IBA's Chairman, Lord Thomson. The normal opportunities to tinker with the content by an official statement here, a bit of balance there, were soon swallowed up by one main issue. After the government's intervention, the question was not in what form the programme should be transmitted, but whether it should go out at all. There were powerful reasons both for and against transmission. The government's stated case was that an inquest into the deaths had already been announced and therefore the matter was 'sub judice'. The programme could only prejudice the proceedings. Under the IBA's own guidelines, the proceedings of a Coroners' Court are just as much affected by the 'sub judice' regulations as any other court. The fact that the inquest was to be held in Gibraltar, under British sovereignty but self-governing, was pleaded by Thames as a reason for going ahead with the programme. Mrs Thatcher herself denounced it as 'trial by television'.

It was virtually unprecedented that a minister of state should request publicly that a programme should not be transmitted.

Political pressures behind the scenes are a fact of daily life, but a public request was another matter. In such cases it should be clear that the final decision must rest with those appointed by the government – in this case the IBA members who acted as the Authority's board. To understand why the IBA allowed 'Death on the Rock' to go out as it did, it is necessary to go back to the beginning of Lord Thomson's stewardship as Chairman.

In the 1980 ITV franchise round presided over by Lady Plowden as IBA chairman and Sir Brian Young as Director General, Southern Television and Westward Television had both lost their licences to broadcast. There had been the usual recriminations from the losers about the arbitrary power of the IBA. When Lord Thomson took over as Chairman in 1982, one of his first public statements was that 'there must be a better way'. In this, most observers heartily agreed with him.

One of the misfortunes of George Thomson's reign as Chairman of the IBA was the fact that Sir Brian Young reached retirement age soon after Thomson took over. A visionary headmaster of Charterhouse, Young had no commercial background but took to the IBA role with a political astuteness and air of authority that belied his lack of experience. In deputies like Colin Shaw as Director of Television and John Thompson as Director of Radio, Young had talent as well as urbanity at his disposal.

In the darkening days ahead, Thompson and Shaw would communicate secretly to each other as 'Brother Television' and 'Brother Radio'. When Shaw finally had had enough and left, Thompson delivered a barbed attack on the new-style IBA in front of the assembled staff that was to seal his own fate.

The omens for the future were not good when Thames Television managing director Bryan Cowgill secured the rights to the next series of *Dallas*, which until that point had been running on the BBC. Much to the bemusement of its American distributors, Lord Thomson's IBA made Thames give *Dallas* back to the BBC on the grounds that a long-standing 'gentlemen's agreement' had been broken when Thames poached the programme. Not only did it cost Thames a lot of money but it led to the replacement of the former BBC hand Cowgill by the relatively unknown and inexperienced Richard Dunn.

In seeking a new Director General, it was widely expected that the IBA would appoint either of its two division heads, Colin Shaw or John Thompson. Thompson had actually been on the shortlist to succeed Alasdair Milne at the BBC, while Shaw was a former Secretary of the BBC. The appointment of either man would have met with general staff approval and there was a degree of more or less friendly rivalry for the job between them.

It was however a time of all change in British public life. In television, as in so much else, the emphasis had moved from programmes to the market place. George Thomson had been particularly impressed by a visit to Capital Radio, when he was entertained by the flamboyant John Whitney, one of the station's founders. Capital, whose Chairman was Sir Richard Attenborough, had an air of glamour and above all was one of the real new success stories in commercial broadcasting. Against his own doubts, Whitney was persuaded to apply for the post of Director General at the IBA.

The IBA members, whose decision it was to make the appointment, were split down the middle. Whitney had undoubted charm and commercial acumen, but the job at the top of the IBA was essentially an administrative grind, relieved by occasional spells as the national Aunt Sally. Undeterred by these doubts, George Thomson used his casting vote to secure Whitney's appointment. 'It's a dotty appointment,' said John Thompson feelingly to his staff on learning of the decision.

The IBA staff muttered darkly that Thomson – a onetime editor of comics like *Dandy* and *Beano* – felt more comfortable with a Director General who like himself was not part of the prevailing Oxbridge and public school ethos that dominated the upper echelons of the Authority. A shrewder guess was that Thomson intended to be much more active in commercial television than was usual in such a part-time role as IBA Chairman. He promptly signalled his intentions by moving permanently with his wife into the ninth-floor flat opposite

Harrods that had been thoughtfully provided for the occasional essential overnight stays of the Chairman or other Authority members.

When George Thomson became Chairman, two things above all were needed at the IBA. The first was some clear policy on how to deal with the ITV franchises next time round in the growing climate of deregulation. The other was how to help equip commercial television for the new age of cross-border television. In particular, the IBA had been charged with overseeing the introduction of direct broadcasting satellite (DBS) television.

The IBA's decisions over the DBS project were even more far-reaching for our story of the Sky Barons than its failure to take the initiative in the matter of the ITV franchises. From the start, the IBA had allowed itself to be unduly influenced by the advice of engineers in the matter of the technical standards for DBS. The IBA's engineering division, subsequently privatised, was then more or less a law to itself. Situated in rural splendour at Crawley Court, near Winchester, it was far from the eye of the Brompton Road. The IBA engineers were strongly influenced by the high picture quality achievable in theory by the D-MAC standard for satellite broadcasting being promoted heavily by the European Community.

In pushing D-MAC, the EC had been heavily lobbied by two state-owned multinational electronics companies, Thomson of France and Philips of the Netherlands. Both companies employ tens of thousands of workers in their home countries and their political importance is considerable. Thomson and Philips had persuaded the EC that a separate European intermediate technical standard, D-MAC, should be inserted between the existing PAL-standard of most European television and the new ultra-high definition systems being developed by the Japanese and the Americans. If they were right, thousands of jobs in electronic components and TV receivers were at stake. If they were wrong, the adoption of D-MAC would be a disaster.

In taking the D-MAC route, DBS in Britain fell between two stools. While the UK government was content to go along with

D-MAC, it made it clear from the outset that it would not put any government money into the satellites that would carry the programmes. This was in complete contrast to France and Germany, where the state had already agreed to pick up the tab for their DBS satellites. As a result, the winning contractor for the DBS franchise in the UK would have to find hundreds of millions of pounds for two satellites before it ever made a programme.

At News International, Rupert Murdoch and Andrew Neil could not believe their luck. At the IBA's insistence, the technical specifications for DBS required the contractor to purchase not just one but two satellites, which must be operational from the outset in order to provide a back-up if one failed. Sky, with its 'low technology' PAL system, was content with just one satellite at the outset. Moreover, Sky had the added luxury of renting its satellite transponders from Astra, based in Luxembourg.

As has been related elsewhere, the IBA's chosen operator, BSB, was singularly ill-equipped to handle the complexities and costs associated with the launch. However, from a technical point of view, the project was doomed from the start. Apart from the £500-million bill for its two Hughes Aircraft satellites, BSB's so-called 'squarial' dish barely saw the light of the High Street, while key manufacturers failed to produce other vital components on time.

The IBA at its top level seemed concerned with other matters. The administrative staff grew almost daily, while the new Director General John Whitney appeared to occupy himself with matters of style rather than substance.

On her first visit to the IBA, Mrs Thatcher had railed against the prevailing 'liberal bias' in broadcasting, banging the dining table for emphasis. When the IBA and the heads of ITV were summoned to a specially convened seminar on the broadcasting industry at 10 Downing Street, Mrs Thatcher listened with barely concealed impatience. 'Oh, do get on with it,' she said as John Whitney expatiated on the qualities and achievements of independent broadcasting. (Told that the stories of overmanning and inefficiency in ITV were really rather exaggerated, she hissed:

'Commercial television is the last bastion of restrictive trade practice.')

By this time, the IBA and ITV were under attack from all quarters. The Authority had patently failed to come up with the promised 'better way' on franchises and the debate had now passed into the hands of radical economists like Cento Veljanovsky and a small but influential group of academics from Brunel University who were advising the Treasury. At the other end of the scale, the ITV companies were seen to be dragging their heels on the demands for access for independent producers. On meeting the ITV chiefs for the first time, Mrs Thatcher had asked: 'Where are the Young Turks?' From the distinctly greying ranks about her, answer came there none.

The fact is that the young Turks had all been too busy trying to make a living 'out there' from sporadic Channel 4 commissions and bits of commercial work to attend important seminars. The independents soon organised themselves into one of the most powerful and effective lobbies of modern times, with direct access to government ministers, including the Prime Minister herself. In radio, likewise, the struggling ILR commercial companies had tired of trying to get sympathy out of what they saw as the fat-cat television culture of the IBA. 'Get the IBA off our backs,' they had begged the Home Secretary.

One other piece of tinder had been thrown into the fire. Under a cosy arrangement, the IBA and the ITV companies had between them managed to persuade the Home Office, which held responsibility for broadcasting, that the levy it paid to the Treasury should change. Since 1974, the Exchequer Levy, as it is known, had been based as a charge on profits. Each company was allowed, free of levy, a slice of profit equal to 2 per cent of its advertising revenue, or £250,000, whichever was the greater. The remainder was subject to levy at 67 per cent. In April 1986, the IBA had managed to persuade the Home Office (who in turn persuaded the Treasury) that the Exchequer Levy on ITV should be reduced to 45 per cent but with an additional new levy on the sale of programmes abroad. Levy only became payable in the first year that a profit was made. It was a cheeky move, which the Home Office somehow swallowed.

It was a windfall for the ITV companies. For the government, the net effect, as calculated in a damning official report, was to deprive the Treasury coffers of several millions of pounds in revenue. There is strong prima facie evidence that the authorities were tipped off to this fact by a member of the IBA's own financial staff, who was subsequently dismissed for the leak.

Into this general powder keg for the IBA was thrown 'Death on the Rock'. In normal circumstances, the programme would have gone out with some kind of health warning and possibly some insistence on certain changes by the IBA itself. But these were not normal circumstances. The IBA was already looking shaky as far as the government's plans for broadcasting were concerned. The decision to remove radio to another body had effectively been taken and it was now a matter of what to do about television.

In 'Death on the Rock', George Thomson had been handed an unexpected farewell gift. With the term of his office due to end that year, he faced the prospect of being remembered as the Chairman who lost the IBA. An astute politician, Thomson must have known, as many insiders already did, that this would almost certainly be the case under plans which the government, egged on by a combination of advertisers, radical economists and Rupert Murdoch, was bringing forward to re-model British television. From the start, he took the line that the Thames programme makers were behaving no differently in seeking to examine what went on in Gibraltar than the authors of articles that had already appeared in the press. 'Death on the Rock' offered the chance for the IBA to sink not ignominiously, but with honour and flags defiantly flying. No editor worth his salt in a similar position would have acted differently. Thomson sanctioned the programme for transmission.

The rest is history, at least for the IBA. The Authority's death throes made a Roman holiday for the *Sunday Times*, whose proprietor Rupert Murdoch had been forced to sell his stake in London Weekend Television, which he had rescued from bankruptcy in the 1970s. Exposure by the *Sunday Times* of

ITV's colossal bureaucracy and overmanning had already had a damaging effect, with ministers resolved to change the system. Downing Street let it be known that the game was up as far as the IBA was concerned. When the Authority came up with a somewhat deficient public explanation of its plans for the future of commercial television, the *Sunday Times* obtained an advance copy, which was roundly lambasted by media editor Jonathan Miller ahead of its release to the press.

The writing was on the wall in August 1988, when an *Insight* editorial, with heavy briefing from Number 10, catalogued the by now bristling portfolio of IBA sins of omission and commission. The Authority would be replaced by a new-style 'Independent Television Commission', which would award TV franchises not on the basis of merit but simply to the highest bidder. In the course of the next few months that stark but in some ways essentially clearcut proposal would be muddied by the usual processes of special pleading by various interested parties. Most of all, the ITC, presenting itself under its Chairman designate George Russell (a former IBA member) as a new broom, managed to wring out the concession of the 'quality threshold'. This would, promised Russell, be a 'Bechers Brook' of a hurdle for those wanting to throw lots of money at the ITC.

There is no doubt that many broadcasters and journalists were deeply opposed to the government's attempts to stifle 'Death on the Rock'. Theirs was a principled stand, which the government of the day and many members of the public found hard to accept. Broadcasters and many others who had doubts about the intrinsic merits of the programme lined up behind it simply because they saw it as another attack on the freedom of speech. For their part, senior ministers simply could not see why the broadcasters took the line they did. It was well known in security circles that the IRA's mainland bombing campaigns in England were conducted for one purpose only. That was what Mrs Thatcher had memorably described as 'the oxygen of publicity'. Time and again, in the view of ministers and the security services, under the argument that they were acting in the public interest, TV and radio reporters would approach 'Sinn Fein spokesmen' – many of them often known to be active IRA members – after some particularly grisly outrage. For Mrs Thatcher and her ministers, most of whom had come within a hair's breadth of death in the Grand Hotel bombing by the IRA in Brighton, or had heard the dull thud of the bomb which blew up Airey Neave outside the Houses of Parliament, the issue was the broadcasters' own failure of imagination. Without 'Death on the Rock', the legislation to bleed ITV of finance might still have gone ahead. With it, the new law was certain.

In retrospect, the period from 1987 to 1991 will go down not just as a watershed but as a revolution in British broadcasting. Among the personal casualties of that revolution must be numbered Alasdair Milne, Bryan Cowgill, George Thomson and John Whitney, James Gatward and Bruce Gyngell. Among the institutional casualties are the IBA, BSB, Thames Television, Gatward's TVS and Gyngell's TV-am.

As for the BBC, its real test is to come when its present charter expires at the end of 1996. As for Bruce Gyngell, he is one of nature's survivors. Perhaps the only person ever to have received an apology from Mrs Thatcher – on learning of the loss of TV-am's franchise – Gyngell has managed to survive both shocks. With a determination that Rupert Murdoch would admire, Gyngell concluded an alliance with the Daily Telegraph Group of Conrad Black and the giant US Time-Warner combine to bid for the UK Channel 5 franchise.

XVI

Wild Colonial Boys

In May 1992, the United States space shuttle *Endeavour* blasted off from Cape Canaveral on its maiden flight, its mission to rescue, repair and relaunch from space orbit one of the world's largest communications satellites, Intelsat VI. Launched in March 1990, one of the booster engines on this four and a half tonne space behemoth capable of relaying up to 120,000 simultaneous telephone calls and three television channels failed to operate and the satellite was left marooned in space. It was to be one of the most difficult and ambitious space rescue missions ever attempted.

On board *Endeavour*, alongside the latest refinements in space technology, the crew of seven carried with them a piece of an old wooden ship's oak sternpost. It came from a 106-foot converted Whitby collier also named *Endeavour* in which Captain James Cook set sail from Plymouth on 25 August 1768 on a voyage which resulted in the 'discovery' and subsequent colonisation of the great Southern Continent of Australia. On 21 August 1770, Cook hoisted the Union Jack on Possession Island and claimed the whole east coast in the name of King George III as 'New South Wales'.

In their quest for global supremacy using all the means of modern space communications technology, the Sky Barons are the new colonisers of the closing decades of the twentieth century. Some of their stories are rich in the ironies of history.

Rupert Murdoch, whose ancestors hailed from the Scottish fishing village of Cruden on the coast road between Aberdeen and Peterhead, set out back from Australia first to colonise large sections of the British media and then on to conquer new worlds across the Atlantic.

The Japanese led by Sony's Akio Morita have been busy buying up chunks of Hollywood four decades after wave after wave of Japanese torpedo and dive bombers destroyed without warning the pride of the United States' Pacific fleet at Pearl Harbor and a century and a quarter after Commodore Matthew Perry sailed into Tokyo Bay with four men-of-war to present credentials from the President of the United States to the Emperor of Japan.

From his headquarters in Mexico City, Emilio Azcárraga is building a new electronic empire in South America nearly five centuries after Hernan Cortes and Francisco Pizarrro colonised Mexico and Peru for Spain. At the same time Azcárraga is looking northwards and using television to help recapture the Spanish speaking population of California, Texas and New Mexico lost to the United States in the war that ended in 1848.

Now there is a newcomer to this band of neo-colonialist barons. Canadian Conrad Black has been travelling Murdoch's route in reverse, going eastwards across the Atlantic from the Americas to the United Kingdom and then onwards to Australia. Black is the latest in a long line of Canadian press barons that has included William Maxwell Aitken (Lord Beaverbrook) and Roy Herbert Thomson (Lord Thomson of Fleet).

Descendants of Australian 'First Fleeters' have similar status in Australia to that accorded in the United States to the descendants of the Pilgrim Fathers who arrived on the *Mayflower* at New Plymouth on the New England coast of the United States in 1620. The Australian 'First Fleet' consisted of eleven vessels carrying seven hundred and thirty-six convicts guarded by three companies of marines. The fleet set sail from Portsmouth on 13 May 1787 to colonise New South Wales. In command was Captain Arthur Phillip on board the fleet flagship, the naval warship the *Sirius*.

Australia has a healthy if radical solution to any overmighty subjects be they First Fleeters or the 'Ten Pound Poms' who flooded to Australia on £10 assisted passages from the United Kingdom in the years following the Second World War. There is a regular cull of any who appear to be growing too tall among the rich and famous 'tall poppies' on the Antipodean horizon.

Riding head and shoulders above the other poppies in the Australian cornfield stands the imposing and substantial (130 kilo) figure of Kerry Packer, the second son of Sir Frank Packer. The family claims descent from Frederick Meredith, a cabin boy aboard the *Sirius* who returned with the Second Fleet to settle in Australia.

Kerry Frances Bullmore Packer was born on 17 December 1937, the younger son of Sir Frank Packer and his wife Gretel. Frank Packer was born in 1905. He earned a reputation as something of a tyrant both as father and as businessman. A skilled amateur boxer, Frank passed the looks of a heavyweight and the guts and skill of the boxing ring to his younger son. Kerry was heavyweight champion at school and a keen cricketer. Later he was to be a single figure handicap golfer as well as a doughty figure on a polo pony.

Now reputedly Australia's richest man, Kerry Packer has so far preferred to build his barony at home rather than set out a-colonising but the story of the Packer family is integral to the history of the down under Sky Barons. One man who knows the Packer family better than most is Bruce Gyngell – the colourful Australian Chairman of Britain's national breakfast time television service TV-am.

Gyngell entered the annals of Australian media history by being the first face to be seen on Australian television. He spent the Sunday before the launch closeted with Frank Packer, the station's proprietor, Mike Ramsden the news editor and Alec Baz who was to become Station Manager. That night Gyngell could not sleep. The next day Frank Packer noticed that his 'announcer feller' was showing the strain. Handing him a sleeping pill Packer sent him home with the admonition 'You'd better wear your dinner suit tonight.' The launch of Australian TV was an historic event and possibly Packer wished to endow it with an echo of Reithian standards of dress. The driver sent to pick Gyngell up later woke him with barely enough time to reach the studio. Gyngell is a tall man and the studio was so cramped it was difficult for the cameraman to get a straight shot. The result was that the angle the camera had to use made Gyngell look like 'Jacques Tati in a gale' as he read the historic words: 'From Channel Nine comes the first television programme in Australia: TCN presents *This is Television.*'

The audience was tiny, no more than three thousand sets in the whole of Sydney, but the build-up to the inauguration of television had been filled with the intense competition that was and remains to this day a hallmark of the Australian media scene. Frank Packer's Channel Nine was launched from an uncompleted building at Willoughby on the outskirts of Sydney that resembled an electricity sub-station and an office with packing cases for desks situated near the city markets. The first modest schedule ran just two hours each evening. Six weeks later, the public service broadcaster (ABC) – always the bridesmaid, never the bride – went on air. It was December before the commercial opposition ATN7, controlled by the Fairfax family, opened for business.

The young Gyngell became almost a member of the Packer family. He recalls how every Saturday he had dinner at Sir Frank's home in the company of such distinguished guests as Lord Attlee, the Rockefellers, Henry Ford III and the Australian Prime Minister and the Federal Treasurer. Sir Frank would tell him 'Don't say a fucking thing, son!'

In 1961, when Sir Frank's wife Gretel, suffering from a thrombosis from which she knew she would not recover, left Sydney for surgery in the United States, Bruce went round to say goodbye. Gretel embraced him. 'Stay with him,' she pleaded. 'Promise me you'll never leave. Frank really needs you.' And, she added, 'You're a good influence on the boys.'

The vast continent of Australia has a landmass over thirty times greater than that of the United Kingdom but a population less than a third of that of the mother country. It has a history of media concentration in the main city centres of Sydney, Melbourne, Brisbane, Adelaide and Perth. Radio was founded from the great press empires built up in the earlier part of the century and television followed suit. One of the first two Sydney channels was awarded to Sir Frank Packer at the time owner of the *Daily* and *Sunday Telegraph*, the other to the owner of the *Sydney Morning Herald* and the *Sun*, John Fairfax.

The Canadian press baron the late Lord Thomson, immortal for his description of the first Scottish Independent Television contract as 'a licence to print your own money', once said 'for enough money, I'd work in hell.' But having looked at the Australian press scene he concluded that it was too dangerous to invest there. 'The inhabitants carried guns and their main occupation seemed to be rape.'[1]

Sir Frank Packer had a reputation as a 'tough old bastard'. He declared a circulation war on Rupert Murdoch's *Mirror* and vowed to send the young interloper 'back to Adelaide with his fookin' tail between his fookin' legs.'[2] But Murdoch held his own and increased circulation and profits.

A year later things were patched up when Packer and Murdoch made a deal to carve up the market for Sydney's suburban papers with the Fairfax-Packer group giving up some of its publications in the north and west for some of Murdoch's in the south. Murdoch's recently acquired Cumberland Newspapers was given the contract to print them all.

Sir Frank Packer's death from pneumonia in 1974 was an event that affected his son Kerry deeply. As a child Kerry was slightly dyslexic and suffered a bout of polio. As a young man he was involved in a serious car accident in which three people died. The accident left him unable to walk for eight months but none of this was to deter him on his route to becoming one of Australia's richest and most powerful men or curtail his lifelong enthusiasm for sport.

In 1977, Packer achieved instant notoriety throughout the English speaking world when he hijacked international cricket and converted it into show business. No mean cricketer himself, he threw out the traditional white flannels and three day events played on lovingly tended grass green pitches and substituted coloured pyjama suits and floodlit stadiums. Packer secretly signed contracts with more than fifty of the world's leading cricketers to play privately sponsored matches for television. The

[1] Quoted in Piers Brendon, *The Life and Death of the Press Barons*.
[2] Quoted in Jerome Tuccille, *Murdoch*.

Long Room at Lords was devastated and cricket authorities around the world were scandalised. It was literally 'not cricket'. But Packer won in the Australian courts and two years later the Australian Cricket Board surrendered and gave his Nine Network exclusive rights for international matches. During one meeting with the Board Packer is reported to have said to the assembled representatives of the Australian cricket establishment: 'There is a little bit of the whore in all of us, gentlemen. What is your price?'

Kerry Packer loved the TV channel his father had launched with Bruce Gyngell back in 1956 but in 1979 he received an offer for it he couldn't refuse. The New South Wales First Fleeter met the Ten-Pound Pom from South Wales. One was to end up in the bankruptcy courts and gaol, the other became a billionaire. A bemused Packer later said he went into the meeting at which he sold his media interests thinking he was buying but he ended up selling. 'You only meet one Alan Bond in your life and I've had mine,' he commented wryly.

When Packer was asked why he was leaving the television industry, he replied: 'It's a good question and I'm not sure I know the answer. Right now I am not sure that I want to sell it, but the deal has been done. He wanted to buy more than I wanted to buy.' Bond's Managing Director, Peter Beckwith, declared with Ted Turnerseque hyperbole, 'We are now world scale operators. The electronic media are one of those rare sectors where big is beautiful. . . . Logically we have to expand. With size comes quality.' Bond said, 'We are now Number One.' The financial analysts said, 'The price paid by Bond for the Packer interests was high.' Packer walked away with a cool thousand million Australian dollars (£425m). Four years later he bought it all back from a near bankrupt Bond for half a million.

Alan Bond's father Frank hailed from the South Wales coal mining village of Cwmtillery at the foot of the Brecon Beacons close by Abertillery in what today is Gwent but was then Monmouthshire. Bond's grandfather Edwin had been a regimental sergeant major in the First World War and then a coal face miner for fifty years. Of Edwin's four sons, all except Frank followed their father down the mine. Frank escaped to London with his elder sister Gladys and after working as a footman for Lord Chelmsford eventually joined the army as a private in the 2nd Middlesex Regiment. Alan's mother, Kathleen Smith, the daughter of a Yorkshire chemist, had also fled to London to seek her fortune. They met by chance at a Christmas party, married in 1934 and set up home at 22 Federal Road, Perivale in the heart of London's western suburbia. Alan, their second child, was born in 1938.

After the war there were summer holidays back in Cwmtillery and legend has it that it was on a visit down the mine with its dank, dark tunnels deep beneath the Welsh mountains populated by straining pit ponies and sweating coal dust encrusted miners that Alan Bond decided that he was going to be a millionaire.

Frank Bond survived the war despite being torpedoed in the Mediterranean but came home with tuberculosis. The winter of 1948 was the worst in living memory and the thick acrid smog of postwar London made Frank's health rapidly deteriorate. Doctors gave him eighteen months to live unless he moved to a drier and warmer climate. The Royal Order of Buffaloes and the Freemasons, of which Frank was a member, clubbed together to buy his fare to Australia early in 1949. Ten months later Alan, at the age of eleven, his sister Geraldine and his mother boarded the SS *Himalaya*, bound for Australia. All were on £10 assisted passages subsidised by the Australian government and had declared assets of just £50 between them when they arrived.

Alan Bond left school at the age of fourteen and became an apprentice signwriter. After three years there he set up in business as a signwriter with his father and, in 1955, he married Eileen Hughes, a vivacious red-haired Fremantle girl from a respected Catholic family. In spite of his father's Masonic links, Alan converted to Catholicism and remains a practising Catholic.

In June 1960, Bond borrowed £13,000 from the Finance Corporation of Australia with a £5 deposit to purchase a five-acre plot of land in the Perth Hills. Thus began the empire that throughout its existence floated on an ocean of debt. During the sixties Bond lurched from one bank-financed deal to another flirting continuously with bankruptcy but by 1967 the money started to come in. Two years later, at the age of twenty-one, he had made his first million. The dreams of the seven-year-old in the darkness of the Welsh coal mine had come true. It was in Australian dollars but it would do! Later it was all to turn to dust. At the end of April 1992, a statement of Bond's financial affairs was filed in the Australian Federal Court. It showed debts and contingent liabilities of over A$700 million (£297 million) and assets of just over a million Australian dollars. Easy come, easy go.

On the same day accountants Price Waterhouse sent a letter to Robert Maxwell's creditors revealing that Maxwell Communication Corporation's liabilities at the end of 1991 exceeded its assets by £763.5 million. Between them these two would-be Sky Barons had managed to lose well over a thousand million pounds that did not belong to them.

In the interim, however, Bond had prospered and in 1983 his yacht *Australia* II wrested the America's Cup from the New York Yacht Club after 132 years of American dominance. 'Bondy' had arrived and became an Australian folk hero. In 1984 he was awarded the Order of Australia. He was a very tall poppy indeed!

He was also one of the 'Mates'. Like Australia's Prime Minister, Bob Hawke, who came to power in 1983, Bond hailed from Western Australia. Hawke was out of a different mould from Australia's traditional leaders. A former President of the Australian Council of Trade Unions he was known as the 'Silver Bodgie'. 'Silver' for his thick silvery grey hair and 'bodgie' after the Australian equivalent of the fifties teddy boy.

Hawke once told the press 'If I see my mates attacked, my mates will find me shoulder to shoulder with them.' The Silver Bodgie's 'Mates' were rich and influential men. They included Sir Peter Abeles, head of TNT (Thomas National Transport) – a vast multinational transport and shipping concern operating in eighty-five countries around the world. Abeles had come to Australia from Hungary in 1949. Together with another of the Mates, Rupert Murdoch who owned much of the press, Abeles owned most of the Australian commercial airline business. TNT trucks helped Murdoch break the siege of Wapping.

Soon after Bob Hawke's election as Prime Minister, for which Murdoch's papers had vigorously campaigned, Murdoch was made a Companion of the Order of Australia for 'services to the media'. As in the United Kingdom there are various ways in which politicians can say thank you to newspaper proprietors and editors for services rendered.

In 1987, Bob Hawke was guest of honour at the 'Businessman of the Year' awards, presented at a lavish dinner at Sydney's massive Regent Hotel. In his speech be said 'I am pleased, as Prime Minister of this country, to count as a close personal friend and to measure as a very great Australian, Kerry Packer . . . and when you talk of Kerry you almost inevitably lead to Alan Bond . . . to you, Alan, congrats for all your achievements and may I thank you for your generous comments about the government.' With that the emotional and sometimes lachrymose Hawke threw his arms around Packer and Bond for the benefit of the television cameras. Packer told his friends 'I wish he'd do those sort of things in private.'[3]

In November of the previous year, the Australian government had quietly changed the ownership rules in the great Australian media race. Cross-ownership between TV and newspapers would no longer be allowed but greater concentration of ownership – up to 60 per cent – would be permissible in the TV networks. It was a change that was to lead to turmoil in the press and broadcasting industries, great profits for some, disaster for others and in the view of many a disastrous decline in the quality of Australian television.

Even before the legislation had gone through Bond made the offer Kerry Packer couldn't refuse, and thus became the owner of Australia's first national TV network. When Bond took over Packer's TCN-9 in Sydney and GTV-9 in Melbourne, he already owned television stations in Perth and Brisbane. In addition he acquired a 27.5 per cent interest in the UK's TV-am (which Packer had bailed out after its disastrous launch in 1983), TV stations in Fiji and Papua New Guinea, together with two satellite

---

[3] See John Pilger, *A Secret Country*.

TV services, ten radio stations, a television film library, a marketing company, and the rights to Australian cricket and Grand Prix motor racing.

On the same day, the Australian Federal Court ruled that, as a US citizen, Rupert Murdoch could be in a position to influence the television stations associated with his Australian companies. Murdoch had just completed a deal with Robert Holmes à Court to carve up between them the Melbourne-based Herald and Weekly Times Group that would leave Murdoch with control of nearly 60 per cent of Australia's major city newspapers as well as substantial television assets to add to the Channel Ten stations he owned in Sydney and Melbourne. The *Herald* and *Weekly Times* had been founded by his father, Sir Keith, who had subsequently lost control in 1952. Rupert felt it was a lost inheritance. One of his associates was reported as saying 'I don't think I've ever seen Rupert so determined before. He'd gone after things and lost them, that was fine. But this time he was determined to win no matter what the cost.'[4]

One of the few to protest at these concentrations of media power was a former New South Wales Supreme Court Judge, Hal Wooten. Chairman of the Press Council, Wooten resigned saying, 'Even if Murdoch were a complete saint I would be opposed to it because there would be no guarantee that he would remain one and no guarantee that his successor would be one.' Journalist Paul Chadwick said the deal would make Murdoch 'dangerously large on a world scale'. Pointing out that Murdoch owned half of a national airline and Bond had huge brewing interests, Chadwick asked whether their editors would run seriously critical stories about their owners' businesses. 'Unlikely,' he concluded. 'The big concern,' said Chris Warren, the acting Secretary of the Australian Journalists Association, 'is that it will make an American citizen more powerful in Australia than the editor of *Pravda* is in the Soviet Union.'

Kerry Packer was one of a percipient few like Sir James Goldsmith who seem to have seen the world-wide October 1987

---

[4] See Jerome Tuccille, *Murdoch*.

stock market crash coming and 'went liquid', exchanging share-holdings for cash. The financial crisis cut a swathe through the fortunes of the world's richest men. An estimated £1,200 billion was wiped off the value of stock markets from Tokyo to Wall Street. Two of the biggest losers were London and Sydney both of which plunged 47 per cent in three weeks. The Sky Barons were among the hardest hit. Entrepreneurs like Alan Bond and Robert Holmes à Court, once the world's greatest corporate raider, whose companies were highly geared and depended on piles of paper assets to keep going, faced extinction. The government of Western Australia was generous in bailing out some of those hardest hit including Alan Bond but Holmes à Court was not so lucky. Having seen almost £240 million wiped off the value of his holdings in his Bell Group he suffered the further indignity of being forced to sell out to Bond. Rupert Murdoch was estimated to have lost £700 million as the market took fright at his News Corporation's borrowings of nearly $2 billion and chopped the value of News International shares by 36 per cent. In the week ending 25 October 1987, the *Sunday Times* estimated losses in personal holdings amounting to £487 million for Rupert Murdoch, £240 million for Holmes à Court, and £25 million each for Michael and David Green of Carlton and Richard Branson of Virgin.

To put these figures in context it should be pointed out that company loss by value for British Petroleum was £3,357 million, for ICI £2,716 million and Reed International £860 million.

In spite of his losses 'Bondy' just carried on trading. Within a month of the stock market crash he 'paid' $49 million plus 15 per cent commission for Van Gogh's 'Irises' at Sotheby's in New York. The purchase was made in traditional Bond style. Sotheby's lent him half the purchase price and most of the rest of the money was borrowed elsewhere.

In 1988, Alan Bond's empire was at its zenith. His world-wide network of interests included brewing (Bond was fifth in the world beer-making league), hotels and office buildings from London to Rome and from Sydney to Hong Kong, banks, oil fields, gold mines, coal mines, the national telephone company in

Chile, a national TV network in Australia, a TV station in Hong Kong and a large stake in Britain's British Satellite Broadcasting (BSB). For the year ended 30 June 1988, Bond Corporation Holdings Ltd figures showed a 70 per cent rise in after tax profits at A$224m on operating revenues of A$4.1 billion. But under-pinning the unwieldy edifice was A$7 billion of debt owed to bankers from the Hongkong and Shanghai to the Bank of Boston.

But 1988 was to be the year when Bond made two mistakes that were to prove fatal. The first mistake was the payment of A$400,000 to Sir John Bjelke-Petersen, the Premier of Queens-land, in an out-of-court settlement over a defamation case. The second mistake was to take on Tiny Rowland.

Early in the year he had bought Robert Holmes à Court's debt laden Bell Group, in trouble after the stock market crash, for US$685 million. He then began building large stakes in the British companies Allied-Lyons – a massive drinks combine – and Roland 'Tiny' Rowland's Lonrho. Allied-Lyons brewed and marketed Bond's Australian beer brands – including Castlemaine XXXX – for the British market.

In October, Bond announced he was buying the St Moritz-on-the-Park Hotel in Manhattan from Donald Trump for $180 million ($150 million more than Trump had paid for it three years previously). In the same month, the Australian Broad-casting Tribunal was investigating the Bjelke-Petersen settle-ment and charges that Bond had personally threatened to use his television stations to expose share dealings by the AMP Society, Australia's largest pension fund and a major institutional investor, if it did not stop blocking his bid for Holmes à Court's Bell Group. As a result, the Tribunal pronounced Bond 'not a fit and proper person' to own broadcasting interests. The finding was set aside almost a year later by a Federal Court which said that the Tribunal 'fell into a serious error of law' – but it had been highly damaging.

Meanwhile Bond's companies were building a 20 per cent stake in the London and Rhodesian Mining & Land Company, Lonrho for short, a giant multinational trading conglomerate. This was done without the approval of its Chairman, Tiny Rowland. To make matters worse, Bond told the *Sunday Times* 'We are the only group in the world that has the management to run Lonhro.'

Rowland had built Lonhro from scratch. He once said of it, 'By God, it has got one thing and that is it has got a protector, and that's me . . . anybody who wants to kill that company has got to have a machine-gun, mortars, guns, all sorts of ammunition because I am going to protect it to the bitter end.'

Rowland, who was christened Roland Walter Furhop, spent most of his childhood in Germany. In 1935, he emigrated to England. Later Sir Edward Heath when Prime Minister was to bestow on Lonhro the title of 'the unacceptable and unpleasant face of capitalism'. In the mid-1980s, Rowland was thwarted in a bid to take over Harrods by the Al Fayed family. 'From 1985, Rowland had with increasing energy devoted his life, the resources of Lonhro, the time of Britain's courts, and the columns of his newspaper, the *Observer*, to damning the Al Fayeds and their supporters.'[5]

In short, Tiny was a formidable adversary for Bond to take on and as it turned out he just did not have the firepower. In the summer of 1988, Bond was holidaying at Antibes in his yacht the *Southern Cross* III. Among the neighbouring yachts were Robert Maxwell's *Ghislaine* and Rowland's *Hansa*. Bond and Rowland visited and appeared to get on well but, in October, Bond launched his hostile bid. The progress of the ensuing battle was faithfully reported in Rowland's *Observer* newspaper with headlines like 'Rowland Couldn't Give A XXXX' (a sarcastic reference to Bond's most successful brand of beer) and details of a 93-page report on Bond's companies that was more thorough than any carried out by Bond's compliant bankers. In brief the report dismissed Bond's companies as 'technically insolvent'.

It was the beginning of the end. Bond was forced to sell back his media interests to Packer and the entire edifice began to crumble.

In January 1990, Bond gave an exclusive interview to Teresa Poole of the Melbourne paper *The Age*. He told her, 'I personally

[5] Paul Barry, *The Rise and Fall of Alan Bond*.

never looked at business for the sake of making money. I looked at business for the challenge of things to be done.' Later in the interview he said that if Bond Corporation went under he would start up again immediately the following day. There are many, many opportunities. The country is full of opportunities. The world is full of opportunities.' Asked if looking back he would like to have been anyone else Bond replied, 'I think I'd be going for one of the great explorers like Captain Cook where they had the opportunity to go out and discover something new. I think that must have been in a period of great challenge. I can relate to that.'

In the late 1980s, Bond Corporation controlled assets worth more than A$10 billion and his personal wealth was estimated at more than A$100 million. Between May 1986 and December 1989 he gave his family cash and gifts valued at nearly A$30 million. On 14 April 1992, Alan Bond was formally declared bankrupt and his passport seized. He was facing criminal charges for fraud (which he denies) and was the subject of enquiries by the Australian Securities Commission and a Royal Commission into alleged corruption in Western Australia. He was also in the early stages of divorce proceedings from his wife Eileen.

Two weeks later, a statement of his financial affairs showed that the man who once bought an entire English village in Oxfordshire did not own a home but was living in an apartment in Cottesloe, Western Australia at a weekly rent of A$200 a week. His assets included A$1,000 in cash, A$2,669 in bank deposits and shares, a wristwatch worth A$1,200 and paintings worth A$1.13m, most of which were claimed by liquidators. His only income was A$195,000 a year in consultancy fees from two UK companies. In 1991, he had paid A$486,441 to lawyers and accountants as he sought to avoid bankruptcy.

Conrad Black's biographer, Peter C. Newman, described him as a 'Roman candle among the wet firecrackers littering Canada's business landscape'.[6] He was, wrote Newman, 'an Inheritor by upbringing, an Acquisitor by temperament' who had

---

[6] Peter C. Newman, *The Establishment Man*.

'come to symbolise Canadian capitalism on the hoof'. Over six foot tall, Black has been described as 'a great bear of a man'.

Black spends seven months of the year in the United Kingdom but keeps a low public profile partly at the persuasion of executives of the Daily Telegraph Group and partly because he did not want to look like 'just another publicity-seeking, self-promoting Commonwealth person, who came rushing over trailing his coat tails in search of a peerage' or 'a materialistic caricature of a North American businessman with no respect for British institutions'. He oversees the running of his papers but is rarely seen on the editorial floor. In Britain, Conrad Black's public face is that of a cultured multi-millionaire, a keen military historian, the author of an exhaustive biography of Maurice Duplessis (the autocratic premier of Quebec), and the proud possessor of a 15,000 book library.

In Canada by contrast he is a 'larger than life' entrepreneur. He is one of the most outspoken and litigious businessmen in the country who brought a dozen-odd libel suits in as many years since 1978. Black himself has a 'talent' for personal invective. He dismissed one critic as 'a slanted supercilious little twit with the professional ethics of a cockroach' and a prominent politician as 'a fat, silly social worker'.

Tony O'Reilly, the Irish millionaire newspaper proprietor and another budding Sky Baron, once said of him, 'If you like strong-minded, interventionist proprietors with Thatcherite views, he's your man.' Black was a firm supporter of both Margaret Thatcher and Ronald Reagan whose speeches he could quote at length from memory. His other heroes include Charles de Gaulle, President Roosevelt, Abraham Lincoln and Napoleon.

Black's entrepreneurial career began at school when, at the age of fifteen, he obtained the key to the Principal's office and made photocopies of the upcoming examination papers and sold the copies to fellow students. This, Newman reveals, raised nearly $5,000 for Black and his young aides before their expulsion from the exclusive Upper Canada College in Toronto.

With seven million dollars inherited from his father he seized control of the Argus Corporation, a conglomerate which had stakes in the Dominion Stores supermarket chain, the engineering giant Massey Ferguson, mining and forestry interests and 48 per cent of Standard Broadcasting which controlled CFRB Toronto and Bushnell Communications. As Peter C. Newman wrote, 'Black and his personal search-and-destroy squad grabbed control of companies worth about four billion dollars in four months of frantic manoeuvring. . . . His name had passed into the language as a generic term signifying either wealth and influence youthfully gained, or corporate manoeuvres too clever by half.' By 1984, Conrad and his brother Montagu had manoeuvred their C$18m inheritance into over C$100m. Black's financial dealings are partly hidden behind private Canadian holding companies.

Conrad Black bought his first newspaper in Quebec in 1969. With two partners he bought an ailing daily newspaper *The Sherbrooke Record* for C$20,000, from which he went on to build a chain of twenty-one publishing businesses – Sterling Newspapers – which by 1981 was making a profit of C$5m a year. Black's great ambition was to own a United Kingdom national newspaper. In 1985 the opportunity was offered him almost on a plate.

The *Daily Telegraph*, which had belonged to the Berry family since 1927, when it was bought by Sir William Berry, was facing serious financial problems. In the early 1980s it had embarked on an ambitious programme to bring its production up to date and to move from Fleet Street to London's Docklands. This involved expenditure of £105 million on new printing plants in London and Manchester and a computerised typesetting system. The switch to new technology involved a further £37 million in redundancy payments and buy outs of the restrictive practices that were then endemic in Fleet Street. Linotype operators were paid extra for correcting mistakes so it was in their interests to make as many as possible. The unions had negotiated an establishment of twenty-two men for presses which needed only ten men to run them and in the Reading Room where the proofs were checked for the mistakes the linotype operators made an elaborate 'sickness' scheme. Up to twenty per cent of the forty-eight readers were allegedly sick at any one time, costing the company £1 million a year.

Lord Hartwell (Michael Berry, the second son of William Berry), the seventy-four-year-old proprietor of the *Telegraph*, and his top management, who were all much of an age, made the mistake of assuming that there would be no difficulty in raising the cash required from the banks. This proved more difficult than expected and in 1984 they enlisted the help of the merchant bank N. M. Rothschild.

Later, Michael Richardson, the senior partner leading the fund raising, was to say: 'To us, as simple merchant bankers, it was barely conceivable that any family could have . . . committed themselves so far if they hadn't got the money to pay. It's rather like you going out and agreeing to buy Blenheim without having any funds. What we were asked to do was to unravel the muddle into which Lord Hartwell had got himself.' Put another way, as David Montagu, a financial expert and director of many companies including London Weekend - Television said, 'Rothschild handed the Berry family's balls to Conrad Black on a plate.'

The paper had committed itself to its new plant and equipment and faced bankruptcy if the extra money could not be found. Ironically as it was to prove later, Fairfax in Australia was being mentioned as a possible saviour. Lord Hartwell had two aims. The first was that the Berry family should remain in control, the second that 'ogres' such as Robert Maxwell and Rupert Murdoch or Sir James Goldsmith should be kept away.

Conrad Black was alerted to the Berry family's plight by Andrew Knight, the Editor of the *Economist*, whose Chairman, Evelyn de Rothschild, was also Chairman of the merchant bank advising the *Telegraph* and knew Black. Black took soundings from another old friend, Rupert Hambro, Chairman of Hambros Bank, and a week later Lord Hartwell and his negotiating team together with a junior executive from Rothschild's boarded Concorde bound for New York. On the same plane was Rupert Hambro who was to advise Black. Conrad Black himself flew down from Toronto in his Challenger company jet. He was alone.

Rupert Hambro made the introductions in a hotel suite overlooking the runways of JFK airport.

After a general and friendly survey of the *Telegraph*'s situation Black expressed his admiration for Margaret Thatcher's policies as Prime Minister and then indicated he might be willing to put up the £10m the *Telegraph* so desperately needed. He said however that he would have to insist on being given first refusal on any further share issue or any future sale of existing shares. Without hesitation, Hartwell said clearly, 'I don't think we can resist that.' With those seven words the *Telegraph*'s fate was sealed and the Berry family heritage lost. Black's ambition was about to be realised.

The deal was sealed as Hartwell, before leaving to board the next Concorde back to London, said to Black, 'I'm flattered by your interest in our newspaper and delighted to have you as a shareholder. I welcome you.' He was to discover that he was welcoming a Trojan horse. It soon became apparent that in spite of the cash injection from Black and the City institutions more money was going to be needed. The conversion from hot-metal typesetting to photocomposition was creating difficulties and mistakes in the paper multiplied. It was clear it was going to cost at least three times the amount estimated.

An investigation by the accountancy firm of Coopers and Lybrand revealed the paper was likely to lose £8.1 million in the financial year to 31 March 1986 (against a previously estimated profit of £5 million) and that there were serious shortcomings in its accounting and control procedures. In spite of a desperate and hopeless rearguard action by Hartwell's son, Nicholas Berry, including a proposal that the Australian newspaper family the Fairfaxes should buy out Black and the other shareholders and put £20 million into the company in exchange for providing the management and holding 50 per cent of the equity, little did the Fairfax negotiators think that six years later Conrad Black was to have them in his sights.

Faced by continuous pressure from the banks, Hartwell borrowed from personal and family funds to the tune of several million pounds on three occasions to ward off threats of foreclosure. He was desperate not to allow Black to take over. He approached the peripatetic Andrew Knight (later to become Rupert Murdoch's London lieutenant), who had been instrumental in bringing Black in in the first place, to come in as Chief Executive. Knight asked him what he had against Conrad. Hartwell replied 'Oh, I like him a lot. He's very helpful, very constructive. But – the Fairfaxes are newspaper people, *our* sort of people.'

The end came on 5 December. The *Telegraph* board agreed terms for a rights issue in which Black's Hollinger Group would acquire 39,907,125 Ordinary Shares giving him 50.1 per cent of the company. Leon Brittan, Secretary of State for Trade and Industry, ruled that since Conrad Black had no other newspaper interests in the United Kingdom the agreement need not be referred to the Monopolies and Mergers Commission.

In an Editorial, Bill (now Lord) Deedes wrote, 'For fifty-eight years we have been in the hands of a family who have thought it more important to run a newspaper honourably than profitably. We salute that.'

In January 1986, Rupert Murdoch made his notorious move to Wapping and showed that he could bring out the *Sunday Times* with no union labour at all. Had his move come earlier it might have saved the *Telegraph* for the Berry family. As it happened Lord Hartwell had to endure the humiliation of seeing the family silver and the Sèvres porcelain – collected by the first Lady Camrose – moved out of the *Telegraph* offices in Fleet Street. The days of the old school newspaper barons, who looked on each other as 'one of us', were over. Hartwell was to say, 'I worked on the papers because they fascinated me. I was always terribly shocked when other people ran their newspapers like biscuit factories, just to make money.' His whole endeavour, he said, had been to make the *Telegraph* a national institution that was respected and admired, 'which would leave the world poorer if it were not there. It sounds awfully boring, but I regarded it as my life's work –that's all.'

Black's team led by Andrew Knight turned the paper around. By 1991, the *Daily Telegraph* made pre-tax profits of £40.5m on turnover of £219m, in spite of the recession. Black had paid £30m for a group now estimated worth up to £1 billion. It was in the words of one commentator 'the deal of the century'.

The board of Conrad Black's Hollinger vehicle and its 'international advisers' have included Sir James Goldsmith, Lord Rothschild, Henry Kissinger, Paul Volcker, Lord Carrington and Lord King of Wartnaby, the Chairman of British Airways. There is, it sometimes seems, an international order of mates whose paths continuously cross and intertwine in business, at dinners and receptions and at the various exclusive 'think tanks' like the annual Bilderberg meeting, at one of which Conrad Black first met Andrew Knight. The interests and political views of this fraternity tend to coincide.

In 1991, Conrad Black owned or controlled in addition to the United Kingdom's *Daily* and *Sunday Telegraph* a range of publications in the United States and Canada and the *Jerusalem Post* in Israel. Hollinger's 1991 annual report set out Black's strategy: 'to acquire newspaper publishing businesses that management believes can be purchased at prices that, if fully financed, will allow sufficient cash flow after about one to three years of ownership – depending on the size and quality of the business – to cover interest expenses plus a reasonable margin'.

Later that year Black's eye lighted on the Fairfax newspaper empire in Australia.

John Fairfax arrived in Sydney in 1838 with a total capital of £10, half of which he won in an on-board lottery on the ship's sailing time from England to Australia. Three years later he had earned enough to become part owner of the *Sydney Herald* – later the *Sydney Morning Herald*. For a century and a half from 1842, when John bought out his partner, until 1991, the Fairfax family controlled the *Herald* and built it into one of Australia's most respected newspapers.

Warwick Fairfax who finally lost the family inheritance was the great-grandson of John from Warwickshire. When he returned from Harvard for his father's funeral, young Warwick's bitterness was turned into a crusade to rescue the Fairfax papers from what he saw as his relatives' incompetence and from the predatory clutches of such as Rupert Murdoch, Kerry Packer and the late Robert Holmes à Court – then king of the world's corporate raiders.

Warwick discovered that the family only controlled 48.6 per cent of Fairfax shares. When his half-brother James and his cousin John refused to buy the extra 1.5 per cent needed to ensure control, Warwick borrowed A$30 million from the Midland Bank and bought them himself. This action left Warwick with a problem. Although he stood to inherit some A$500 million, he had no significant income and no way to keep up the interest payments on the loan. The only way out was to gain control of the company and with it access to its cash flow. Having been warned against this course by several merchant bankers and his mother Lady Mary, Warwick turned to an entrepreneurial Perth businessman Laurie Connell who had converted a small Queensland menswear concern into the Rothwell merchant bank. The strategy was to borrow A$1.3 billion to buy out all the non-family shareholders and then repay the debt by selling assets including the *Australian Financial Review* and floating 55 per cent of the subsidiary company which published the *Age*.

Warwick sprung the plot on his relations late one Sunday night in August 1987 on the eve of the public announcement. Contempt between the relatives was mutual. James and John accepted the bid but pushed up the price from A$1.3 to A$2.1 billion. In the middle of negotiations in October 1987, the world stock market crashed, halving the value of the Australian All Ordinaries Index. Despite protests from his mother Lady Mary, Warwick decided at a meeting in the penthouse of Sydney's Regent Hotel to carry on with his bid.

Later Lady Mary backed her son and when the crash finally came she said, 'I admit my son made an "A-Grade" mistake and so did I and it is one we have paid dearly for but it is ridiculous to suggest Warwick alone engineered the collapse. Warwick did not try to steal the company from his family: he went to his half-brother James and his cousin John first but he could not convince them with the offer.' Lady Mary said she only agreed when her son approached her and she realised she was 'the last cab off the rank'.

There was no difficulty in buying out the small shareholders anxious to sell following the crash but the same crash wiped out most of the deals Connell had made to cover the cost with Holmes à Court, Packer and Murdoch. Soon after, the Rothwell merchant bank collapsed and had to be bailed out by the Western Australian government and Alan Bond. Bond sued Warwick for the A$100m fee claimed by Rothwell's and the banks brought an action claiming that any funds raised through asset sales should be used to repay the existing Fairfax debt.

Warwick turned to Michael Milken, the United States king of the junk bond, later sentenced to ten years in jail for US securities violations. A bond issue raised enough for Warwick to pay for all the shares he had bought. He settled out of court with Alan Bond for A$27m. Brother James walked away with A$163m and Cousin John and his father Sir Vincent with A$306m.

The Australian economy slid deeper into recession following the crash, and Warwick's problems mounted as revenue growth slowed. He continued to refuse to give up control and new bidders started to circle the nearly moribund company as the receivers moved in.

When Warwick began his play, Rupert Murdoch, possibly with tongue in cheek, congratulated him saying he wished he had had the guts to do something like it when he was twenty-six. In Murdoch's *Telegraph Mirror*, Terry McCrann put it this way: 'The fall of the House of Fairfax can be sheeted home directly to the stupidity and impatience of one immature and pampered young man, aided and abetted by some equally foolish and ambitious bankers.'

As so often it was the bankers, managers, advisers and lawyers who gained the most. On 14 December 1990, the *Australian Financial Review* estimated that the bill for their services had already reached a staggering A$150 million. The *Review* commented, 'The grotesque size of the bill for what was presumably meant to be inspired advice and competent management must surely stand as a high watermark of stupidity in recent Australian corporate life.' 'It is,' the leader continued, 'a simple matter of avarice pandering to greed.'

In 1991, Conrad Black and Kerry Packer formed a consortium to pick up the pieces of the Fairfax empire. There was considerable opposition to Packer's involvement even though his stake in the Tourang Consortium would be limited to 14.9 per cent because of Australian restrictions on cross-media ownership. 'It would,' wrote Fred Brenchley in the *Sydney Morning Herald*, 'be widely condemned as the ultimate, cynical outcome of the Government's media policies . . . for the health of the media industry, and the credibility of the Government in running a media policy in the national interest rather than that of a few media owners, the best advice Hawke and Keating can give Kerry Packer is "don't".'

Freda Whitlam, former Prime Minister Gough Whitlam's sister, wrote from New South Wales to the *Independent* in London to protest. She pointed out that Packer and Murdoch already owned 85 per cent by circulation of Australia's top thirty magazines. Murdoch owned 62 per cent by circulation of metropolitan newspapers and Packer was the most powerful television operator in Australia. 'In Australia,' Freda Whitlam wrote, 'with a small population and few media proprietors, a change in media ownership can have far-reaching effects. Once you control the media you control not only all people who are now working and voting but those in their formative years.' If Tourang with Packer took over she concluded, 'it will mean two very rich, unelected men can run our society because of their huge media power. They can set the political agenda, make or break governments and oppositions, promote or disparage the Prime Minister and the leader of the opposition, can vilify any citizen and undermine any institution.'

The 'Friends of Fairfax' group issued a statement that while 'Australian ownership is to be preferred' it 'would rather tolerate a level of foreign ownership than editorial interference'. Another group, 'The Age Independence Committee', also preferred 'a reasonable increase in the level of foreign ownership' to being 'forced to accept an interventionist proprietor and a greater concentration of media ownership.'

Packer withdrew from the Tourang Consortium rather than

submit to the inevitable enquiries into the ownership issue. The consortium paid £640 million (A$1.5 billion) for Fairfax. Black's Daily Telegraph Group has a 15 per cent stake, Hellman and Friedman the American investment bank 5 per cent and the rest is split between Australian financial institutions. Black has operational control.

The decision to award the Fairfax empire to Tourang and Black angered former Liberal Prime Minister Malcolm Fraser. Saying that Australia had been let down by a 'stupid government' he went on, 'It's got nothing to do with personalities but it now means that 90 per cent of important print media in Australia is owned by foreigners. So far as the Government and the Opposition are concerned, they have made it perfectly plain there is not a single Australian asset that they would not sell to foreigners if the price were high enough.'

The saga ended when, on 17 December 1991, Conrad Black arrived in Sydney, wearing a blue tie dotted with boxing kangaroos, to take over his new acquisition.

In the summer of 1992, the Daily Telegraph Group, 83 per cent owned by Black through his international holding company Hollinger, sought stock exchange approval for an agreement that would divide his world-wide spheres of interest. The arrangements proposed included a flotation that was expected to value the Telegraph Group at between £400m and £500m. The flotation would reduce Hollinger's stake in the Telegraph Group to 70 per cent. In compensation, a special 10p dividend as a means of 'rewarding existing shareholders ahead of the proposed flotation' would net £11.1 million for Black's other pocket – Hollinger.

Hollinger and the Daily Telegraph would have a world-wide cooperation agreement under which Hollinger would concentrate its activities on North and South America and the Daily Telegraph on the United Kingdom and Australia. The rest of the world would be conveniently divided up 'in a manner acceptable to the Stock Exchange'. It was reminiscent of the Borgia Pope Alexander VI's allocation of the 'world yet to be discovered' between Spain and Portugal except that Black plays the role of Pope as well as those of the monarchs of the two states.

At the end of April 1992, Conrad Black was back in America putting together a deal to buy the *New York Daily News* in the remnant sale of the Maxwell empire. At the same time he joined a consortium including Bruce Gyngell's TV-am, David Frost and Time-Warner to bid for the United Kingdom's fifth television channel. Meanwhile the computer giant IBM was reported to be considering making a substantial investment in Time-Warner Entertainment and creating a large scale joint venture to offer 'interactive multi-media services' to homes and businesses throughout the United States. The venture would also include an electronics manufacturer such as Toshiba, which, together with the Japanese trading company C. Itoh, recently agreed to take a 12.5 per cent equity stake in Time-Warner Entertainment.

Back in London an even more extraordinary relationship was being forged between Rupert Murdoch and the BBC. In June 1992, this bizarre couple snatched rights to English football's Premier League from under the noses of ITV in a deal which removed live matches from the free public channels to place them on the satellite subscription and pay channels of Sky, while preserving for the BBC the pittance of showing recorded highlights. Next, discussions began on cooperation in a new joint BBC/Sky all-news satellite chanel to rival CNN. Other deals, it was made clear, were in the pipeline.

The complex dance to be positioned for the next stage in communications technology has begun. New alliances are being forged as the deals continue.

XVII

1992 and All That

For Silvio Berlusconi, and for many of the principal characters of our story, 23 October 1990 was a date rich in significance. If Sky Barons have a god, he was working overtime that day. For on that day and in the three weeks or so that followed, an extraordinary unravelling of many key threads of our story took place.

Once again, the focus was Italy. But from Rome and Milan the strands ran outwards via Monte Carlo and Paris to Rio de Janeiro and Hollywood. On another axis they stretched from Sydney to Luxembourg and New York. In Italy, 23 October 1990 was the day appointed by the Italian government for thousands of television and radio station owners who had opened up the unregulated frontiers of commercial broadcasting in the past twenty years to stake their claim for a licence. From one-man-and-a-dog operations in Naples, to the giant corporations of Northern Italy, the applications flooded in.

23 October was a particularly important day for Giancarlo Parretti. It was the day on which he was due to stump up the balance of $1.3 billion to purchase the MGM studios in Hollywood.

But first to Rome, where Thursday 23 October is a day that many observers of the Italian media thought would never arrive. Certainly, for the Milan based Fininvest empire of Silvio Berlusconi, which had dominated Italian television for the last ten years, it threatened to be the end of an era.

A few weeks earlier, after years of seemingly endless legal contortions and a final crisis which nearly brought down the government, the Italian senate had passed a new television law which at last promised to impose some limitation on the media monopolies. 'La Leggia Mammi' ('The Mammi Law'), named after Minister of Posts and Telecommunications Oscar Mammi, was better known among the government legislators and the Italian press corps as 'the Berlusconi law'. It was so called because Berlusconi's domination of commercial television had become such that even his traditional supporters, Craxi's socialists, recognised the time had come for some restraint. Not content with all three national commercial TV networks, Berlusconi has added a fourth, an embryo pay-TV service called Telepiu, modelled along the lines of France's successful Canal Plus. Berlusconi was also heavily embroiled in film and TV production and had created Italy's largest cinema theatre circuit, Cine 5, in partnership with leading distributors Mario and Vittorio Cecchi Gori.

As we have seen, Parretti was reported in the world's press on 23 October 1990 to have completed his acquisition of MGM/UA. Even the acounts in publications like *The Wall Street Journal* and the *Financial Times* seemed to leave many questions unanswered. Parretti, it was said, had done a last-minute deal with Ted Turner, always one to spot a man in the water, whereby Turner had acquired rights to 1,000 UA films for $200 million, thus completing Turner's 1986 purchase from Kerkorian. Very unclear at the time, however, was the status of the $600 million deal with Warner Brothers, the subsidiary of Time-Warner, on which the financing of Parretti's MGM acquisition was said to depend.

23 October also saw a drawn and tired-looking Rupert Murdoch in Sydney explaining to investors what he proposed to do about News Corporation's massive A$10.5 billion debt burden. By a delicious coincidence – or was it? – an extremely bouncy Robert Maxwell had put out a press statement the previous evening saying that the Maxwell Communications Corporations had repaid US$990 million in short-term debt incurred during its 1989 purchase of Macmillan Inc. and Official Airline Guides. While Murdoch was telling *The Wall Street Journal* that News Corporation would in future be increasingly dominated by film and electronic media rather than the newspapers and magazines on which he had built the company, Maxwell was letting it be

known that he saw the MCC's future mainly in terms of print. An ebullient Maxwell told the *FT*'s Raymond Snoddy: 'There were those saying we would be bankrupt by now. Where are they now? For all of its forty years this company has honoured its commitments on time.' On the same day, a largely unnoticed item in the *Daily Mail* business pages noted that 'large amounts of Mirror Group pension fund money have been invested in companies in which publisher Robert Maxwell is interested'.

All this was overshadowed by the rapidly escalating Gulf crisis, where Saddam Hussein had kept hundreds of foreign workers hostage in Iraq after his invasion of Kuwait.

Thursday 23 October 1990 – 'Sweet Thursday' for some Sky Barons but not others – also saw a significant development in the story of France's troubled La Cinq television station, in which Berlusconi held a 25 per cent stake. Publishing giant Hachette, rapidly expanding into audiovisual media, had got the go-ahead from the French CSA media watchdog to take control of La Cinq, ending an eighteen-month battle. Robert Hersant, the controversial owner of the right-wing daily, *Le Figaro*, sold his 25 per cent interest to Hachette, who had support from others holding another 20 per cent.

Back on the Italian scene, it was again almost unnoticed that Rizzoli/Corriere della Sera, the media ancillary of Gianni Agnelli's massive FIAT combine, had joined Roberto Marinho's Globo as a partner in Telemontecarlo, simultaneously bidding for one of the new national licences. At the same time, Silvio Berlusconi was reported as having sold his three pay-TV channels on Telepiu to a group of 'nine Italian business executives' to comply with the Mammi law. 'The Telepiu Nine' turned out later to be mostly long-standing business associates of Berlusconi.

Berlusconi's home base of Milan is the home of the La Scala opera and some of Italy's most powerful fashion empires. It is also one of the centres of the New Socialism – sometimes called 'Gucci Socialism' – that has emerged in Italian politics in recent years and spread to other countries in Europe. The new political climate has been a feature of Silvio Berlusconi's rise to prominence and power not only in Italy, but in France and Spain.

The connections between Berlusconi and the Socialist Party in Italy are well documented. We have seen how Socialist leader Benito Craxi used his influence to rescind legal judgments made against Berlusconi by the courts – a quite breathtaking use of presidential power against the judiciary.

The power of the New Socialists in Europe has been dependent on a very high degree of state involvement in the cultural, commercial and artistic life of Italy, Spain and, in particular, France. All of those countries operate significant quota systems for domestic production in television and film and provide significant state subsidies for them. When it comes to appointments to the top posts in broadcasting, they are almost invariably made directly by the government.

There is also a powerful kind of 'networking' that operates between the Socialist Parties in France, Italy and Spain which has benefited Berlusconi's plans for expansion in Europe and led, directly or indirectly, to Giancarlo Parretti's support by the state-owned French bank Crédit Lyonnais.

The story goes back to February 1987. It was then that Robert Hersant formed what was seen as an unholy alliance with the two men who had started France's newest television channel La Cinq – Italy's Berlusconi and the Chargeurs company head, Jérôme Seydoux. Berlusconi had gained the concession for La Cinq in partnership with Seydoux under the left-wing administration of François Mitterand. When conservative Jacques Chirac became Prime Minister, it was expected that matters would be made more favourable to Hersant. So they were. The Hersant/Berlusconi/Seydoux consortium was duly successful in gaining the new franchise for La Cinq. Hersant became Chairman with 25 per cent and Berlusconi Vice-Chairman, also with a 25 per cent stake while Seydoux retained 10 per cent.

Hersant was the price Berlusconi and Seydoux had to pay to keep their interest in La Cinq. It was an uneasy alliance. The consortium promised to invest a billion francs in the station and forecast it would reach break-even by 1990. With privatisation looming over TF1, the state network, La Cinq at first succeeded in wooing away some of TF1's leading talent, including light entertainment chief Marie-France Briere and on-air personalities such as Patrick Sabatier. In a coup reminiscent of the ill-fated Thames raid on the BBC, La Cinq also acquired the rights for *Dallas* previously held by TF1.

The award of TF1 in May 1987 to a group headed by cement king Francis Bouygues signalled a raising of the stakes. Bouygues' team demonstrated unexpected fluency with the media game. TF1 countered La Cinq's privateering raids with the signing of top-line names such as newsreader Christine Ockrent.

The struggle was always unequal. TF1 had an established inroad into French households with its national coverage. La Cinq's transmitters could only reach about half the population. There was competition from three other services, notably from the subscription channel Canal Plus. With television advertising in France only a quarter of the total national spend (compared with a third in the UK and US and a massive one half in Italy), it was a risky business.

La Cinq was its own worst enemy. Its first schedule was a flop. La Cinq had promised advertisers it would cut rates if it failed to increase its 10 per cent audience share significantly. This it was forced to do when the Médiametrie ratings showed TF1 had actually increased its audience domination. La Cinq had made no impact. Recriminations between the Berlusconi and Hersant camps followed, with the Italians focussing on what they saw as Hersant's failure to make the transition from the world of press to that of television. Losses mounted. By autumn of 1989 the rift had developed into a full-blown court battle for control between Hersant on the one side and Berlusconi and Seydoux on the other. By December, the position had reached stalemate.

As so often with Berlusconi, the impasse was resolved quite suddenly in a flurry of activity towards the end of January between Milan and Paris. A deal was struck in which La Cinq's director general, Hersant's Philippe Ramond, agreed to stand down. In his place, La Cinq would be run by two general managers, Berlusconi's long-standing French representative Angelo Codignoni and Yves de Chaisemartin, the Hersant group's Chief Executive and legal expert. Seydoux, whose stake in the channel had slipped to about seven per cent, at first refused to sign the agreement.

In Paris, the question being asked was which of the two – Codignoni or de Chaisemartin – would emerge as top dog? For the moment, both men were making soothing noises, with Codignoni talking smoothly of his friend Yves and de Chaisemartin curbing the Hersant camp's habitual references to 'Les Italiens'.

The revitalised TF1 was meanwhile still in the ascendant, while La Cinq nursed estimated losses of some 2.2 billion francs.

The pact for shared control put together in a flurry of activity between Milan and Paris harnessed two rising names on the French broadcasting scene. As joint general managers, Angelo Codignoni and Yves de Chaisemartin were very different champions of their respective lords. On the one hand, Codignoni was the very model of the modern Milanese media man. As Berlusconi's ambassador to France, Codignoni had the suavity of the diplomat: fluent in French, able to lever open the doors of power, with an apartment on the Avenue Montaigne. Then there was de Chaisemartin: the Hersant company *notaire*, a little severe and formal, rising to notice in the courtroom battles that had dogged the fortunes of La Cinq for months.

For a while, Berlusconi and Hersant, the two predators in the same pond, stuck it out together. Before long, they were at loggerheads in the courts over who should control La Cinq. Hersant eventually sold out to Hachette, but the issue became academic when La Cinq became bankrupt in December 1991.

Silvio Berlusconi's success in gaining one of the three national commercial TV licences in Spain likewise represented part of a cherished dream for the Milan based Fininvest empire. Berlusconi was on record as saying that his ambitions were to build a new European television network. There was no doubting his supremacy in the Italian market, where Fininvest controlled the channels, sold the advertising and a short while before had bought one of its main retail clients, the Standa chain. But his ventures outside Italy, in France and Germany, had so far had mixed success.

Berlusconi had prepared the ground much more carefully in

Spain than he was able to do in France. One of Fininvest's first acquisitions outside Italy was the purchase of the huge Roma film studios in Madrid in the mid-1980s. This facility gave Berlusconi a production base in the country's capital and a potential site for his new channel.

There were close parallels too between the situation in Spain and that in Italy when Berlusconi made his entry into private TV. The key factor was the strength of the advertising market. In Spain, as in Italy before it, the market had so far been dominated by press and radio. Before Berlusconi, radio in Italy had accounted for as much as 10–12 per cent of the national 'spend'. This figure gradually shrank to around 4–5 per cent with the advent of the three Berlusconi commercial TV channels and the increase in advertising on the state channels of RAI. In Spain, press and radio had an even stronger grip on the market. Commercial radio had existed since before the Civil War. Its share of all advertising was around 13–14 per cent. Broadcasting was about to be shaken up.

There could be few more telling reminders of Spain's postwar legacy than the recent travails of its state broadcasting corporation, Radio Television Española. The abrupt sacking of RTVE's director general Luis Solana after charges of persistent political bias showed how relatively fragile and new was the growth of democracy and independence. The appointment of a professional journalist Jordi Candau gave RTVE its third chief in as many years.

Born in the province of Castellon, Jordi Garcia Candau started as a journalist in the state radio service RNE. He rose to become editor of one of the big network news programmes but had never worked in television. Candau marked an abrupt change of direction from his two predecessors. He was judged as having a much more developed sense of editorial issues than Solana, who became known as 'The Commissar' for his bureaucratic and high-handed way of dealing. Previously the head of the state telecommunications service, Solana was essentially a business-man whose appointment was regarded as an insult by many RTVE hands. Candau also had another advantage: an established line of communication with the governing board of RTVE, of which he was already a member.

Things had been going downhill for RTVE for some time. The nadir was reached in the celebrated Pilar Miro administration. Miro, a film director, had been forced to quit her post in January 1989 because of allegations (subsequently disproved) of excessive personal spending at her employers' expense. Among Miro's legacies to Solana was a bill from the government for £30,000 in bonus payments made by Miro to a handful of top executives.

Solana's first reaction was to freeze his own salary. A few months later, Solana succeeded in winning approval for a massive pay increase of 60 per cent for RTVE's top management. The reason given was to prevent the poaching of talent by the new commercial television networks licensed by the government. At the same time Solana promised a streamlining of RTVE's operations and staff, following a study recommending that 6,000 jobs should go. Candau was to find that RTVE remained an overstaffed company, top-heavy with administrators from the old Franco years who had simply clung on to their posts. At the same time, said RTVE staff, the organisation was short of key people such as engineers. 'We badly need technical people,' said one insider. 'The best are leaving RTVE to work for the new commercial television companies.'

Politically, Candau is a well-known member of the Socialist Party. While it is still taken for granted that the government of the day will choose one of its own men for such a post, the reign of Solana had been heavily criticised for its outright bias to the ruling Socialist PSOE administration of Felipe Gonzalez. Matters came to a head over RTVE's treatment of the European and general elections. The final straw was Solana's decision not to give live coverage to a parliamentary debate on the Juan Guerra scandal involving a brother of the Deputy Prime Minister. Every single autonomous television region transmitted the debate except the RTVE network – 'a disgrace' in the words of one of its own top executives.

Normally the government would have shaken off such criticisms. But the elections left the Gonzalez administration with a wafer-thin majority. As a result, opposition parties such as Partido Popular saw the chance to press for a change to the RTVE articles of association concerning the political appointments to the board. With discussions deadlocked, Gonzalez's PSOE caved in to pressure for Solana's head. Candau was the compromise candidate.

Candau still faces a difficult tightrope act. Apart from fending off government interference, Candau has the more immediate task of streamlining the RTVE for the continued onslaught of commercial television. He will need to find the financial resources from savings within the company in order to hang on to big-name stars. He must also restore some of the dignity and self respect lost in the past two administrations. The three commercial networks started by Berlusconi and others in Spain are no longer at a formative stage.

The basic problem however remains: a system inherited from the Franco days where the politicians rather than an independent board of governors appoint the chief executive. Until that is changed, Candau or any other director general may be removed at the drop of a prime ministerial hat.

At a press conference in Brussels in June 1989 attended personally by Silvio Berlusconi, representatives of Europe's most powerful commercial broadcasters announced the formation of a new Association of European Commercial TV. The five private broadcasters – UK's ITV, Luxembourg's CLT, Fininvest of Italy, West Germany's SAT 1 and TF1 of France – together commanded a total of more than 250 million viewers. Their aim was to break the stranglehold of the traditional national television organisations represented in the European Broadcasting Union. The move was widely seen as likely to lead to the break-up of the EBU, which had introduced Eurovision and represented the interests of national broadcasting organisations.

It was the culmination to mounting frustration by the European commercial television community at the role of the EBU. The commercial TV companies had always felt they played second fiddle to national TV organisations within the EBU.

Matters had come to a head following the formation of a consortium between leading EBU members, including the BBC, and Rupert Murdoch's newly launched Sky Television. The grouping, calling itself Eurosport, was effectively a cartel aimed at cornering the rights to important sporting events to the exclusion of the existing commercial TV channels. The unholy alliance with Murdoch had infuriated the commercial broadcasters, who already paid hefty membership fees to the EBU.

The EBU was also criticised for having been ineffective in the negotiations to produce workable cross-frontier guidelines for European television. 'We're associated with broadcasters whose countries are blocking the directive,' complained the chief executive of the UK ITV Association, referring to the EC's policy on cross-frontier broadcasting.

The new organisation – ACT – brought together Italy's 'Pope of Television' Silvio Berlusconi, France's 'Cement King' Francis Bouygues who owns the majority of TF1, and the head of the German Beta Taurus group, Leo Kirch. Berlusconi's Fininvest group had long been prevented by the opposition of the state RAI-TV from holding full EBU membership.

In order to comply with EC legislation, the five commercial television organisations registered the new association as a European economic interest group. This was intended to give it important lobbying status in the Brussels and Strasbourg corridors of power.

Most of the European media combines are close to saturation level within their own territories in terms of competition law. Silvio Berlusconi is under attack in Italy for his domination of the country's advertising market. Bertelsmann cannot easily expand further on its own territory because of the national monopoly and anti-trust legislation, though the unification of East and West Germany offers new opportunities. Increasingly tough European Community laws restrict its growth in a wider Europe. Like all the Sky Barons, Bertelsmann is looking for expansion in other parts of the world, through diversification within the ever-growing range of possibilities offered by new communications technologies and by new alliances with fellow Barons.

Hachette in France, under its chairman Jean-Luc Lagardere, is one of the world's biggest publishers and has expanded rapidly into audiovisual media, not without some pain. Both Lagardere and his counterpart Francis Bouygues, who has added new film ventures to his TF1 networks, have pursued a policy of growing fast through acquisitions in the United States to prepare for what is shaping up to be an increasingly bitter struggle of global rather than continental proportions.

Feature films and sport are two of the most powerful weapons in the Sky Barons' armouries. The coverage of sport in Europe was once the exclusive preserve of the national public service members of the EBU. But in a ruling that holds great significance for the future, the EC has condemned the Eurosport venture as anti-competitive.

The cost of rights to sporting events rocketed during the 1980s. The EBU paid $5.95 million for the 1980 Summer Olympics in Moscow and NBC paid $85 million for the American rights. These figures rose to $19 million (EBU) and $225 million (ABC in the US) for Los Angeles in 1984. For Seoul in 1988 the Olympic rights were $28 million (EBU) and $300 million (ABC). By 1992 the EBU was forced to bid $75 million and NBC $401 million for the rights to the Barcelona Games. In 1992 the EBU faced the formidable resources of Bertelsmann in the contest for the European rights to cover the 1996 Olympiad in Ted Turner's base, Atlanta, Georgia. At the time of writing, the American rights had not been settled but were likely to fetch at least $550 million.

In 1988 Bertelsmann and its partners in the pay-TV service RTL-Plus had purchased the rights to broadcast coverage of the German Bundesliga soccer league matches for $84 million. In 1991, Kirch and Springer's rival SAT-1 channel raised the ante to $437 million. In 1989, Bertelsmann, 40 per cent owner of the RTL-Plus channel, secured exclusive rights in Germany to the Wimbledon tennis championships, the year in which German players won both the Men's and Women's singles finals.

Until the 1990s it would have been unthinkable that the BBC should not televise any major cricketing event anywhere in the world, but in 1992 Rupert Murdoch secured the rights to the Cricket World Cup in Australia for his Sky Sports satellite channel. Millions of British viewers and MPs of all parties protested vociferously at being deprived of coverage which was only available to the less than three million viewers owning satellite dishes or connected to cable systems. Sky refused to allow the BBC anything more than the most limited news access to the event and edited highlights of the final involving England. Murdoch's triumph was hardly soured when the Australian team was knocked out of the competition before the semi-finals.

A new feature of television programming in Europe is the practice of barter syndication. Barter – the practice whereby a programme provider retains some of the advertising time within programmes instead of cash payment – is seen by a growing number of television producers in Europe as the answer to the problem of future programme funding. Barter syndication has grown phenomenally in the US local networks over the last few years. It accounts for over $1 billion of television business in America.

Paul Styles, former Director of the UK Independent Producers' Association and now Head of Media with Peat Marwick McClintock, told us: 'There's going to be a major crisis in programme financing in Europe in the early 1990s, with a massive increase in the number of hours. How is that going to be paid for? All sorts of new means have got to be found to finance the programming that will be needed.' Styles acknowledges that considerable confusion exists about the respective boundaries and definitions of sponsorship, barter and syndication. In UK television, sponsorship is still a relatively new area. Barter syndication is even more unfamiliar.

The US Advertiser Syndicated Television Association has its own definition: 'Advertiser supported (or barter) syndication is a system whereby the syndicator gives the station a show in return for some of the commercial time within the show rather than cash.' According to ASTA, of all the changes taking place in US television, 'the rise of advertiser-supported syndication as a broad and vital programming marketplace is the most dramatic'. ASTA cites the fact that not only has syndication in the US grown from almost nothing in 1980 to its current billion-dollar status, but along the way it has captured over 25 per cent of the national TV audience and become the biggest and most direct competitor to the US networks.

The practice of barter syndication grew up in the US on the off-network local TV stations. Originally designed to make network quality second-run series affordable to local stations, barter syndication now has its own first-run market. Virtually all first-run shows are now sold locally on either a barter or cash/barter basis.

In Europe, now too, there is increasing activity. The Carat Espace group set up a new division 'to exploit opportunities in the funding and control of television programming.' Former head of Carat Entertainment, Justin Bodle, was credited with what is claimed to be Europe's first barter deal during his time at Henson International, the Muppets on Super Channel. Bodle has predicted a 'massive increase' in independent production – the powerhouse of barter syndication – in Europe over the next few years.

The Europeans will receive strong competition from the Americans. US syndicators King World opened its first international office in London and concluded a deal with Unilever through the Lintas ad agency to produce local versions of the *Jeopardy* game show for TF1 in France and of *Wheel Of Fortune* with West Germany's SAT-1 and Berlusconi's Reteitalia. Shortly after, the UK ITV companies Central, Thames and Yorkshire announced a landmark agreement with the ABC network, MGM/UA and DL Taffner to exploit barter syndication in Europe.

Accusations that syndication is just a means for the dumping of large quantities of undistinguished American programming are challenged by the ASTA. There are the dubious gems such as *Tabloid* and *On Trial* ('great programmes – great demographics'). But the ASTA also points to material such as Turner Programme Syndication's *Rediscovery of the World* and *National Geographic – On Assignment*, the latter a first-run prime time series airing in 48 of the top 50 US TV markets and covering 90 per cent of US TV homes.

For the advertising industry, sponsorship, barter and their various combinations are all part of a new concept called 'media broking'. The words look set to become a catchphrase of the European television industry in the next couple of years. The key to media broking is that it is research based and encompasses the whole range of related sponsorship and advertising opportunities on a targeted basis. It is no surprise then that it is the advertising agencies who have taken the lead in gearing themselves up for the expected take-off. Young and Rubicam and Ogilvy and Mather are just two of the leading agencies which have already created specialist units to deal with sponsorship and barter syndication opportunities. Young and Rubicam opened its Media Europe office with the specific brief of researching European markets for TV sponsorship and barter syndication.

Ogilvy and Mather undertook a reorganisation of its international media resources, with Stephen Stokes joining from Leo Burnett to develop programme sponsorship and barter syndication. Stokes is cautious about the prospects for barter syndication. Like other observers, he stresses the historical differences of the largely homogeneous US market compared with Europe's cultural hotchpotch. Stokes believes that 'the primary route of interest' for advertisers in Europe will be actual sponsorship of TV programmes. With the increase in the number of channels and hours in European TV, Stokes points out, there will also be a corresponding increase in advertising time. 'There is a fairly limited pot of money out there. Barter syndication will only arrive once sponsorship has got itself very much established.' However, Stokes concedes: 'Once you have your sponsored programme there are "a variety" of ways of getting it on air – ranging from straight cash deals, programme giveaways and exchange of programmes for airtime.'

It all points to an inevitable showdown between the producers and advertisers. The producers see some form of barter as a means of securing funds while holding onto their editorial independence. At the same time there would seem to be a substantial body of advertisers and agencies who see the deregulated future as one in which the advertiser rather than the programmer will be in the driving seat.

The UK government has relaxed significantly the provisions against sponsorship and barter in its Broadcasting Act. With the EC and European Council widely expected to take a neutral stance on the issue, the practice is expected to spread rapidly in Europe.

XVIII

Whose Finger on the News?

Broadcast news has come a long way since Lord Reith's BBC radio announcers wore dinner jackets to read the evening bulletins. Few would argue that it has all been downhill. However, in the supply of global news and information, the trend towards concentration in a few hands is becoming ever more marked. While it is possible to dismiss much of TV as mere entertainment – a view with which Rupert Murdoch would vehemently disagree – there is no doubt that television is the most powerful information medium ever seen, creating as well as reporting news events, sometimes of global significance.

Two issues dominate. The first is the strategic and political importance of news and information supply. The second is the content of news, whether it is shaped or twisted for political, commercial and other ends.

Advances in recording equipment and mobile satellite technology have transformed TV newsgathering. Live television pictures of events throughout the globe dominate the newsgathering routines. Ted Turner's prediction – 'we're gonna be all over the globe' – has come true.

Television rather than newspapers 'sets the agenda' for the great issues of the day. And pictures – their availability or otherwise – set the agenda for television news. It was television reports, some of them live by satellite, from famine-stricken Ethiopia and Sudan that awakened the conscience of millions and resulted in globally televised concerts and appeals for assistance. It was the widespread broadcasts of live television reports from the Soviet Union that prevented the organisers of the Kremlin putsch from establishing their customary clampdown on information.

'I believe that national newspapers now cannot compete with television for news in any way at all,' commented TV-am's programme director Bill Ludford, a newspaper veteran, at the time of the Iraqi invasion of Kuwait. During that crisis, viewers in Europe became accustomed to waking up to hear the overnight round-ups and first-hand reports of television reporters from the Middle Eastern capitals. When the Allies transformed Desert Shield into Desert Storm and the bombs and cruise missiles began to fall on Baghdad, millions of viewers in Europe and elsewhere for the first time became conscious of an organisation called CNN, the world-wide news service pioneered by Ted Turner.

The conduct of CNN and its chief reporter Peter Arnett after Saddam Hussein expelled other TV reporters from Baghdad became itself a cause célèbre. But the early domination of the Gulf crisis coverage by CNN caused a reaction amounting to total panic in the heads of other broadcasting services, making them bring forward plans to provide their own transnational news channels. The BBC quickly dusted off its plans for a TV equivalent of its radio World Service, entering into an agreement with an Asian satellite service where it launched its World Service Television. In the European corridors of power, the European Broadcasting Union received EC backing for its Euronews channel which the French government, ever-conscious of Anglo-Saxon linguistic dominance, has given a home in Lyon.

Because of the intrinsic and some would say intrusive presence of television, the medium shapes and participates in the news in a way undreamt of by the old press barons. In Brazil Roberto Marinho has used the power and influence of his Globo empire to change political systems. In Mexico, Azcárraga's Televisa has consistently and openly supported the ruling PRI party to the virtual exclusion of the representatives of the opposition. Newspapers on the whole have never been expected to demonstrate political impartiality, by reason of the fact that the multiplicity of supply should be sufficient to ensure that a broad range of views is heard. In television news, the scarcity of channels has hitherto prompted more enlightened governments to write in fairness doctrines or impartiality requirements in the legislation governing television. Rupert Murdoch's News

Corporation, whose British newspapers robustly supported the Conservative administrations of Margaret Thatcher and John Major from 1979–92, has willingly subscribed to the impartiality codes for his Sky Television networks, albeit they fall outside UK legislation. Similarly Ted Turner's CNN adheres to the fairness doctrines familiar to the US.

Elsewhere, even in Europe, the concept of fairness and impartiality in television is a somewhat more fragile flower. In Italy the heads of the three state RAI networks are appointed on the basis of their political allegiance – one for each of the three main parties. Silvio Berlusconi was prepared to use his own illegal television stations to drum up resistance against court moves to close them down. In France and Spain, there are constant accusations about news bias on the main TV channels.

Roberto Marinho, who comes from a similar newspaper background to Rupert Murdoch, does not agree with the latter's vision of the remorseless logic of interrelated communications. 'Newspapers and TV are irreconcilable enemies,' he likes to say. Like Murdoch, however, Marinho is wont to play down the significance of his role. Pressed on the proprietorial influence he exercises over his newspaper and television news, he draws a distinction between the two. 'We have strong politics in the Globo newspaper, but not in the television. TV gives the facts and incidents but has no editorial.'

'When I started TV Globo I thought that every day in the newspapers there are political, economic comments on matters of national interest and it should be the same with the TV. But then I stopped because I did not want to have, through TV Globo, influence that others did not have.'

'Where do you think Globo will be in ten years' time,' we asked, 'in the year 2000? Will it continue to grow?'

'I think so,' says Marinho easily, 'I think so because our only interest is the common good. That is easy to say and not so easy to prove, but I can only say that it is absolutely true.'

Like Rupert Murdoch and Roberto Marinho, Emilio Azcárraga Milmo is a survivor and a fighter, as his recent US adventures proved. It is a family trait all three have inherited from their fathers in one way or another. In the case of Azcárraga, he seems impervious to the continual criticism from Mexico's liberals and intellectuals.

The Azcárragas are also extremely rich and powerful, as was recognised by the United States Embassy fifty years ago in its urgent message to the State Department warning Washington of the potential dangers of crossing their path. But even the Azcárraga family must have been surprised by a column in Mexico's English language newspaper *The News*, owned and operated by no less than Miguel Alemán and Rómulo O'Farrill Junior – former partners in the Televisa troika. On 24 January 1992, *The News* columnist Richard Seid recalled Ronald Reagan's description of the old Soviet Union as an 'Evil Empire' and how Mikhail Gorbachev's policy of glasnost had introduced the possibility of and even encouraged 'criticism of governmental policies, actions, inactions and personalities' in all media including newspapers, radio and television.

'In no way, of course, is Mexico an evil empire,' wrote Seid, 'but evil empires do lurk within. In the last century, the Catholic Church was an "Evil Empire" until a liberal President Benito Juarez curbed it. Today the evil empires are . . . well, let's just say that the private television monopoly, Televisa, is one of them. It's not number one – but it's right up there.'

Televisa had a virtual monopoly throughout the whole country, continued Seid, and a vast majority of Mexico's citizens got their news and had their opinions formed by Televisa's programming. 'Televisa knows on which side of the bread the butter is,' continued the columnist. 'Televisa doesn't need to be censored. Never has it allowed any opinion to be aired against, or even questioning, the government or the party which has held power for more than sixty years.' Continued Seid: 'Televisa claims that it has complete freedom of speech and that it simply supports the candidate of its choice. Is it just a coincidence that it is always the ruling party's candidate who gets almost all the coverage from Televisa? During the 1988 presidential campaign why was the voice of the leading opposition candidate, Cuauhhtemoc Cardenas, never heard on any of Televisa's channels? Doesn't

Televisa (and the government) realise that the people aren't completely gullible? That a backlash is almost inevitable?'

Seid summed up his argument with this forcible swipe: 'Televisa has ignored the fact that a television concession implies a public trust. For Televisa to retain its licence to broadcast, honest reporting and a fair editorial policy should be obligatory. Unfortunately, "honesty", "fairness" and "objectivity" are not in Televisa's vocabulary.'

'Right now,' he concluded, 'Televisa is an obstacle to Mexico's democracy. It is an evil empire.'

At the press launch of the UK's Sky Television in June 1988, Rupert Murdoch invited questions. A journalist from Channel 4's news programme was the first to stand up.

'May I ask about the standards of journalism you would use. Are we going to expect the kind of journalism we've seen in the *Sun* and *News of the World*, the fabrication of stories. . . ?'

'We don't fabricate,' retorted Murdoch. 'I'm very proud of all my newspapers and I'm sure I'm going to be proud of what we do on this channel, thank you.'

'Is it going to be the same kind of standard of journalism we see in the USA?' the journalist persisted.

'It'll be totally different and I can tell you it'll be absolutely first class,' replied Murdoch.

'In America, your network [Fox Television] showed a man demonstrating how he strangled his girlfriend. Is that the kind of current affairs we can expect on your channels here?'

Murdoch rolled a baleful eye, visibly rattled. 'You'll have to ask the editor,' he snapped.

It was hardly the appropriate time to raise such an issue but the implication was clear. It was the same issue that had come up when Ted Turner attempted to take over CBS.

Turner had revelled in the impact he had made on the New York financial and broadcasting establishment. He seemed to see himself as some defiant Confederate general. 'It is really a war with CBS,' he told a Rotarian lunch. 'I love it because I feel like I'm on the side of right and they are on the side of wrong. When I believe something is right, I fight it to the death. CBS has tried to smear me by saying that I'd manage the news, put a right-wing slant on it. I've been endorsed by the Right and the Left. I think we'd be in a hell of a mess in a free society if we didn't have a Right Wing.'

Lawsuits began to fly between CBS and Turner Broadcasting, and following them came the mud. In a letter to shareholders rejecting the bid at the end of April mainly for financial reasons, CBS alluded to matters of a more personal nature: 'In the light of a number of pejorative statements by Mr Turner about various minority, religious and ethnic groups, we believe that TBS's acquisition of CBS would undermine the CBS network's present broad acceptance by the American public.' Meanwhile the CBS chairman Tom Wyman said publicly that Ted Turner did not have the 'conscience' nor was he 'moral enough' to run CBS.

'We will not dignify the mudslinging by CBS with a response,' retorted Arthur Sando, Turner's spokesman. He pointed out that Turner had received a number of awards from community, ethnic and religious groups and that he was to receive the Tree of Life award in Atlanta the following week from the National Jewish Fund for 'outstanding professional and community leadership and service to humanitarian causes.'

On his side Turner had frequently criticised the three networks in the past for their 'sleazy programs' that focus on 'stupidity, sex and violence'. He had also criticised network newscasts for 'too much sensationalism' and not enough balance.

On 3 May 1985, Sally Bedell Smith wrote in the *New York Times*: 'What effect can an executive's controversial public statements have on his or her ability to operate a broadcasting business? How should the "conscience" of a broadcaster be judged, and should that judgment be a factor in determining who should control a station or a network?'

The policy of the Federal Communications Commission was clear. A licence applicant was judged only on whether he or she had violated criminal or civil laws relating to felonies, combinations in restraint of trade, unfair competition, fraud, unfair labour practices or discrimination. But the FCC specifically did not take into account 'philosophical viewpoints'. A Supreme

Court in 1943 said 'Congress did not authorise the Commission to choose among applicants on the basis of their political, economic or social views, or upon any other capricious basis.'

According to Turner Broadcasting, CBS hired four firms of lawyers to track down and question past business associates, acquaintances and employees of WTBS and CNN about employment practices and news policies.

Turner's supporters accepted that he was notorious for his sometimes outrageous utterances, but claimed that controversial statements such as those cited by CBS had no effect on his employment policies, nor on the programmes he transmitted. Documents filed at the FCC showed that Turner's record on employment for minorities and women at WTBS-TV was roughly on a par with that of CBS. In 1984, WTBS (Turner's Super Station) had 36 minority employees out of a full-time staff of 171 – of whom 118 were men and 53 were women. In a CBS station of comparable size, KMOX-TV in St Louis, there were 37 minority members on staff of 167 full-time employees – 106 men and 61 women. At WTBS there were about 12 out of 33 women in the officials and managers category and 6 members of minority groups. For the CBS station the figures were 11 women and 8 minority out of 30.

WTBS largely followed Turner's stated ideals for programming and reflected his concern about the environment and the nuclear arms race. In 1984 Turner broadcast the BBC television drama *Threads* about the aftermath of a nuclear war. In the same year he gave three hours of WTBS primetime to a telethon for the United Negro College Fund.

Employees of CNN state that Turner imposes no political slant on their coverage. 'We are very straight-arrow as opposed to being on the flamboyant or tabloid side,' says Ed Turner (no relation), the Executive Vice-President of Turner Broadcasting. 'Ted plays a very limited role at CNN. He has never ordered a story killed or a story run. He does have story ideas from time to time. After all he knows a lot of interesting people.'

'The Tube' column in *The Village Voice* entered the fray. In an article entitled 'How good is CNN?', editor Richard Goldstein poured scorn on Turner as 'the Attila of Atlanta'. Referring to an interview Turner had given on CNN about baseball and his team the Atlanta Braves, Goldstein sneered: 'No one expects a cable TV mogul to be modest; but imagine the founder of a real network taking to the airwaves for personal publicity. Imagine a broadcast industry in which such gall were regarded as the mark of heroism. That may be what Ronald Reagan envisioned when he proclaimed this the age of the entrepreneur, but it also suggests the distinction between Turner's 24-hour Cable News Network and a major news operation.'

'The difference,' Goldstein went on, 'has more to do with sensibility than scale. Even if CNN had a bureau in every bush, its approach to reporting would be provincial; Ted Turner's New South values would pervade its coverage if he were looking down Sixth Avenue from a corner office. Those values include a rigid optimism – the most ominous events are served sunny side up on CNN; a hurricane becomes a warning to wear your rubbers – and a preoccupation with sex. It's no accident that CNN's most brutal error, broadcasting the name of a sexual assault victim, occurred in its haste to cover a notorious rape trial live. Though it feigns discretion, CNN thrives on the very prurience Turner condemns elsewhere on TV.'

Goldstein went on to accuse CNN of 'pilfering formats invented elsewhere', of seeing journalism as 'a common carrier', as 'the perfect format for elevators and waiting rooms: newzak'. He concluded: 'What a network this could be if the dominant on-air personality weren't its owner.'

The passions aroused in the battle for CBS may now seem hard to understand. Today, CBS is dogged by debt and cutbacks, its reputation as the most authoritative news source under serious challenge. Ted Turner's attempted purchase of CBS was a key turning-point. By failing in his attempt to take over the network, Turner was instead forced to transform CNN itself. Today, it is CNN rather than CBS which is spreading its tentacles over the world.

One of the specific accusations made against CNN during the Gulf War was that the network received favourable treatment from Saddam Hussein because it was less overtly antagonistic to Iraq than many of the other major foreign news organisations. What made these accusations more bitter was the behaviour of CNN's chief correspondent Peter Arnett, who had been the first to get reports back of the Allied attacks on Baghdad.

Only Arnett had permanent access to a 24-hour line, or 'Four-Wire', which allowed him to get his reports out of Iraq and up via the satellite. This facility had been provided by the Iraqi government to the CNN man and caused resentment among the other correspondents.

In his book on the Gulf War, the BBC's distinguished foreign editor John Simpson specifically criticises Arnett's coverage of the hostage crisis and the outbreak of hostilities.[1] Arnett made his reputation as a war correspondent in Vietnam and won a Pulitzer Prize with the Associated Press news agency. In Baghdad, Arnett refused to allow virtually the only other journalist left beside himself, a newspaper correspondent from Madrid, access to the Four-Wire. What raised the ire of Simpson and others was that CNN then promoted themselves as the only Western news organisation in Baghdad.

Whether Arnett had lost his objectivity, as Simpson suggests, is more doubtful. As a colleague says: 'I never knew that of Arnett and Arnett survived Vietnam and won a Pulitzer. It's obvious that they weren't the only Western news organisation there and it's obvious that they could have helped out the correspondent from a Madrid newspaper and didn't. . . . Those were not the shining moments in their efforts, I would think.'

What really caught the other news organisations flatfooted was the fact that CNN had some time previously installed the CNN service in Saddam Hussein's office. Similar relationships have been created by CNN all over the world as a way to enhance their newsgathering and their reach. This hardly amounted to a 'special relationship' with Saddam, as the former CNN staffer told us. 'They dealt similarly there as they did elsewhere and therefore he

---

[1] John Simpson, *From the House of War*.

watched the network. It was the network where he could see himself and he could see Bush. They were talking back and forth to each other. . . . It was the same with Thatcher, she ordered it installed in Downing Street. You wouldn't say that Ted Turner did a slimy deal to get in there. That's the network Saddam saw himself on and therefore he found that network important.'

Not since Rothschild's couriers brought the tidings of the defeat of Napoleon at Waterloo to London before it reached the government of the day has there been such a giant leap in the development of newsgathering and distribution. CNN's operation is not only ahead of traditional diplomatic and other channels of information, it sometimes replaces them. President Bush, it is reliably reported, once told other world leaders: 'I learn more from CNN than I do from the CIA.' Even Archbishop John Foley, president of the Pontifical Council for Social Communications, is said to rise at 6.00 am to watch CNN 'to know what to pray about'.

Time magazine reported that during the Gulf War, whenever CIA director William Webster learnt through a spy satellite that an Iraqi Scud missile had been launched, he would ask National Security Adviser Brent Snowcroft to watch CNN 'to see where it lands'.

In December 1950, CBS launched a new radio programme with Ed Murrow called *Hear It Now*. Less than a year later, on 15 September 1951, CBS Television followed on with *See It Now*, which included live pictures from both the Atlantic and Pacific coasts of the United States to demonstrate for the first time the ability of television to span the continent. Today the invitation to 'see it now' has become a reality. News is no longer a question of reporting what happened – it *is* what is happening now. And seeing what happens now can change what happens next. In crisis situations world leaders have seconds instead of days to make decisions that may affect the future of mankind.

We have reached the stage where newspapers and even other television services rely on one network as a prime source. There are few self-respecting newsrooms or financial dealing houses that do not have a monitor displaying CNN's 24-hour news service.

The veteran CBS newscaster Charles Morrow told *Time*: 'What I fear is that in their straitened economic conditions, the [US] networks will find CNN an excuse to shuck some of their own responsibilities. I can conceive that as the situation grows worse the networks may say: "The public is being served by CNN. We don't have to be there." '

CNN landmarks have included the explosion of the Challenger spacecraft shortly after lift-off at Cape Canaveral in January 1986, the Tiananmen Square massacre in June 1989, the fall of the Berlin Wall in November 1989, the release of Nelson Mandela in February 1990, the Gulf War and the Soviet Coup in January and August 1991 and the Senate hearings on the Anita Hill and Supreme Court nominee Clarence Thomas sexual harassment charges and the Kennedy rape trial in 1992.

In this light the question of news selection assumes massive importance and the question 'whose finger on the button?' suddenly acquires a new relevance in the field of communications. One, or at best a handful of men and women, have control over the switch that may have to decide whether to go from live coverage of the William Kennedy Smith trial for rape to live coverage of the release of the Associated Press correspondent Terry Anderson. Given the reliance of world leaders on CNN as a source of news and its influence on world opinion, it is not difficult to envisage situations and issues of far greater import. The death of a President, the meltdown of a nuclear reactor, the mid-air collision of two jumbo jets, an earthquake measuring seven on the Richter scale, a famine in Africa, a revolution in Venezuela – a handful of men in Atlanta may be the arbiters of such priorities.

Bernard Ostry of TV Ontario told us: 'There have to be ground rules – television is in every home, in every schoolroom . . . it is too pervasive and powerful to be left simply to discussion about can we trust "Joe" to do this job.'

The world may appear to be a safer place than it was in the mid-1980s but is it acceptable that decisions such as this should be left to the judgment of a few proprietors who may have their own agenda or who are beholden to advertisers who pay for large audiences and expect their commercials to come up on time?

In spite of rivals such as Sky News it is difficult to see how CNN can be toppled from the position of television news pre-eminence it has established. CNN is owned by a consortium in which Time-Warner, *Time* magazine's parent company and the world's largest media conglomerate, has a 21.9 per cent stake. They and the cable owners have first refusal on any sale of CNN.

A determined attempt to provide a Spanish language alternative is being made by Mexico's Televisa with its ECO service. Japan's NHK carried out extensive studies of a global television news service but dropped out when it saw the costs.

The BBC started a service on the STAR-TV satellite system in Asia alongside Li Kashing, Hong Kong's wealthiest entrepreneur. The service reaches thirty-eight Asian nations comprising half of the world's total population but few among them have the means to receive the service – even when it is partially relayed through local television stations. The BBC is looking to extend the service to Africa and the Americas and it is already available in Europe. The Middle East Broadcasting Centre, backed by the Saudi royal family, has similarly launched a satellite-delivered news channel to the Arab nations and provides the service to Arabs living in Europe.

In 1982, the United Kingdom's Independent Broadcasting Authority led a satellite TV experiment supported by the European Broadcasting Union, the European Commission and the Council of Europe, involving fifteen European national public broadcasting services. The experiment was intended to provide the blueprint for a multilingual pan-European satellite service along public service lines that might challenge the burgeoning CNN. Five individual weeks spread across the year were broadcast on five separate language channels across Europe by satellite by the IBA in the UK, RAI in Italy, NOS in Holland, ORF in Austria and ARD in Germany.

The experiment was not followed through, partly because of the problems of differences in style and common language it highlighted, but more importantly because of the national preoccupations and ambitions of the participating broadcasters.

Ten years later, in 1992, the European Broadcasting Union announced the projected start of a satellite-delivered news channel involving ten European broadcasters. . . .

XIX

The Big Picture

'We live in a society, in a civilisation that is unmatched in history for its energy, its vitality, its sheer capacity to change,' Rupert Murdoch told the Business of Entertainment Conference in New York in March 1992.

In an extraordinary performance, Murdoch outlined his vision of society's future, one in which News Corporation, with its film studios, programme libraries, TV networks, newspapers, print, publishing and electronic data interests will have a major – perhaps dominant – role. It was, he said, borrowing from the theme of the conference, 'The Big Picture'. 'Presently, we are engaged in the production and dissemination of information and entertainment on five continents around the globe. . . . I honestly believe that no other company is positioned as well as we are to take advantage of the global growth we expect to see in the next decade. . . .'

Murdoch continued: 'We do not seek partners, and while we have sold a piece of some of our assets, none of our core assets will ever be sold. As a result of our recent restructuring, our finances are in first-class shape, our balance sheet is strong and we intend to continue moving confidently, building our businesses to be even better positioned in the years ahead.'

His vision of a global media empire outlined four years earlier was as strong as ever, he said. 'Because of our uniquely independent and international situation, we will have the flexibility to more fully integrate all our media operations and respond to new technologies as they become available in the years ahead. . . . Our film and television businesses in the United States and United Kingdom are performing very well, and they will only get stronger in the years ahead. Our newspapers, magazines and book publishing interests are highly profitable and well-positioned to take advantage of any upswing in the economy.'

However, said Murdoch, he was not here just to sing the praises of News Corporation, as he admitted he had been forced to do with investors on many occasions over the previous fraught eighteen months. He wanted instead to 'focus for a few minutes on some fundamentals of the information and entertainment business'.

At the heart of his vision, said Murdoch, was consumer choice. 'Choice in all things, including news and entertainment, is an unstoppable force spreading across the world. And as this is happening, so we must protect and enhance this choice here at the centre.' What this meant was soon made abundantly clear. 'In other words,' Murdoch said, 'we must make the needs and interests of the consumer in the United States our number one priority, and above all we must strive to achieve and preserve a free market in intellectual property rights, including in particular, television programming.'

There was far too much emphasis by the media industry on its own interest and on peripheral matters of technology rather than the substantive issues, he said. 'We must abandon our historical delusions of media self-importance. In their place, we must embrace a new populism in which the marketing of television resembles the marketing of other consumer goods and services. Like other marketeers, we've got to focus on product quality, and brand-name identity.' In this New Jerusalem, said Murdoch: 'Television products will have names – brand names that trigger an instant mental image in the minds of consumers. The cable people took the lead with identifiable brands like CNN and MTV. At Fox [his US Fox Television network], we believe we have created the first true brand name in broadcast television. Consumers know that the Fox brand stands for innovative, younger programming. And, in the next phase of our growth, we intend to create the same kind of brand-name identity for Fox news and information services.

'As sure as I'm standing here, we must, and we will, find ways to make the television menu more democratic and more responsive to consumer demand. We must let the viewers choose what they want and let their dollars flow to nourish the services that they choose. In the end, it is the programming – the content of our information and entertainment products – that counts. You would never know it from our endless distribution wars, but people don't really know or care how a programme they like makes its way to their home.'

Murdoch went on to liken the New Age viewer to a consumer standing in a supermarket 'choosing her [*sic*] favourite soap powder' who is 'completely indifferent' to how the box got there. 'And ultimately the viewer cares not one whit whether a programme comes from an analogue broadcast signal, a digital broadcast signal, a coaxial cable, a glass fibre owned by TCI, a glass fibre owned by Bell South, a satellite, a microwave system or a microwave oven. . . . What the viewer cares about is the programme.'

What this meant, Murdoch went on to conclude, was that: 'Ultimately, what our business gets down to is ideas. Those ideas have to be relevant to our consumers – the viewing public – whether they be in front of a television set in their home or a seventy-millimetre screen in a movie theatre. If we succeed in that challenge, we have every right to expect fair compensation for the value we provide. It's a simple concept, and one that will ensure a prosperous, diversified broadcast industry for decades to come.'

Murdoch recalled an interview he had given to the *New York Times* two years previously. He had made the observation then that 'modernisation is Americanisation'. *The Times*, thought Murdoch, had been somewhat embarrassed by his ringing endorsement of America and all it stood for – 'weaselly' he described their reaction. But his views had been given support by a new book called *Rebirth of the West: The Americanization of the Democratic World*. 'That title says it all,' said Murdoch. 'Events of the past few years have left this country's media in an unrivalled position as suppliers of news and entertainment. The force of events round the world has clearly shown the demand for choice and the demand for modernisation. And I stand firm in my belief that modernisation is Americanisation.'

Whether Murdoch is right or wrong, the issue of Americanisation of culture is a hot topic in the USA's nearest Latin neighbour, Mexico. When Televisa decided to run the Spanish version of *Sesame Street* ('Plaza Sesamo') in 1973, its publicity for the show was intended to express the organisation's view of its duties to its childhood audience. It expressed sentiments worthy of Voltaire's *Candide* and is reminiscent of Silvio Berlusconi's saccharine programme philosophy:

> A healthy mind on a healthy screen, or rather a healthy mind on . . . *Plaza Sesamo*. A programme that is part of our daily message – the message that we have developed with such care because it is aimed at children. Children – the most sensitive section of our community and the one on which we pin all our hopes for the future. To capture their attention, give direction to their boundless capacity for wonder and hold their interest, all in a spirit of happiness and entertainment – that's the task we've set ourselves on Televisa channels 2, 4, 5 and 8. With *Plaza Sesamo* we are beginning the changes that we've decided on to give more depth, more real content to Mexican television. Televisa. The Sign for Mexico, the Sign For Progress.

Whether Big Bird and Elmo have lived up to this billing is debatable. In the intervening twenty years, Televisa's programmes for children have moved on but not the underlying principles. In 1992, Mexico's most popular TV game show for children – *TV-O* – features ten pre-teenage girls with snub noses, white cheeks and long fair hair led by two nubile and equally blonde young female announcers. 'What comes across on the screen,' wrote one critic, 'is an imposition of a "perfect image" for girls: good, happy, friendly and above all blonde.' From time to time the camera pans to the invited audience of children. They are, as is most of the population of Mexico, almost entirely composed of children of Indian or Mestizo (mixed blood) descent. The diversity of their black haired, brown eyed, dark skinned looks contrasts bizarrely with the blonde moppets and bimbos on stage.

In the year celebrating the 'discovery' of the Americas by Columbus, the show is creating no little controversy among the descendants of the original inhabitants of Latin America. Those who see the arrival of the Europeans as the prelude to the conquest and destruction of the ancient civilisations of the Aztec and the Maya will recall the Aztec princess Malintzin who acted as interpreter for, and later bore a son to, the conqueror of Mexico, Hernan Cortes. She is known as 'La Malinche'. 'Malinchismo' – the denial and betrayal of Mexico's racial heritage through the imposition of alien products and standards – is a charge frequently heard in Mexico these days. But while the Mexican government is promoting plans to strengthen respect for Mexico's ethnic diversity and giving Indians and Mestizos greater access to natural resources, the 'guero' or blonde is a hot property on TV and with advertisers. Fair haired models with Anglo-Saxon features advertise motor cars, airlines and banks. Even an advertisement for a government public works project is sung by 'fresas' ('strawberries' or young white schoolgirls), although intended to benefit Mestizo and Indian communities.

It is said that as Mexico, Canada and the United States negotiate the terms of a North American common market, investors from the North would prefer to 'put their dollars in a country that looks whiter'. The suggestion is that 'white' and 'blonde' are synonymous with beauty and superiority. It is a fact that no more than 1,000 families of Spanish and fair-skinned descent control most of the wealth and power in this nation of 85 million people of whom 90 per cent are of Indian or mixed blood. But the perpetuation of colonial ideas continues through open and covert systems of domination – racial, social and economic.

'Nose jobs' – plastic surgery to change the shape of the nose – have been popular in Mexico for more than a decade. Cosmetic surgeons vie with gynaecologists in the columns of the city telephone directories. For $25 you can buy an orthopaedic nose uplift insert that is supposed to make flat Mestizo nostrils look more like an Anglo-Saxon nose. It is marketed as 'nariz bella' or 'pretty nose'. The maker, who is a Mestizo himself, predicted sales volume would double in 1992 to more than 100,000. The inventor, Ruben Lazcano Vergara, claimed in a telling commentary on the divisions in Mexican society: 'Now the maid can have a nose as pretty as the housewife she works for.'

There would seem then to be no brooking of Murdoch's vision of America in excelsis. 'In the film industry, for example, international markets are becoming increasingly important as they contribute a larger percentage of overall revenues for both theatrical releases and video. At the same time, there is a continually expanding market for American product with the growth of satellite and deregulation in the industrialised countries, and the opening up of less-developed markets in Eastern Europe, Asia and Latin America. And this demand for American product continues despite active movie industries in places such as India, France and China not to speak of active politicians trying to lock us [*sic*] out.'

If it had taken the Australian grandson of a Scottish Presbyterian minister to reaffirm how the West was won, the implication was clear: 'Pure and simple, the world wants American entertainment and the American way of life,' said Murdoch.

Murdoch rounded off his remarkable Media Gettysburg address in New York with a canny reminder that America need not worry about its film and television industry slipping into the hands of others. He had read recently that the Japanese wanted to buy an American baseball club. 'What a business! It's better than selling a movie studio! The US parts with no tangible assets, there's nothing involved except a handful of contracts and a chance to participate – literally as well as metaphorically – in the American game. No other country is in that position. And no other industry is in a better position than the entertainment industry. . . . Perhaps we have found the philosophers' stone: we can make dreams into gold.'

A persuasive voice expressing a very different point of view from Rupert Murdoch's is that of Bernard Ostry, former chairman and chief executive of TV Ontario. We went to see him in his Toronto apartment.

'Freedom,' Ostry claims, 'is the supreme value in culture as in politics, and a range of choice is essential to it. But practical experience shows that competition in the marketplace tends to make rival products more or less identical. There is no realm where the copycat or follow-my-leader mentality prevails more than in commercial television. And when it enters its truly transnational phase it will have to become increasingly bland, value-free and abstract.'

Bernard Ostry deplores 'the increasingly accepted subversion for profit of television, the socially most useful technology for disseminating information, education and culture in democracies, on the false excuse that it is for freedom.'

Clearly a staunch defender of beleaguered public broadcasting values, Ostry believes that multinationals must be tackled on the international level. 'Hopes of regulating the mega-corporations are vain. We have taken the route of regulation in Canada and found it a dead end. The new super-novas in any event are beyond the reach of mere national laws, looping the loop in the regulatory void of outer space. Our best hope is to respond to this international challenge by international cooperation and collaboration.'

Yet how do you intervene in a process of popular culture that is zinging about the world with the merry gusto of a genie let out of the bottle? Is it not a form of cultural imperialism even to consider to do so?

Take the 'telenovela', the uniquely Latin and South American form of soap opera that has swept all before it. Alan Riding wrote in *Inside the Volcano* that some politicians argue privately that banal telenovelas and the like contribute to stability by diverting attention away from social problems. 'It's better to use tearjerkers than tear gas,' one politician told him. 'If the nanny keeps the children quiet, why change her?'

Emilio Balli, one of Azcárraga's executives, said of the Televisa Group's radio programmes in 1956: 'We have given the audience what they ask for and that is why we have progressed. What the public wants is comedies, sketches, shows, music, bullfights. That is how we serve the public and the advertisers because with a big audience the commercial is more effective. That is the task for those who run the radio industry.'

The first telenovelas in Mexico date back to 1957 but it was the arrival of videotape and electronic editing that gave them impetus. Today, like CNN's news, Mexican and Brazilian soap operas are 'all over the world'. A Mexican diplomat arriving in Beijing was greeted at the airport recently not with the strains of the Mexican national anthem but with the theme music from *Rosa Salvaje* ('Wild Rose'). Programmes like this and *Los Ricos Tambien Lloran* ('The Rich Also Cry') are popular from Istanbul to Seoul and from Spain to Argentina.

The telenovela is made on a factory production line basis. Actors are equipped with radio earpieces through which they hear and repeat their lines to avoid the waste of time involved in learning or rehearsing them. Make-up is specially designed to resist tears, which are heavily in demand.

Matt Moffett of *The Wall Street Journal* recounted the story of a visit to the set of Televisa's latest hit telenovela, *La Picara Sonadora* ('The Mischievous Dreamer'). A five-year-old actor committed the cardinal sin of not crying on cue. 'An impatient starlet tapped her high heels. The leading man's aplomb is slipping – as is the silk jacket draped over his shoulders. Finally the director gives up and tells the make-up man to apply drops to the boy's cheeks. "Unless this boy learns how to cry," says the starlet petulantly, "his possibilities for advancement in Mexican television will be extremely limited." '

The distinguished author Carlos Fuentes, in the course of an interview with Patricia de la Peña for the BBC series *Mexico Viva*, argued that the telenovela was like melodrama defined as comedy without humour. It was what Susan Sontag called camp – 'some of them are so bad they're good – like old "B" movies or "penny dreadful" novels.' This kind of television, said Fuentes, was like a Saturn that instead of devouring its children devoured itself. The telenovela spins on and on night after night without even the form of the 'B' movie. 'They confirm people in their worst habits of mental laziness,' Fuentes told de la Peña. 'They contain every imaginable cliché: the good will triumph, the bad will perish . . . the mothers are always good . . . the rich are sometimes egoistical but finally we discover they have a heart of gold . . . the poor in spite of having no education also turn out to be good people as well. It's a Manichean world, unreal, dripping with sentimentalism.'

The worst was that there was no choice. Fuentes said that he didn't mind if people sat watching telenovelas all day. He had nothing against them and even found them entertaining and amusing. But there had to be a choice. There must be the option of viewing something else that was educational, something that was challenging, something above all that reflected the political and economic realities of the country. Those who transmit nothing of value beyond the telenovela were pouring rubbish into the mouths of millions of viewers who deserved and were hungry for better.

Holding up the BBC as an example of what television should provide, Fuentes said that those who provide a diet consisting entirely of the kind of television represented by the telenovela were the very worst kind of elitists: 'The people are ignorant. Let's carry on giving them this so that they are kept amused and keep quiet.'

XX

The Future

What makes a Sky Baron?

When Ted Turner was starting CNN he said: 'I am the right man in the right place at the right time. Not me alone, but all the people who think that the world can be brought together by telecommunications.'

Bruce Gyngell, who has worked with or for many of them, from those of the old school like Sir Charles Moses, Sir Frank Packer and Lord Grade, to the new generation from Alan Bond to Conrad Black, painted the following portrait:

> They are all powerful men who run their businesses with the same obsessive care and attention as the owner of a corner store. They are all individualists prepared to break every rule in every management rulebook ever written. They are clearly focussed on their ultimate objectives. They are prepared to work as hard or harder than anyone else in their organisations. They are committed and dedicated to their empires. They all have a very human streak and the same frailties as other men.
>
> They all desperately want to be liked. They can be generous to a fault. They are easily irritated if things go against them. They like people to stand up to them but find it uncomfortable. They can be arrogant, merciless, aggressive, but deep down they want to be liked and loved and held in high esteem – provided it isn't inconvenient or detrimental to their business.

There are certain characteristics which the Hollywood moguls and press barons of the past share with today's Sky Barons. Lord Beaverbrook felt he had been rejected by 'polite society' in London because of his small stature and his Canadian roots. As we have seen, in many cases the drive to power and wealth of the Sky Barons seems to have been based on a similar sense of rejection or on perceived wrongs done to their fathers or families.

Rupert Murdoch for many years nursed an inherited sense of an injustice meted out to his father and exacted his revenge. Ted Turner reclaimed his father's bankrupt company from the creditors and built a world-wide news network. The teenage Roberto Marinho set about building the empire started by his father, who had died prematurely. Akio Morita, head of Sony, is typical of a generation of Japanese whose determination to rebuild their country's power was kindled in the flames of Hiroshima and Nagasaki. Out of the ruins of postwar Germany Reinhard Mohn rebuilt his family empire, Bertelsmann, and Robert Maxwell, whose family died at the hands of the Nazis, embarked on his unique rise and fall.

'To men eager for a sort of power and status, men who had often been rejected by orthodox politics, circulation was an index of public acclaim,' wrote Simon Jenkins of the Barons of Fleet Street. The new index of acclaim is ratings rather than circulation and is measured in hundreds of millions.

Like the old-style press barons and Hollywood moguls, a certain preoccupation with their immortal souls and the future of mankind will be seen to creep into their conversation and actions from time to time.

The days of the movie moguls and the press barons have faded and gone. The Northcliffes, Harmsworths and Beaverbrooks no longer rule in Fleet Street. Sam Goldwyn and Louis B. Mayer left only their names to MGM, which along with the other great film companies has seen its assets stripped.

The old school of proprietors like Scripps and Hearst in newspapers or Warner and Goldwyn in the cinema saw themselves as running self-contained empires. In many cases they were deeply involved in and knowledgeable about their products. The

Sky Barons are a different breed, prepared to play across the board. They are businessmen first.

Yet the two most powerful inheritors of the 'old school' – Rupert Murdoch and Roberto Marinho – have successfully developed their original press empires into television and films. 'This is a new age we believe we're bringing,' announced Rupert Murdoch at the launch of his Sky Television project in the United Kingdom on 9 June 1988. 'Our record in this country has been to create competition and indeed to enhance it and we think that we'll do the same thing for television. We're seeing, I think, the dawn of an age of freedom for viewing and freedom for advertising.'

What then is the danger? Gyngell suggested that the principal danger stems from financial considerations. There is, he said, 'no doubt that money does corrupt and the more money, the more right-wing you get because you want to protect your assets.' At the same time, the constant search for profitability means that media owners are not going to produce something that the public does not want to buy because that would 'erode their financial power base.' The danger is a lowering of standards, a tendency to avoid anything that might raise the awareness of the audiences – and, it would seem, less choice rather than more.

Satellite communications, glass-fibre optical cables and semiconductors are the hardware that has taken away the ability of individual nations to control the last bastion of state-regulated information supply – the television broadcast. The world-wide and instantaneous transmission of information of all kinds, from newspapers to financial data, means that censorship is no longer possible. By the time the plug is pulled the message has gone.

It is no novelty for the rich and powerful to seek to control a communications outlet to boost their fortunes, to impose their views or to attempt to influence the course of history. But never before have so few men been in a position to wield so much influence beyond national boundaries and on a world-wide scale.

Concentrations of ownership in the communications media raise important issues of public interest and civil liberty. Freedom of information and opinion is essential to the survival of democracy. There is as yet no First Amendment to the United

Nations Charter or the Treaty of Rome guaranteeing free
expression and no mechanism to safeguard the free flow of
information in a world in which a handful of giant multinational
corporations control the world supply.

Privileged and quasi-monopolistic enterprises on this scale are
uniquely placed to lobby governments for industrial and commercial policies that favour their own interests. In return, they are
in a position to grant governments a favourable view of their
activities. When the same enterprises are also suppliers of goods
and services of strategic economic or military importance to the
governments concerned, the risks of abuse are evident.

The proponents of pure market-led controls claim that such
policies guarantee freedom and individual choice. The evidence
would suggest they are leading directly to a new and insidious
form of licensing imposed in part by the very magnitude of the
resources required to run modern media.

A handful of large corporations whose concern is the generation
of profit and whose communications activities may be ancillary to
their main business have a disproportionate influence on the basic
freedoms of choice and expression. The interest of such corporations lies in supporting the status quo and any government that
guarantees their continuing existence. Whatever protestations are
made as to editorial freedom, the content of the media they
control invariably reflects their own interests.

The future would seem to beckon for the Sky Barons. New
hardware will enable them to exploit the new generation of multi-
media, interactive software with its vast potential for information,
education and entertainment. Their conglomerates will own
privileged channels for the advertising of their own products
placed by their own advertising agency. Conglomerates which
also publish newspapers and magazines in which are printed
favourable reviews of their own films, books and television
programmes and other products. Conglomerates which also
manufacture arms and strategic electronics and provide public
services from money to transport to water supply. Conglomerates
which have the ear and the favour of the government in power.

The prospect is Orwellian. It would have pleased the young
Edward Willis Scripps.

Appendix:
Elements of a Modern Media Empire

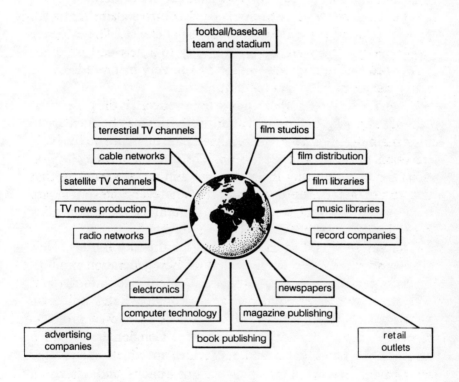

Bibliography

Abramson, Albert, *The History of Television*, London: McFarland, 1988.

Alemán Valdés, Miguel, *Remembranzas y Testimonios*, Mexico: Editorial Grijalbo, 1987.

Alemán Velasco, Miguel, *Copilli: Corona Real*, Mexico: Diana, 1981.

——, *El Héroe Desconocido*, Mexico: Diana, 1983.

——, *La Isla de Los Perros*, Mexico: Grijalbo, 1984.

Allen, Frederick Lewis, *Only Yesterday*, New York: Harper & Brothers, 1931.

Allen, G. C., *The Japanese Economy*, London: Weidenfeld, 1981.

Altschull, J. Herbert, *Agents of Power*, New York: Longman, 1984.

Article 19, *Information, Freedom & Censorship*, London: Longman, 1988.

Auletta, Ken, *The Art of Corporate Success*, New York: Penguin, 1985.

Baily, Leslie, *Scrapbook for the Twenties*, London: Frederick Muller, 1959.

Barry, Paul, *The Rise and Fall of Alan Bond*, London: Doubleday, 1990.

Barnouw, Erik, *The Image Empire*, New York: Oxford University Press, 1970.

Barzini, Luigi, *The Italians*, New York, Atheneum, 1985.

Bernal Sahagún, Victor M., et al., *Espacios de Silencio. La Televisión Mexicana*, Mexico: Nuestro Tiempo, 1988.

Bohmann, Karin, *Medios de Comunicación y Sistemas informativos en México*, Mexico: Alianza Editorial, 1989.

Boller, Paul P., *Hollywood Anecdotes*, New York: Wm. Morrow, 1987.

Bower, Tom, *Maxwell: The Outsider*, London: Aurum Press, 1988.

Boyer, Peter J., *Who Killed CBS?*, New York: St Martin's Press, 1989.

Brendon, Piers, *The Life and Death of the Press Barons*, London: Secker & Warburg, 1982.

Briggs, Asa & Spicer, Joanna, *The Franchise Affair*, London: Century, 1986.

Buendia, Manuel, *Los Empresarios*, Mexico: Océano, 1988.

Bunce, Richard, *Television in the Corporate Interest*, New York: Praeger, 1976.

Campagnac, Elisabeth, *Citizen Bouygues*, Paris: Belfond, 1988.

Caplan, Gerald L. & Sauvageau, *Report of the Task Force on Ottawa Broadcasting Policy*, Canada: Minister of Supply & Services, 1986.

Carrandi Ortiz, Gabino, *Testimonio de la Televisión Mexicana*, Mexico: Editorial Diana, 1986.

Collier, Peter & Horowitz, David, *The Fords. An American Epic*, London: Futura, 1987.

Cooke, Alistair, *America Observed*, London: Penguin, 1989.

Cremoux, Raúl, *Televisión o Prisión Electrónica*, Mexico: Archivo del Fondo, 1974.

Cudlipp, Hugh, *The Prerogative of the Harlot*, London: The Bodley Head, 1980.

Curran, James & Seaton, Jean, *Power Without Responsibility*, London: Routledge, 1988.

Davis, William, *The Innovators*, London: Ebury Press, 1987.

Drosnin, Michael, *Citizen Hughes*, London: Hutchinson, 1985.

Enkelaar, Carel, *Behind the Screen*, Hilversum: NOS, 1979.

Ernst, Morris L., *The First Freedom*, New York: Macmillan, 1946.

Evans, Harold, *Good Times, Bad Times*, London: Weidenfeld & Nicolson, 1983.

Fernández Christlieb, Fátima, *Los Medios de Difusión*, Mexico: Juan Pablos, 1989.

Freedland, Michael, *The Goldwyn Touch*, London: Harrap, 1986.

——, *The Warner Brothers*, London: Harrap, 1985.

Friedman, Alan, *Agnelli and the Network of Italian Power*, London: Harrap, 1988.

Friedrich, Otto, *City of Nets*, London: Headline, 1987.

Fuentes, Carlos, *La Muerte de Artemio Cruz*, Mexico: Fondo de Cultura Económico, 1990.

Fuentes Navarro, Raúl, *La Investigación de Comunicación en México 1956–1986*, Mexico: Ediciones Comunicación, 1988.

Gabler, Neal, *An Empire of Their Own*, USA: Crown, 1988.

Galeano, Eduardo, *Las Venas Abiertas de América Latina*, Mexico: Siglo Veintiuno, 1987.

Goldenberg, Susan, *The Thomson Empire*, London: Sidgwick & Jackson, 1985.

Grade, Lew, *Still Dancing*, London: Collins, 1987.

Graham-White, Claude, *Flying*, London: Chatto & Windus, 1930.

Greber, Dave, *Rising to Power*, Canada: Methuen, 1987.

Greenslade, Roy, *Maxwell's Fall*, London: Simon & Schuster, 1992.

Guimares, Cesar & Amaral, Roberto, *Brazilian Television: A Rapid Conversion*, London: Sage, 1988.

Haines, Joe, *Maxwell*, London: Futura, 1988.

Haley, Sir William, Evans, Harold, Lord Windelsham & Graham, Katherine, *The Freedom of the Press, The Granada Guildhall Lectures 1974*, London: Granada, 1974.

Hamelink, Cees, *Finanzas e Información*, Mexico: Editorial Nueva Imagen, 1984.

Hart-Davis, Duff, *The House the Berrys Built*, London: Hodder & Stoughton, 1990.

Hay, Peter, *MGM – When the Lion Roars*, Atlanta: Turner Publishing, 1991.

Hobsbawm, F. J., *The Age of Capital. 1848–1875*, London: Abacus, 1985.

Hughes, Robert, *The Fatal Shore*, London: Collins Harvill, 1987.

Ishihara, Shintaro, *The Japan That Can Say No*, London: Simon & Shuster, 1991.

Jameson, Derek, *Touched by Angels*, London: Penguin, 1989.

Kempowski, Walter et al., *1835–1985. 150 Jahre Bertelsmann*, Munich: Bertelsmann, 1985.

King, Cecil H., *With Malice Toward None*, London: Sidgwick & Jackson, 1970.

Kobayashi, Koji, *Rising to the Challenge*, Tokyo: Harcourt Brace Jovanovich, 1989.

Larsen, Egon, *Spotlight on Films*, London: Max Parrish & Co., 1950.

Laver, James, *Between the Wars*, London: Vista Books, 1961.

Leapman, Michael, *The Last Days of the Beeb*, London: Coronet, 1987.

Levinson, Charles, *Vodka Cola*, London: Gordon & Cremonesi, 1978.

Lhoest, Holde, *The Interdependence of the Media*, Strasbourg: Council of Europe, 1983.

Martín Moreno, Francisco, *México Negro*, Mexico: Joaquin Mortiz, 1989.

Matsushita, Konosuke, *Quest for Prosperity*, Kyoto: PHP Institute, 1988.

Mattelart, Armand, *Communication and Information Technologies – Choices for Latin America*, London: ABLEX, 1985.

——, *La Cultura como Empresa Multinacional*, Mexico: Biblioteca Era, 1989.

——, *Multinational Corporations and the Control of Culture*, Sussex: Harvester Press, 1979.

Mohn, Heinrich, *Carl Bertelsmann*, Gütersloh: Bertelsmann, 1935.

Molina, Gabriel, 'Mexican Television News: the Imperatives of Corporate Rationale', in *Media, Culture and Society*, vol. 9, no. 2, April 1987.

Montgomery, John, *The Twenties*, London: George Allen & Unwin, 1957.

Mordden, Ethan, *The Hollywood Studios*, New York: Knopf, 1988.

Morita, Akio, *Made in Japan*, London: Fontana/Collins, 1989.

Mosely, Sydney, *John Baird*, London: Odhams Press, 1952.

Mosley, Leonard, *The Real Walt Disney*, London: Grafton, 1986.

Munster, George, *Rupert Murdoch. A Paper Prince*, London: Viking, 1985.

Musch, Hans-Dieter, *Gütersloh in Westfalen*, Gütersloh: Flottmann, 1985.

Newman, Peter C., *The Establishment Man*, Toronto: McClelland & Stewart, 1982.

Ogilvie, Vivien, *Our Times*, London: B. T. Batsford, 1953.

Ortiz Garza, José Luis, *México en Guerra*, Mexico: Planeta, 1989.

Paper, Lewis J., *Empire. William S. Paley and the Making of CBS*, New York: St Martin's Press, 1987.

Paulu, Burton, *Radio and Television Broadcasting in Eastern Europe*, USA: University of Minnesota, 1974.

Pilger, John, *Secret Country*, London: Jonathan Cape, 1988.

Pragnell, Anthony, *Television in Europe: Quality and Values in a time of Change*, Manchester: European Institute for the Media, 1985.

Pye, Michael, *Moguls*, London: Temple Smith, 1980.

Ramsey, Douglas K., *The Corporate Warriors*, London: Grafton, 1987.

Random, Michael, *Japan. Strategy of the Unseen*, London: Crucible, 1987.

Riding, Alan, *Mexico. Inside the Volcano*, London: I. B. Tauris, 1987.

Righter, Rosemary, *Whose News. Politics, the Press and the Third World*, London: Burnett/Deutsch, 1978.

Robinson, Jeffrey, *The Risk Takers*, London: George Allen & Unwin, 1986.

Ruiz Castañeda, Carmen, Maria del et al., *La Prensa Pasado y Presente de México*, Mexico: Universidad Autonomo de México, 1987.

Sampson, Anthony, *The Midas Touch*, London: Hodder & Stoughton, 1989.

Sánchez Ruiz, Enrique E., *La Investigación de la Comunicación*, Mexico: Ediciones de Comunicación, 1988.

Schiller, Herbert, *Mass Communications & American Empire*, New York: A. M. Kelly, 1969.

Scott Berg, A., *Goldwyn*, London: Hamish Hamilton, 1989.

Sédillot, René, *Les Deux Cent Familles*, Paris: Perrin, 1988.

Simpson, John, *From the House of War*, London: Hutchinson, 1991.

Sloan, Alfred P., *Adventures of a White Collar Man*, New York: Doubleday, Doran & Co., 1941.

Smith, Adam, *The Wealth of Nations*, London: Penguin, 1986.

Sperber, A. M., *Murrow: His Life and Times*, New York: Bantam Books, 1986.

Swanberg, W. A., *Citizen Hearst*, New York: Scribner's, 1964.

——, *Luce and his Empire*, New York: Scribner's, 1972.

Sykes, Trevor, *Operation Dynasty*, Australia: Greenhouse Publications, 1989.

Thompson, Peter & Delano, Anthony, *Maxwell. A Portrait of Power*, London: Bantam Press, 1988.

Toffler, Alvin, *The Third Wave*, London: Bantam, 1980.

Trejo Delarbre, Raúl et al., *Televisa. El Quinto Poder*, Mexico: Claves Latinoamericanas, 1987.

——, *Las Redes de Televisa*, Mexico: Claves Latinoamericanas, 1988.

Tuccille, Jerome, *Murdoch*, London, Piatkus, 1990.

Tunstall, Jeremy & Palmer, Michael, *Media Moguls*, London: Routledge, 1991.

Wansell, Geoffrey, *Tycoon*, London: Grafton, 1988.

Whittemore, Hank, *CNN. The Inside Story*, London: Little Brown, 1990.

Wintour, Charles, *The Rise and Fall of Fleet Street*, London: Hutchinson, 1989.

Witherspoon, John & Kovitz, Roselle, *The History of Public Broadcasting*, Washington: Current Newspaper, 1987.

Wright, Basil, *The Long View. An International History of Cinema*, London: Paladin, 1976.

——, *The Role and Functions of the Australian Broadcasting Tribunal*, Australia: Commonwealth of Australia, 1988.

——, *Self-regulation for Broadcasters*, Australia: Commonwealth of Australia, 1977.

——, *The Public Service Idea in British Broadcasting*, London: BRU (Broadcasting Research Unit), 1988.

Index

Index

Index

Index

Index